THE HANDBOOK OF

PORTERS & STOUTS

THE ULTIMATE, COMPLETE & DEFINITIVE Guide

INTRODUCTION *by* STEPHEN BEAUMONT
SPECIAL TASTING SECTION *by* JOSHUA M. BERNSTEIN

JOSH CHRISTIE & CHAD POLENZ

CIDER MILL PRESS

BOOK PUBLISHERS

Kennebunkport, Maine

The Handbook of Porters & Stouts

Copyright © 2014 by Appleseed Press Book Publishers LLC

This is an official licensed edition by Cider Mill Press Book Publishers LLC

All reviews by Zach Fowle were originally published in
the *Phoenix New Times* and on www.phxfood.com.

A version of the article "Culinary Stouts" on page 161
was published originally in *Draft* magazine.

13-Digit ISBN: 9781604334777
10-Digit ISBN: 1604334770

This book may be ordered by mail from the publisher. Please include $4.95 for postage
and handling. Please support your local bookseller first!

Books published by Cider Mill Press Book Publishers are available at special discounts
for bulk purchases in the United States by corporations, institutions, and other organizations.
For more information, please contact the publisher.

Cider Mill Press Book Publishers
"Where good books are ready for press"
12 Spring Street
PO Box 454
Kennebunkport, Maine 04046

Visit us on the Web!
www.cidermillpress.com

Cover design: Whitney Cookman
Interior design: Corinda Cook and Alicia Freile, Tango Media
Typography: Arno, Destroy, Franklin Gothic

Printed in China

1 2 3 4 5 6 7 8 9 0
First Edition

To Katy. I'm forever in your debt for introducing me to beer.

—Josh Christie

For the true fans and friends who have supported me over the years. I wouldn't have gotten this far without you. Thanks!

—Chad Polenz

CONTENTS

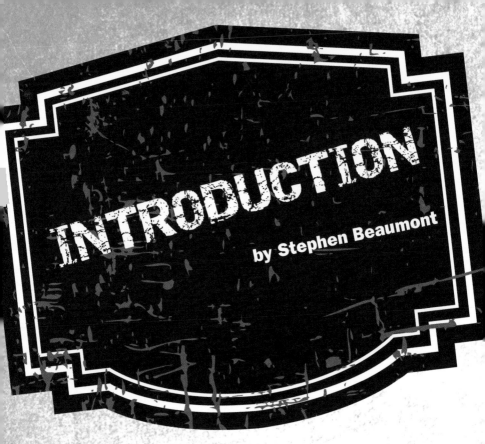

INTRODUCTION

by Stephen Beaumont

We've come a long way since "I don't like dark beer."

That lament, once a common refrain in bars and restaurants where beer was afforded more than token representation, is far less common in this modern age of black-hued India Pale Ales (IPAs) and Belgian-inspired brown ales, dark lagers, and especially stouts and porters. No longer is it a beer-savvy server's duty to painstakingly explain that an ale or lager's color has nothing to do with its strength or weight or calorie count. The modern beer consumer, for the most part, gets it.

Difficulties still arise, however, when we begin to dig a little more deeply into style. Stout? Why, that's simply Guinness, right? And porter is like stout but lighter in body, or maybe it's less hoppy, or it's sweeter and more chocolaty. Imperial stouts are simply strong stouts, and the early ones had something to do with Russia. Baltic porters are basically the same as Imperials, aren't they? Unless, of course, they're not.

In other words, most beer drinkers know stouts and porters, but few truly understand them. This is no slight against collective beer knowledge, just confirmation of how confusing the different styles can be.

One thing we do know for certain, however, is that porters came first. Often mistakenly believed to be the descendant of a beer blend known as three threads—a tale with its origins in a nonbrewing book, *The Picture of London*, written by John Feltham in 1802—porter is now known to date from the early eighteenth century and to have been an offshoot of the sweet brown ale that was ubiquitous in London during the late seventeenth century. Its rise was attributable not to a mixing of ales as in the three threads story but to the rise of new malting and brewing techniques that lent themselves to the creation of a drier, more roasty form of beer.

Two aspects of the porter story that do appear to be true, according to the British beer historian Martyn Cornell, are that it was named after the London porters who favored a pint of the dark brew as a restorative and that it was a brewery-aged beer, often maturing for months or even years in massive vats. It also is thought to have been the world's first global beer style.

Around the time of independence, porter was a popular brew in the United States, a fact evidenced by any number of modern black beers said to have been inspired by the recipes of Thomas Jefferson, Samuel Adams, and George Washington. When Australia was established as a penal colony in 1788, according to Cornell in his definitive book on British beers, *Amber, Gold & Black*, the settlement was toasted with glasses of porter. Contrary to widespread belief, barrels of porter were being successfully shipped to British colonists in India well before the popularization of "Pale Ale as prepared for India," or IPA as it is known today.

Stout, of course, evolved from the nearly ubiquitous porter, but the word originally meant only "strong beer," much as brewers today are wont to use the term *Imperial*. When applied to porter, the strongest became "stout porter" or sometimes "brown stout" and eventually just "stout," thus co-opting the term in perpetuity.

In Dublin, courtesy of a famously generous and long-term brewery lease, there arose the world's most famous brewer of stout, Guinness, although it took a pair of world wars and the corresponding grain shortages for the celebrated beer's strength to descend to the present (and, in the original sense of the term, very unstoutlike) 4.2% alcohol. Then as now, the principal difference between Irish stouts and porters and their across-the-Channel cousins was the use of only pale and roasted malt in the former and the habitual addition of brown malt to the mix in the latter, a nod to its brown ale roots. As a result, English- or London-style porters and stouts tend to be slightly sweeter and notably more rounded than those inspired by Irish brewing traditions.

Although Ireland broadly, and Guinness specifically, has come to define stout for most of the world, other variations have continued to grow and flourish, often after nearly fading away entirely. Notable among them is Imperial stout.

So named because of its popularity in the imperial court of the Russian czar, Imperial stouts were strong and well hopped, as many remain today. However, except for a handful of occasionally brewed hangers-on, the style had all but vanished by the mid-twentieth century before being resuscitated in the 1980s by the Samuel Smith Brewery of Tadcaster, England, at the behest of its American importer, Merchant du Vin. Today, of course, Imperial stouts are commonplace, as is the use—abuse?—of the Imperial designation as a catchall for a strong version of an otherwise moderate beer style.

The Imperial stout's closest cousin is the Baltic porter, a strong and sweet brew that originated in eastern Europe, principally the Baltic states. As the region's large, mass-production breweries switched wholesale from darker ales to golden lagers, the desire to maintain a vestige of their collective history resulted in a bottom-fermented version of the beer, cold-conditioned and as strong as many Imperial stouts but sweeter, less roasty, and generally equipped with a lower degree of malty complexity. A similar evolution in the West Indies, where "export-strength" Guinness remains popular, resulted in the similarly styled Caribbean stout.

Also common today is oatmeal stout, a self-defining style that includes oats among the grains used in its brewing, resulting in a creamy texture and often a slight porridgelike sweetness. Less prevalent is that era's other main stout derivative, milk or sweet stout, made with nonfermenting lactose (milk sugar) for extra body and sweetness and once billed as a restorative that "Does You Good."

In light of its use of what is in essence a flavoring ingredient, lactose,

it is possible to consider milk stout the spiritual predecessor of today's multitude of flavored stouts and porters, beers spiked with everything from cherries and spices to coffee, chocolate, and oysters. Although such inventiveness has without question been pursued with vigor in the United States, probably the world's most widely recognized flavored stout is the English ale Young's Double Chocolate Stout, and the country with the strongest claim to the title of stout nation of the future might well be black beer–happy Denmark.

Finally, we must address those stouts and porters which are not billed as such, the most obvious among them being the black IPA sometimes known as Cascadian dark ale. (Cascadia is an imagined land consisting of Washington State, Oregon, the Canadian province of British Columbia, and sometimes parts of Alaska, Utah, and other neighboring states, and Cascadian dark ale, or CDA, is so named because its proponents claim Cascadia as its point of origin.) Although, like many other styles, it is riding the wave of popularity currently sweeping along India Pale Ales of all sorts, the black IPA is in essence merely a hoppy porter; that is why some examples are included in the following pages. Likewise, certain strong ales with predominant roasted malt characters straddle the line between Imperial stouts and barley wines, and sometimes other styles as well, and so merit occasional notation here and there.

In the end, although it is best to remember that while not all black beers are stouts and porters, all stouts and potters are indeed black beers, or at very least dark brown ones, although of vastly differing strengths, textures, aromas, and of course flavors. Notwithstanding the rare and frivolous sighting of a modern "white stout," that is the way it is likely to stay, barring the improbable return to the use of *stout* as an adjective meaning "strong" and the repositioning of the FedEx driver as a porter.

THE ORIGINS OF PORTER

by Martyn Cornell

Fly back three centuries, to the reign of Queen Anne (1702–14), when (according to a "good pub guide" from that time called the *Vade Mecum for Malt-Worms*) the drinks you would be most likely to find in a London alehouse would be mild beer and stale beer (both made from brown malt), amber beer (made from pale malt), ale (including strong Twopenny pale ale, Derby ale, Burton ale, Oxford ale, Nottingham ale, and York pale ale), and stout.

Those names do not mean what they do today. "Mild" beer was fresh and recently brewed. "Stale" beer wasn't actually stale; it was the mild beer aged and matured. "Ale" meant very specifically a less hopped drink than beer, while "stout" could be any color, as long as it was strong. In addition, the ale brewers and the beer brewers were still two different groups of people.

London's drinkers, then and for centuries to come, liked to mix their brews: One group of pub-goers would order stale beer, which cost four old pence a pot (or quart), but stale beer and mild beer together was a popular drink. Others—according to a by-then elderly brewery worker calling himself "Obadiah Poundage" and writing in 1760—drank a mixture called "three-threads," costing three pence a pot.

Fermenting vats in the 1830s.

A great deal has been written about three-threads, because a man called John Feltham, writing in 1802, claimed that three-threads was a popular drink made up of "a third of ale, beer and twopenny," for which "the publican had the trouble to go to three casks and turn three cocks for a pint of liquor." According to Feltham, porter was invented to taste like three-threads, but because it came from one cask, it saved the publicans the trouble and waste of mixing the drink afresh every order from three separate casks. Feltham's description of what went into three-threads, and his statement that porter was designed to copy it as a single beer that would not need to be served from three different casks, has been repeated by almost every writer on beer for two centuries.

However, Feltham was writing eighty years or so after the time when three-threads was most popular, and he seems to have gotten it entirely wrong. The (admittedly obscure) *A New Dictionary of the Terms Ancient and Modern of the Canting Crew* by B. E. Gent (the "canting crew" being those who spoke in "cant," or slang), published around 1697/1699, called three-threads "half common Ale and the rest Stout or Double Beer" (both "stout" and "double beer" meaning "strong beer"). This definition was repeated in Nathan Bailey's *Universal Etymological English Dictionary* of 1737, which again said that three-threads was "half common Ale and half Stout or double Beer."

What three-threads actually was, was a tax cheat. There were only two grades of tax on beer and ale in Britain at the start of the eighteenth century, one on "strong" beer at five shillings a barrel and one on "small" beer at one shilling and four pence a barrel. However, if you brewed a barrel of "super-strong" beer, you still only paid the five shillings strong beer tax on it. But if you mixed that super-strong beer with a barrel of small beer, you now had two barrels of strong beer, on which you had only paid six shillings and four pence tax, not ten shillings. This was, unsurprisingly, illegal, but landlords did it, and the mixed beer was called "three-threads."

The truth is that porter was not actually a new beer, or a beer designed to imitate any other, but ordinary London brown beer, the stuff previously sold as mild and stale, revitalized and improved under the pressure of the competition it was receiving from other ales and beers. One threat came from the growing popularity of Twopenny pale ale, originally introduced to the London market, according to Poundage, by the country gentry, who had brewed and drunk pale ales (nothing like our modern pale ales, but lightly hopped and very strong) and were spending more time in the capital in Queen Anne's time than they had in the past. They brought the fashion for this strong pale, lightly hopped ale with them, and it retailed for four pence a quart, two pence a pint.

Another pressure on London's brown beer brewers, Poundage revealed forty years later, was that middle-men were buying the mild beer cheaply from the brewers, storing it, and then selling it to the publicans and ale-house keepers as more expensive and more flavorsome stale beer, thus depriving the brewers of profit.

The London beer brewers worked on their brown beer, hopping it more, lengthening the storage times, improving the ways they stored it, surmising, according to Poundage, that "beer well brewed, kept its proper time, became racy and mellow, that is neither new nor stale, such would recommend itself to the public." This improved brew sold at three pence a quart, the same price as three-threads and less than stale beer or Twopenny. Although "at first it was slow in making its way... in the end the experiment succeeded beyond expectation," Poundage declared.

That porter was London brown beer by another name is confirmed by several writers in the eighteenth century: An advertisement in a Sheffield newspaper in 1744 used "London Brew'd Porter" and "brown Beer" as synonyms. Michael Combrune, in his book *Theory and Practice of Brewing*, first published in 1762, continually referred to "Porter or Brown Beer." And in 1768, the anonymous author of a book called *Every Man His Own Brewer* talked about "London Brown Beer," which was "usually called Porter."

The improved brown beer found an eager market among London's working classes, thousands of whom worked as porters. These men moved goods around the streets of London and on and off the ships moored in the Thames, either informally or for the two main organized por-tering groups: the Fellowship Porters (who did most of the loading and unloading of ships) and the Ticket Porters (who did most of the "street portering"—you can see a Ticket Porter draining a quart pot of beer in William Hogarth's etching "Beer Street"). Theirs was hot, tiring work, and they drank a lot of beer, even while working. From the improved brown beer's popularity with London's porters "came its appellation of porter" wrote Poundage in 1760.

The earliest known mention of porter by name is in a pamphlet by the political journalist and poet Nicholas Amhurst dated May 22, 1721, which talks about dining at a cook's shop "upon beef, cabbage and porter." In November 1726, the Swiss traveller César de Saussure, describing

The Brick Lane Brewery, shown here, was the largest brewery in the mid-nineteenth century.

London in a letter home, said that "nothing but beer is drunk and it is made in several qualities. Small beer is what everyone drinks when thirsty; it is used even in the best houses and costs only a penny a pot. Another kind of beer is called porter . . . because the greater quantity of this beer is consumed by the working classes. It is a thick and strong beverage, and the effect it produces if drunk in excess, is the same as that of wine; this porter costs 3d the pot. In London there are a number of houses where nothing but this sort of beer is sold."

Although the public picked up on the name, the London brewers themselves do not appear to have called the beer "porter" until the early 1760s. Instead, they generally referred to it as "entire" or "entire butt" beer. "Entire" was the standard term for any brew made from the complete run of mashes on one piece of "goods," or malt, all mixed together, e.g., "entire small beer," was small beer made from all the mashes off one mash-tun full of grain, and "butt beer" was beer matured in butts, or 108-gallon

A 1950s brewery.

casks. So "entire butt" was a brew made from a complete set of mashes and matured in butts.

This certainly seems to have been how porter was originally brewed: For several decades the big London porter brewers hired cellars all over the city to store butts full of maturing porter in. Eventually they learned to mature the porter in giant vats on the brewery premises, though the fashion for building ever-bigger vats ended when the hoops on one huge vessel at the Meux brewery on Tottenham Court Road, London, burst and five hundred tons of maturing porter smashed down the back wall and roared out into the slums behind, killing eight people.

PORTERS

961 BEER PORTER

961 BEER

The wealthy Lebanese entrepreneur Mazen Hajjar encountered a book titled *Beer School*. He read it and was soon brewing. This was in 2006, in the middle of a war. Mazen ran and still runs the first and only micro-brewery in the Middle East. When 961 Beer officially began brewing, it was one of the smallest breweries in the world, and today it brews nearly 2 million liters per year. 961 Beer, the trade name for this brand, comes from the country's telephone code.

961 Beer is a traditional English-style porter that uses dark roasted malts with a hefty addition of crystal malts. It is also hopped with several English varieties. It pours a fairly opaque dark-brown color with a few highlights of garnet. This medium-bodied beer pours beautifully with nice carbonation and produces a solid head in the glass. At 5.6% ABV, it has a nose that is chock-a-block with hints of smoke, burnt sugar, dark chocolate-covered caramel malts, French roast coffee, raisins, nut, and toast, with undercurrents of dark cherries and raspberries for a nice mild finish.

AMON AMARTH RAGNARÖK

THREE FLOYDS BREWING COMPANY

The label of this beer from Three Floyds of Munster, Indiana, features the Swedish metal band Amon Amarth. There seems to be a growing trend in craft beer of brewers collaborating with nonbrewers for special one-off releases. These brews can seem a little gimmicky. But hopes are high for Three Floyds Amon Amarth Ragnarök because it is a collaboration between one of the best American craft brewers and one of the biggest names on the heavy metal music scene. What they came up with is an Imperial porter that is certainly unique, and this is a very tasty, enjoyable beer.

There is a typical porter or stout complexion of a nearly jet black color with slightly ruby red edges. It forms a large dark khaki frothy head that laces and retains extremely well. Very true to the porter style, there are sweeter notes of chocolate, cocoa nibs, and raisins (chocolate-covered raisins, actually) and a subtle but noticeable smell of coconut and a general earthiness.

In the world of brewing, a strong porter is technically a stout, but there's a distinct difference in taste, especially in the case of Amon Amarth Ragnarök. This beer has all the sweeter flavor notes you find in a porter: a slight milky/dairy flavor, milk chocolate, dark cherry, and raisins, plus some earthy roughage on the back end to provide bitterness.

As it warms, this beer grows even more complex, imparting a slight smoky taste, a hint of coffee bitterness, and a slight sourness or tang. You might chalk this up to the alcohol accentuating the components often found in the palate of more traditional pub-style porters.

Although this beer is rather hefty at 8.2% ABV, it would be difficult to detect that. There's no alcohol presence, and the beer doesn't feel all that heavy. It's supersmooth with a lovely but light chocolate and raisin aftertaste. Though sweet, it's never cloying. Its drinkability is a great reason to love it. (This beer is no longer in production.)

CP

ANCHOR PORTER

ANCHOR BREWING COMPANY

There's a strong case to be made that Anchor Brewing Company kicked off the era of microbreweries (or as they're called these days, craft breweries) in the United States. Originally founded during the Gold Rush era by George Breckle, the brewery managed to survive earthquakes, fires, and even Prohibition. When Anchor was on the brink of closure in 1965, it was purchased by Fritz Maytag. Maytag turned the failing brewery around and went on to introduce American drinkers to myriad styles that had never been brewed in the United States.

One of those styles was porter. Although the styles of stout and porter are popular these days, at one time porter very nearly went extinct. By the 1970s, no English breweries were brewing porter; they all had ceded that space to the more popular style of stout. In stepped Anchor, which brewed the first post-Prohibition porter in the United States in 1972.

(It should be noted that by 1979, a handful of English brewers had started experimenting with the style again.)

Fermented with Anchor's top-fermenting yeast and brewed with a mélange of roasted malts, Anchor Porter falls right in the sweet spot between the sweet malts of a brown ale and the dark roastiness of a stout. The flavor is largely toffee sweetness, with bitter coffee and caramel maltiness rounding out either side. Even with these rich notes, Anchor Porter is light in body and easy to drink at 5.6% ABV. More than four decades after its debut, it remains the quintessential American porter.

JC

AVERY NEW WORLD PORTER

AVERY BREWERY CO.

This is a pretty-looking porter with a dense black body (when held up to the light, it's deep brown with a splash of red wine color) under a compact, fluffy mud-brown head.

There are thick smells of dark chocolate, dark-roasted coffee reminiscent of the small intense cups of café noir served in French cafés, brown sugar, salty licorice, caramel fudge, and nuts. There's also an underlying whiff of wood, earth, and citrus (more like the peel of lemons than the juice) from the tag team of Columbus and Fuggles hops. You can sniff this beer for ages before drinking it.

This brew draws you in with its oily texture, coating the mouth with sweet flavors of dark fruit, orange, and chocolate. Then it suddenly turns on you, delivering a bitter slap in the face of pine needles, licorice, and sap. There's a load of roasted flavors that border on being burnt and induce a long drying finish. Perhaps the body is a little skinny.

This porter would pair well with a sweet chocolate cake such as *kladdkaka* as its dry and bitter roasted character would balance out the sweetness of the cake perfectly.

Avery New World Porter owes its intense hop aroma and taste to the fact that it has been dry-hopped, which means that dry hops are introduced into the beer after fermentation. Dry hops add no bitterness, but the technique often gives back some aromatic oils that normally are lost in the boiling process.

DP

BENCHWARMER PORTER

COOPERSTOWN BREWING CO.

The Cooperstown Brewing Co. is a very small operation just south of the Baseball Hall of Fame in upstate New York. Not surprisingly, there is a baseball theme to all of its beers. I decided to start with the possibly ironically named Benchwarmer Porter. In sports terms a benchwarmer is a lousy player, but in the case of this beer it's a solid performer. If this is the benchwarmer, the rest of the team must be outstanding.

When poured, this beer flowed out of the bottle like water and produced next to no head. What developed was a coating of tan soapy suds, although you can generate a thicker head with a forceful swirl of the glass. The color was typical for a porter: nearly opaque black but with dark ruby red highlights around the edges. The aroma was standard for a porter: malty with a touch of dark fruit and yeast. It was fairly sweet and had no alcohol notes.

The brewers describe this beer as being made in the tradition of English porters, and you can tell this is the case on the first sip. Much like its brethren from across the pond, Benchwarmer Porter is noticeably mild with a surprisingly light body as soon as it hits the palate. There's a dark fruit flavor and a slightly yeasty texture followed by a strong milk chocolate and coffee aftertaste.

This beer is somewhat like Samuel Smith's Taddy Porter throughout the first half of the glass. As I continued to drink, the chocolate and coffee flavors seemed to weaken but the fruits and malts from the front became more prominent. Eventually it all became a mélange of flavors typically found in British pub beers. The palate was pleasing even though it was mild.

British pub ales are known for their high drinkability, and Benchwarmer Porter follows the formula with its extreme smoothness. The mouthfeel is light and thin, and the beer almost doesn't seem carbonated as it goes down like water. The sweet aftertaste is pleasant, although it becomes quite dry as the beer warms.

For a beer with a potency of 6.3% ABV, this drinks like a much lighter brew. Between the mild body and the mild palate it's impressive how well the alcohol is hidden both in the palate and in your system. This beer would pair well with a red meat dinner; two bottles could substitute for dessert.

Cooperstown Brewing's Benchwarmer is so drinkable, it's the kind of beer you could see yourself buying often.

BLACK BUTTE PORTER

DESCHUTES BREWERY

Deschutes in Oregon brews a huge volume of beer, but its products are not distributed nationwide. Black Butte is one of its better-known offerings, perhaps even its flagship beer. It's a good porter with a reputation that precedes it.

Porter is a style that brewers tend not to mess with. That's not to say that if you've had one you've had them all, just that the style is solid, so why tamper with it? That seems to be the approach taken with Deschutes Black Butte Porter. It plays it very safe with a tasty, well-balanced, and smooth palate.

Black Butte has an extremely dark blood-red maroon to black complexion that is noticeably ruby red around the edges and forms a large, dark-khaki, tightly compacted foamy head that retains and laces quite well. The classic porter aroma of dairy aisle milkiness has some additional dark fruit notes such as cherry and prune and a hint of chocolate candy.

Black Butte begins like most porters do with a mild, lightly sweet taste of milk chocolate at the beginning. It transitions to something more fruity, authentic, and rich through the middle of the palate, like a Dr Pepper crossed with a Trappist quad. There's the classic cough syrup component many porters tend to have, but prune and dark cherry are the main attraction. The finish is quite nice, with a toasty, roasty malt taste plus some dark chocolate sweetness. There's a light coffeelike bitterness and dryness as well, but it's barely noticeable until the beer reaches a warmer temperature.

This beer is tasty and satisfying all around, but what's really interesting and impressive is the drinking experience. Although porters tend to be thinner and lighter than stouts, Deschutes Black Butte has noticeably finely carbonation and a thin, wet mouthfeel. It's not quite a creamy or velvety texture, but it does go down smooth. The 5.2% ABV is right where it should be: big enough to give it genuine energy but small enough to keep it under wraps.

CP

BREWFIST X-RAY IMPERIAL PORTER

BREWFIST ITALIAN ALES

X-Ray is an American porter–style beer brewed by Brewfist in Codogno, Italy. Brewfist wanted to make porter that would go deep into your bones. It's a big fat porter with a lusty 8.5% ABV, a rich and complex beer that is brewed with traditional English malts such as pale, crystal, chocolate, brown, and Monaco and topped off with Magnum hops. It pours an opaque dark-brown color and is well-balanced with a small amount of sugar and a touch of bitter hops. Chocolate absolutely dominates.

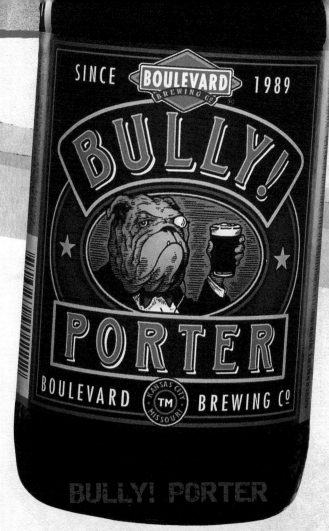

BOULEVARD BREWING CO.

The intense flavors of dark-roasted malt in Boulevard's rendition of the classic English porter are perfectly balanced by a generous and complex hop character. This porter was made using pale malt, Cara 300 and Cara 120 malts, malted wheat, chocolate, and hops that include Magnum, Bravo, Cascade, and Ahtanum. This is a dark-colored, medium-bodied beer with a prominent burnt, roasted malt aroma and flavor and an equally prominent hop aroma, flavor, and bitterness. Bully! is a big, robust English-style porter that comes in at an even 6% ABV.

JC

CAMBA BAVARIA ERIC'S PORTER

CAMBA BAVARIA

At the beginning of industrial age in the eighteenth century, people poured into London to earn money in the factories and markets. Their days were long and hard. Many of the workers coming out of those hot buildings crowned with smokestacks had an unslakable thirst. Many preferred drinking to buying what little food their money could get them. Porter was like a meal in a glass, and this porter is a classic instance. Now Camba Bavaria makes this beer in Germany.

Brewed according to the recipe of the master brewer Eric Toft from the Schönramer Brewery, Eric's Porter (6.5% ABV) provides a big whiff of chocolate and caramel that soon is replaced by *Kaminwurz* (smoked sausage) and subtly smoked bacon. There is a velvety creaminess to the beer, which also has a hint of black pepper followed by the earthy spiciness of the classic English hop varieties Fuggles and Goldings.

CHATHAM BREWING PORTER

CHATHAM BREWING

Chatham Brewing is run by garagistes. They started brewing in an old garage just off Main Street in Chatham, New York. There was a small sign on the sidewalk that pointed visitors to the brewery down a crooked alley. In an old garage, there were several mash tuns, several tanks, tons of small and large kegs, and boxes of growlers. There they brewed their beer and sold it in kegs and growlers. People lined up, tasted the beer, and whatever beer they wanted, Chatham filled a growler with it. It was a rustic scene with no tasting room or pretty setting. It was garage beer, and the beer was great. Word spread, and Chatham became more and more popular.

In 2013, the brewery moved across the street into its current digs. One morning, armed with large tractors with forklifts on their fronts, the entire brewing operation was moved 600 feet. It might as well have been six miles for all that was needed to move the copper works. They did it early on a Sunday morning while traffic was low and people were still asleep.

Since then, their expansion has skyrocketed. The old brew works are now on display in the tasting room. They are making small-batch seasonal beers. The new brewery out back dwarfs the old machinery. Chatham

UNION STATION, CHATHAM, N.Y.

Brewing has taken a huge step forward to the big leagues of New England brewing.

One of the throwbacks to the old days is the porter, the beer that made Chatham famous. The label shows a big puff of black smoke billowing from an old steam locomotive. The porter is a nod to Chatham's railroading past, when it was a rail hub for northeastern New York. The porter derives its deep color and flavor from chocolate malt.

When poured into a pint glass, the beer shows a good deep dark rich brown-black color. It has a nice frothy beige head that sticks around a while and provides a pretty lacing as you drink it. Very nice.

Chatham Porter smells almost like an iced coffee at first whiff. Roasted coffee and dark baking cocoa come through big. There's also a touch of hops and a nice smokiness, with a small amount of spice and a hint of anise. The flavor is excellent, with medium body and low carbonation. It starts off with a lovely chocolate malted note, but at a second taste, rich coffee and dark chocolate notes come through loud and clear. A hint of toffee or brown sugar is also present. This is a dry porter with very little or no hint of sweetness. A beautiful, creamy finish lingers on the palate. Coffee and chocolate come through on a nice long finish that lasts and lasts. This is a very easy-drinking beer.

COCOA PORTER WINTER WARMER

COLORADO MOUNTAIN TOWN CRAFT BEER

TOMMYKNOCKER BREWERY

COCOA PORTER

THE ADDITION OF COCOA POWDER AND HONEY MAKE FOR A SPECIAL BREW

WINTER WARMER

COLORADO

5.7% ALC/VOL   IBU 18   12 FL OZ (355ML)

ALE BREWED WITH COCOA AND HONEY

TOMMYKNOCKER BREWERY

Tommyknocker Brewery can be found in Idaho Springs, Colorado. Their Cocoa Porter is a popular seasonal beer; a smooth, classic dark-brown ale with milk chocolate and coffee flavors as well a gorgeous aromas of roasted malt. A light addition of domestic Perle and Willimette hops balances the complexity of this beer. The addition of pure cocoa powder and Colorado honey elevates it from good, to classic. At 5.7% ABV this beer is a very drinkable session beer that is highly acclaimed and worth seeking out.

DARK
ARTS
PORTER

TROUBLE BREWING

This porter by Trouble Brewing, a brewery in Kill, Co. Kildare, Ireland, pours almost black. It is brewed using a big shock of black malt and chocolate malt, as well as crystal, black patent, pale ale, Caramalt, and flaked barley. These all add intense and roasty flavors. It's hopped with Northdown, Challenger, and Cascade. This 4.4% ABV ale explodes with coffee, cocoa, and toffee. The hops balance the whole body of the beer out, for a nice, complex but drinkable brew.

DRAYMAN'S PORTER

BERKSHIRE BREWING COMPANY

In 1992, Chris Lalli and Gary Bogoff of Montgomery, Massachusetts, came to the conclusion that they both had a similar purpose in life—to make beer. After three long years of planning and test brewing and many months of hunting the Pioneer Valley to pick the right location, Berkshire Brewing Company found a home in historic South Deerfield, Massachusetts. They opened the building and started brewing at the end of 1994, and since then, they've grown and grown into a solid, quality regional craft brewer.

A full-bodied, dark ruby-brown ale, Drayman's Porter is slightly sweet with notes of chocolate malt and coffee, which combine with a very nice hop bitterness at the end. It has nice carbonation and good complexity and balance. It's a great porter from a superior regional brewer. And, at 6.2% ABV, you can have a few!

THE DUCK-RABBIT PORTER

DUCK-RABBIT CRAFT BREWERY

The Duck-Rabbit Craft Brewery is a small packaging microbrewery in Farmville, North Carolina, that sold its first beer in August 2004. It specializes in beautiful, delicious full-flavored dark beers. These beers are highly rated and hard to find because they are so highly coveted.

The Duck-Rabbit Porter is very dark in color. This robust porter has a pronounced flavor of roasted grains reminiscent of dark chocolate. The brewers add oats to the grist to give a subtle round silkiness to the mouthfeel. You can be confident that you'll love this impressive porter.

EDMUND FITZGERALD PORTER

GREAT LAKES BREWING CO.

Porters have always been safe bets for me, and Great Lakes' Edmund Fitzgerald Porter is one of the best. This is a beer with the light body of a porter but the robustness of a stout.

The body appears to be black but is actually dark ruby red. It forms a generous dark tan soapy head that dissipates slowly and leaves a little lacing on the glass. The aroma is inviting with roasted malts, coffee, dark chocolate, oatmeal, and the dairy scent most stouts and porters seem to have.

Before I came to appreciate craft beer and especially stouts and porters, I always found beers like this to have a cough medicine–like taste. With Edmund Fitzgerald I still find that flavor, but now I enjoy it. That taste is a combination of roasty malts and the sweetness of

Edmund Fitzgerald

chocolate. Not that this is a chocolate beer per se, but there definitely is a confectionary flavor.

The first half of the beer is rather mild, but the second half is quite robust. Whereas most American porters tend to have just a hint of chocolate and coffee on the finish, those flavors are overt here. There's not much bitterness and certainly no lazy hops hanging around on the tongue afterward. The coffeelike taste and bitterness are only momentary, and the aftertaste is short and sweet (literally).

Porter has been a "working man's beer" for centuries, and this beer follows the trend. For such a seemingly strong palate, it has a very thin, light mouthfeel. It also seems to be more highly carbonated than most porters, to point of having a sodalike feel. At 5.8% ABV Edmund Fitzgerald Porter is something of an all-purpose beer. It probably would work best as a pub beverage, but I could see pairing it with meals that don't have a lot of spice. It also would work well as a session beer or an after-dinner liquid dessert.

CP

ELEMENTAL PORTER ALE

RENAISSANCE
BREWING COMPANY

MARLBOROUGH · NEW ZEALAND

Elemental

PORTER ALE
A dark, rich and mellow
balance of hops
and roasted malts

500ml   1 PT .9 FL OZ

RENAISSANCE BREWING COMPANY

Located in Blenheim, in the heart of the province of Marlborough, New Zealand, the Renaissance Brewing Company is situated at the old grove mill on Dodson St., which is the oldest commercial building in Blenheim. Over the years it has housed an ice cream factory, a malt house, two very famous Marlborough wineries (Grove Mill and Whitehaven), and more recently a craft brewery.

Elemental is a 6% ABV export porter and is Renaissance's most awarded beer. Originally the beer of choice for workers in London's produce markets, porters would drink beer when they clocked out at dawn. Brewed in a more modern robust style, Elemental Porter is rich and full bodied.

Dry dark chocolate and roasty malt start this porter off well. The ale eventually levels off with a refreshing hop-driven finish. It is a good session beer.

ELEVATOR HORNY GOAT

ELEVATOR BREWING CO.

This beer from a brewery in Columbus, Ohio, claims to be a classic-styled porter that's been aged in whiskey barrels. It is dark ruby red to brown in color, with fine carbonation bubbles noticeable around the edges. It forms a very large tan foamy head that does dissipate but not completely and leaves some lacing on the glass. It has a sourish smell in that good Belgian-style way, not in a spoiled way. There is a noticeable whiskey scent but not much porter aroma.

Beers that are aged in whiskey or bourbon barrels tend to be amazing, but in the case of Elevator's Horny Goat porter, the result is a plain good beer. There's a lot of whiskey character to this brew, perhaps a little too much. A great barrel-aged beer maintains the characteristics of the original brew with the spirit flavor as a complement, but here the whiskey flavor is the star of the show.

The palate is similar to that of a standard porter, and so it has a sweeter, more fine maltiness than a stout. There are some colalike flavors at the beginning with hints of prune and dark cherry and a slight tartness. It seems to change on a dime as the whiskey taste comes out of nowhere to smack your tongue. It's sweet with just a hint of vanilla and traces of woodiness.

At 7.5% ABV the mouthfeel is rather thin and highly effervescent for a brew of this style and weight. However, the fact that there's noticeable heat and an accompanying booze taste and sensation makes this feel like a much bigger brew than it is. Still, Elevator Horny Goat Porter goes down pretty smoothly and finishes mostly clean with just a slight aftertaste of whiskey or vanilla extract. It is a good after-dinner beer on a weeknight.

FOUNDERS PORTER

FOUNDERS BREWING COMPANY

All porters should be Founders Porter! It has that rare combination of hearty and robust but retains the qualities of a porter. The aroma has roasted barley, dairy, and a hint of alcohol. The palate is, for lack of a better description, that of a typical porter with toasted malt, a milky-dairy sweetness across the middle, and a little milk chocolate on the finish. It's not a particularly bitter or dry beer as is common with stouts, and so there is next to no coffee flavor or bitterness. The finish is surprisingly clean, with a hint of confectionary sweetness (I wouldn't have minded some aftertaste). The silky smooth and soft texture doesn't coat the entire mouth the way an Imperial stout does, but it definitely covers the tongue from start to finish.

Founders Porter is one of the most quaffable beers. Between the flavorful but tame palate, the gentle mouthfeel, and the smooth finish, it's difficult not to throw this beer down as if it were a shot. But it's a fun beer to savor. The 6.5% ABV feels right but might be a tad higher than drinkers prefer in a porter; I would love to session this brew but think I'd get overwhelmed quickly.

Overall, it's the best porter I've ever had and an excellent beer in its own right.

CP

FULLER'S LONDON PORTER

FULLER, SMITH & TURNER

I often mock the British beer scene for being boring and archaic, but sometimes a traditional British brew really hits the spot. A case in point is Fuller's London Porter. Although not the most robust or complex beer ever made, it is impressive for its ability to be so tasty and so smooth for an Old World–style brew.

The deep dark ruby red appearance is seemingly opaque black with a huge tan frothy head that lingers and leaves gorgeous lacing on the glass. It has a classic porter aroma of black licorice, milk chocolate, and dark malts.

There isn't a lot happening with the palate, but what's there is very good. A blend of slight confectionery sweetness, a hint of coffee bitterness, and a lingering chocolate candy aftertaste are the three main components of this brew. It's simple, but they're enjoyable for their distinctiveness and the way they transition together. This beer is not quite as sickly sweet as many stouts and has less bitterness as well. I think this may be the absolute best beer to give to someone to show that dark beers can be flavorful but not intimidating. Light sweetness and light bitterness create a perfectly balanced, delectable body.

As satisfying as the palate is, what makes this such a good beer is how drinkable it is. The body is on the thinner side for a dark beer, but it's not watery. It's velvety smooth across the tongue and might even be considered refreshing for a moment. The aftertaste isn't completely clean, but there is just enough to leave a pleasing flavor that doesn't dry out the mouth. At 5.4% ABV, Fuller's London Porter is dangerously drinkable because it could be sessioned all day even though it's technically a tad too big to be a session beer.

CP

GASPAR'S PORTER

FLORIDA BEER COMPANY

This beer has a typical opaque black body. It forms a large light brown spongy head that doesn't completely dissipate and leaves minor lacing. It has a mostly standard porter aroma but with an odd scent of cherry and possibly chalk.

The first few sips are quite good. The nose is a good indicator of the taste. There is the dark malt flavor here you expect in a porter. It is on the sweeter end with only light bitterness and no roasted or burnt malt character, which makes it a true porter rather than a stout. There is some distinct dark cherry flavor on the second half coupled with a chalky taste and sensation. They may play around with the cherry character and make it the star of the show, but as it stands, the net result is a pretty good beer.

Although Gasper's Porter may not break new ground in the taste department, it's a high achiever as far as drinkability goes. The mouthfeel is full, soft, and slightly energetic. It's not thick, sticky, or chewy in any way. It goes down silky smooth and leaves just a lightly bitter dark chocolate aftertaste. At 6.1% ABV, it's full-bodied but not obese. It is probably best enjoyed with or as a dessert, though it's tempting to throw back two in a row.

CP

GREEN MAN PORTER

ROBUST

Dark, full-bodied, and rich in flavor, Green Man Porter is wonderfully easy to drink. It offers a creamy, smooth mouthfeel and finishes with distinctive chocolate notes. This traditionally crafted, award-winning British-style Porter, like a true rock star, enjoys a legendary following.

DISCOVER.SAVOR.REPEAT

CONCEIVED IN ASHEVILLE

GREEN MAN

PORTER
rich dark ale

Brewed and Bottled at Green Man Brewing Co, LLC, Asheville, NC

Alc. by Vol. 6.0%   40 IBU   Vol. 12 FL. OZ.

Legendary Ales :: Since 1997

GOVERNMENT WARNING: (1) ACCORDING TO THE SURGEON GENERAL, WOMEN SHOULD NOT DRINK ALCOHOLIC BEVERAGES DURING PREGNANCY BECAUSE OF THE RISK OF BIRTH DEFECTS. (2) CONSUMPTION OF ALCOHOLIC BEVERAGES IMPAIRS YOUR ABILITY TO DRIVE A CAR OR OPERATE MACHINERY, AND MAY CAUSE HEALTH PROBLEMS.

GREENMANBREWERY.COM

GREEN MAN BREWERY

Brewing award-winning ales since 1997, Green Man was founded in downtown Asheville, North Carolina, as a brewpub. New ownership and a fresh approach spurred evolutionary change in 2010, allowing Green Man to focus on production, distribution, and growth. With the help of the original brewer, John Stuart, and his team, Green Man has evolved into a respected and well-known brewery.

The Green Man motif has many variations. Found in many cultures around the world, the Green Man is related to natural vegetative deities in different cultures through the ages. Primarily it is interpreted as a symbol of rebirth or renaissance, representing the cycle of growth each spring.

Green Man Porter is a classic rich, dark, big-bodied, and flavorful porter that has a loyal following. Roasty notes dominate the nose. The idea was to make a traditional London pub–style easy-drinking dark beer. Creamy and smooth, this delicious porter finishes with chocolate notes and has a soft ending that makes it eminently drinkable.

KETO REPORTER

BIRRA DEL BORGO

Birra del Borgo owner and visionary Leonardo Di Vincenzo was a home-brewer from 1999 to 2004. Traveling in Europe, he discovered ancient beer styles and fell in love with German and Belgian ales. He thought the English beers were more interesting and more representative of their culture and place. In 2005, Birra del Borgo was born in Borgorose, a small village in the province of Rieti, on the border between Lazio and Abruzzo in the nature reserve of the Mountains of the Duchess. This brewery remains the laboratory of the mad genius himself.

By 2009, they inaugurated a new brewery in Spedino, not far from the original one. In the same year, in collaboration with his friend Teo Musso of Baladin and other partners, Di Vincenzo debuted his new gastronomic brewpub, Open Baladin, in Rome, a few steps from the Campo de' Fiori. In 2011, with Teo Musso and Sam Calagione of Dogfish Head, Leonardo opened the brewpub on the top floor of Eataly in Manhattan.

Meanwhile, he brews a mean beer, and one of his masterpieces is this excellent example of an extreme beer. The idea that Keto Reporter is a smoky porter is stretching things, but this 5% ABV porter was brewed with the addition of aromatic tobacco during the brewing process. Birra del Borgo used two types of tobacco leaves: King Porter tobacco from Kentucky and a classic cigar tobacco named Toscano.

This beer pours black with a dark beige head. It is creamy with nice lacing. The nose has dark and roasty chocolate and coffee, caramel, dark-brown sugar, molasses, licorice, and spices with an added kick of earthiness from the tobacco. There's lots of spice, mainly from the tobacco leaves; it's as aromatic and flavorful as beer gets.

MAINE BEER COMPANY

FREEPORT, MAINE

King Titus

Porter

Do what's right.

KING TITUS PORTER

MAINE BEER COMPANY

As always at Maine Beer Company in Freeport, Maine, there is a story behind the beer. Titus was a bold silverback gorilla that led with its heart. The Dian Fossey Gorilla Fund International studies and protects these magnificent animals in the Virunga Mountains in Rwanda, and the Maine Beer Company proudly supports their efforts.

This 7.5% ABV beer is the brewery's take on an American robust porter. Made with American two-row, Caramel 40L, Caramel 80L, Munich 10L, chocolate, roasted wheat, and flaked oats malts, it is hopped with Centennial and Columbus for complexity and good balance. It is dark, thick, chewy, chocolaty, and generously hopped. This is an amazing giant silverback of a beer, appropriately named.

KLEIN DUIMPJE PORTER

HUISBROUWERIJ KLEIN DUIMPJE

Klein Duimpje Porter is made by Huisbrouwerij Klein Duimpje in Hillegom, Netherlands. Brewed with chocolate malts and East Kent Golding hops, it has a hoppy bitterness of 38 European bittering units EBU. It pours black, brown with a beige head, and the palate is dark chocolate and coffee followed by sweeter grains and some dark molasses, too. A slight smokiness can be detected in this well-balanced beer of great complexity.

LONDON PORTER

MEANTIME BREWING COMPANY LIMITED

Meantime Brewing Company is an award-winning brewery based in Greenwich, England. It was founded in 2000 by brewmaster Alastair Hook, a graduate of the world-famous brewing school at the Technical University of Munich in Weihenstephan. The Greenwich Brewery originally was located at 0° 2' 12" east of the Greenwich Meridian before moving to a site on nearby Blackwall Lane in 2010.

Hook is driven to help consumers rediscover their cultural and culinary beer heritage. Since its establishment, Meantime has built a worldwide reputation for both quality and the authentic re-creation of several of the world's iconic and pivotal beer styles.

Meantime has matched its reputation for authenticity with one for innovation. It was the first British brewery to win medals at the World Beer Cup in 2004 and the only British brewery to have won medals at every WBC since then. In 2007, Meantime had no fewer than four beers ranked in the World's 50 Best Beers compiled by the UK-based International Beer Challenge, a feat it repeated in 2008. Hook was named the 2008 Brewer of the Year by the British Guild of Beer Writers.

With all its notoriety, it's easy to figure out that Meantime London Porter is a special treat.

MAYFLOWER PORTER

MAYFLOWER BREWING COMPANY

Mayflower Brewing Company is a craft-beer microbrewery located in historic Plymouth, Massachusetts. Founded in 2007 by a tenth great-grandson of John Alden, the beer barrel cooper onboard the Mayflower, they are dedicated to celebrating the history and legacy of the Pilgrims by creating unique, high-quality ales for the New England market. One hundred years after the Mayflower landed at Plymouth, a new beer style, the porter, emerged in England and traveled to the colonies where it was heartily accepted.

Their porter is brewed using yeast the brewery cultivates itself, malts such as 2-row pale, caramel Munich, chocolate, peated, and brown. It is hopped with Pilgrim and Glacier hops. At 5.2% ABV, it is rich and drinkable. Complex and well-balanced, it features a nose bursting with roasted coffee beans and bittersweet chocolate with a hint of smokiness. Very solid.

NARRAGANSETT PORTER

NARRAGANSETT BREWING COMPANY

Few breweries in the United States can claim a history as rich as that of Narragansett. Founded in 1890 with just $150,000 (much more money in those days, mind you), 'Gansett is one of the few American breweries that survived Prohibition. The brewery changed hands many times in the century after its incorporation, with ownership residing in Rhode Island and Massachusetts and as far afield as San Francisco. After the closing

of the Rhode Island brewery in 1981, the brand survived but suffered from middling quality for decades. In 2005, a group of local Rhode Island investors led by Mark Hellendrung purchased the brand and essentially revived it. The brewing of a few of their seasonal beers, including the porter, was moved back to Providence, Rhode Island, and quality has seen a sharp increase in the last decade.

Narragansett was never a name that most people associated with high-quality craft brews—it was more of a regional Schlitz/Pabst/Old Milwaukee alternative—but its seasonal releases have been dynamite.

The porter, the brewery's winter seasonal, is a crisp, easy-drinking take on the style. It's a practically black beer that pours with a thick tan head and has a heavy coffee character with hints of cocoa. Despite the rich flavors and creamy texture, the porter drinks very light, and the 7% ABV can sneak up on you when you're drinking it one 16-ounce can at a time. The subtle smokiness lurking in the Narragansett Porter makes it a perfect beer to pair with smoky barbeque.

JC

NIGHTMARE YORKSHIRE PORTER

NICK STAFFORD'S HAMBLETON ALES

Nick Stafford's Hambleton Ales was established in 1991 in the hamlet of Holme on Swale, situated on the banks of the River Swale in the Vale of Mowbray, England. (The white horse on the Hambleton labels has been seen from the brewery.) Nick was made laid off twice within seven months during the worst recession in England since World War II. So, he started his own, under-funded brewing company. By 1997, the company had revenues of $2.1 million. That's success!

Hambleton Nightmare (Yorkshire Porter) is an English porter–style beer with 5% ABV. It pours dark, with a dark beige head and nice lacing. The nose is a big dose of toffee and caramel with a touch of honey and smokiness. Dark fruits such as prunes, plums, and cherries come across, too. It is smooth and creamy on the palate with good dose of chocolate and coffee coming through in the taste as well as the smell as you drink it. This is a well-built beer and a solid porter with a good handle. And at 5% ABV you can drink a few. A very nice beer.

ODELL FERNET AGED PORTER

ODELL BREWING COMPANY

On almost any subject, you'll find a group of nerds willing to fight to the death to defend its awesomeness. Every day across the land, beer nerds write sloppily constructed brew reviews, but it's not often that nerds' interests intersect. However, occasionally there comes a product that can please members of multiple groups, and Odell's Fernet Aged Porter is one of them.

Cocktail craftsmen know Fernet well. The bitter, aromatic Italian spirit made with spices that range from chamomile and cardamom to saffron and myrrh is having something of a moment. The version popular among the cocktail set right now is Fernet Branca, invented in 1845 as a stomach medicine and used today to add a bold, bitter black-licorice flavor to drinks. Fernet isn't a spirit to be trifled with; the flavor is assertive, almost angry. Most cocktails use only a drop or two.

This isn't the first time Odell has experimented with the bitter medicinal spirit. In July 2012, the brewery premiered a Fernet-aged version of its popular Cutthroat Porter. That brew was interesting but too dry and bitter and too heavy on the Fernet. I pined for more malt flavor and sweetness, for the brew tasted a bit too much like toothpaste.

In this new porter, Odell has made all the right adjustments. To create it, brewers cooked up a batch of strong porter and then separated it into two halves. The first half was sent to the calm, cool confines of stainless steel; the second was placed in oaken barrels that once held

Fernet from Colorado's Leopold Bros. distillery, which blends bold notes of aloe and peppermint with about twenty other botanicals, including lavender, honeysuckle, ginger, dandelion, chamomile, and rose petals. The result is a brew that's like brushing your teeth with mint chocolate ice cream.

In a snifter, Fernet Aged Porter is thin yet dark, a deep ebony liquid beneath a sandy tan head composed of large, fragile bubbles that pop away quickly, giving up beautiful aromatics. Chocolate is noticeable in multiple forms: cocoa powder, milk chocolate squares, and mint chocolate chips. Herbal mint, anise, and alcohol swirl in the background.

The flavor is much more Fernet-forward. Peppermint zings around the mouth, balancing the bitter dark chocolate notes of the base porter. Floral imprints are apparent, decorating the darker beer and liqueur with licorice and lavender designs. An oaky char is met with flavors of molasses and gingerbread. The body's a little thin and the lively, fizzy carbonation is much higher than it needs to be, but the strange, pleasantly discordant sensation of cooling aloe and mint combined with the warmth of alcohol makes up for this.

I wouldn't be surprised if this porter was the same base used in Odell's decadent beer-wine hybrid Amuste; its rich chocolate notes and pungency are nearly the same. The funky, herbal bitterness, however, is very different. Get a bottle to settle your stomach or to give you and your cocktail-nerd friends something to agree about.

ZF

OKKARA
PORTARI

OKKARA

Okkara Portari is an Imperial, strong porter beer made by Okkara, a brewery in Velbastaður, Faroe Islands. The Faroes are an archipelago that is an autonomous country within the kingdom of Denmark, situated between the Norwegian Sea and the North Atlantic Ocean, approximately halfway between Norway and Iceland.

This 7.9% ABV beer pours dark but has a big creamy head that is long-lasting. Lots of roasted grain and dark bittersweet chocolate come across on the nose. Licorice, smoke, peat, and spices also come through. There is a hint of sweetness on the palate, which coffee and chocolate dominate. There is a nice, warm finish.

OLD ENGINE OIL

HARVIESTOUN BREWERY LTD.

This 6% ABV black ale is just the thing for anyone who appreciates beautifully engineered stuff that used to be made properly. It is a truly great British beer. Old Engine Oil is a smooth and rich and luxurious, with a beautiful velvety mouthfeel. There are flavors of coffee, slightly buttered toffee, dark chocolate, and earthy hops. You may find some mild cherry fruit within the residual sweetness accompanying the roasted flavors that last to the finish. It is thick and pours like old engine oil, but it develops a nicer head and tastes a lot better.

ORIGINAL FLAG PORTER 1825

ELGOOD AND SONS (DARWIN)

Elgood's is a family regional brewery in Wisbech, Cambridgeshire, United Kingdom. The North Brink Brewery was established in 1795 and was purchased by the Elgood family in 1878.

Flag Porter is based on a traditional nineteenth-century British recipe that included yeast that was salvaged from containers or barrels in a ship that sank in the English Channel in 1825. In 1988, several bottles of the brew were obtained from the sunken ship. They were in their original containers, with the wood stoppers and wax seals intact. When opened, the beer was said to taste like wet boots according to the renowned brewer and micro-biologist Dr. Keith Thomas. Upon examining the beer under a microscope, he found that a small percentage of the yeast was still alive. He spent months growing the yeast to brew a porter using an 1850 recipe.

This beer pours jet black with little head or lacing. Coffee and roasty notes come first, followed by a cookie dough–like aroma that also resembles freshly baked brownies. The taste is slightly sweet at first but then evens out. Not a creamy stout, this one is a bit thin, which makes it a good session beer. It is very drinkable, and it's fun to discuss this bit of history in a bottle.

PERNŠTEJN PORTER

PARDUBICE BREWERY

Pernštejn Porter is a premium dark beer. At 8% ABV
it is the strongest Czech beer, with a brewing tradition
dating back to 1890. The beer was brewed for those
who wanted a bigger drinking experience. It has
a dark mahogany color with a medium beige head.
The aroma is roasted malt, caramel, and coffee.
The taste is roasted malt, coffee, caramel,
and some dark cherry. This is a complex,
well-built beer with big taste up front,
nice complexity, and a dry finish.

PORTER

SIERRA NEVADA BREWING CO.

Ken Grossman learned to homebrew from the father of a close friend. From an early age, he was enamored by the sights and smells of the fermenting jugs of bubbling beer, wine, and sake. Originally from Southern California, Ken Grossman fell in love with the Northern California culture and decided to move to Chico. He founded the brewery in 1979.

As history goes, porters were invented as a fortifying drink for the rough-and-tumble working class of London's bustling markets. So Sierra Nevada wanted to keep that in mind, when they brewed it for good folks with calluses on their hands. This is a classic Porter, brewed in the hop-forward American style pours dark brown-black. The head foams nicely, but settles relatively quickly and leaves a nice lacing. There's nice big malt and a hint of sweetness up front and complexity with roasted notes of black coffee and cocoa. The aggressive hops leave a clean, refreshing finish. And at 5.6% ABV, you can drink a few of them.

SIERRA NEVADA®

PORTER

Before Sierra Nevada was a reality, brew recipes and dreaming of starting porter. Made before roasted malts were kitchen roasting barley for our own to this rich, bittersweet and roasted

nights were spent perfecting home-a brewery. One of our favorites was a readily available, we spent time in the malt. This handcrafted dedication led gem that quickly became a classic.

SIX 12 OZ. BOTTLES

PORTER ALON

NEGEV BREWERY

בירה דרומית

**NEGEV
BREWERY**

נגב הינה מבשלות בוטיק דרומית המייצרת
בירה עדייה. ייחודית ועשירה בטעם חרומה.
לצורך בישול הבירה בחרנו את המרכיבים
הטובים ביותר ולייחנו אותה בכל שלבי
ההכנה. לך נשאר רק
ליהנות ממנה...

פורטר אלון - בירה מעורפלת בגוון
שחור עמוק המוויישנת עם שבבי עץ
אלון המעניקים לה מרקם קרמי וטעם
עשיר וקטיפתי. בעלת מרירות נעימה,
ניכוחות וגוף מלא.

יצרן: מבשלות הנגב בע"מ
בקרוב: כפליו 23 ק, גת
www.negevbrewery.coil

רכיבים: מים, לתת (מכל גלוזן)
כשות, שמרים ופחמן דו חמצני

סימון תזונתי ל- 100 מ"ל
אנרגיה (קלוריות): 53

חייב בפקדון 30 א ל

יש לאחסן במקום קרר ויבש.
עדיף להשתמש לפני ך

כשר

Oak Porter   **פורטר אלון**
330 ml | alc. by volume 5%   אלכוהול בנפח 5% מ"ל

since 2008

NEGEV BREWERY

This traditionally styled porter is brewed at the Negev Brewery in Kiryat Gat, Israel, one of that country's leading microbreweries. The brewery opened its current facility in 2010.

This dark black English-style porter is aged with oak shavings, which contribute to its creamy texture and intense rich flavor. It pours black with a big generous head that doesn't stay long but leaves excellent lacing. The beer is creamy and chocolaty. It is characterized by nice roastiness, a light bitterness, and a dominant body.

YEASTIE BOYS

Pot Kettle Black

ALE   6% ALC/VOL   11.2 FL OZ

POT KETTLE BLACK

YEASTIE BOYS

Pot Kettle Black is an award-winning black IPA that some call a hoppy porter. The different names convey the fact that this beer is a contradiction of styles: fresh and hoppy yet dark and rich. Most important, it is a complete original. The New Zealand brewery uses almost the same malt base with every vintage, though recent vintages have seen increases in chocolate and orange. It also has been made with more local Cascade hops and a zesty fistful or ten of imported Styrian Goldings. At 6% ABV, it's very drinkable.

PROPELLER LONDON STYLE PORTER

PROPELLER BREWING COMPANY

Propeller is brewed in Halifax, Nova Scotia. It has won a ton of medals, including two gold medals and three silvers in national and world competitions. It is jet black with a nice head that is an off-white or eggshell color and two fingers high or so. It seemed to last, and there is a nice light creaminess to the head.

It smells really good, with a typical porter scent, almost like a milk scent.

From the first sip it's pretty much everything you look for in a porter: nice and malty but not too heavy. At 5.7 ABV you would think the flavor would be a little too mild, but for a smaller beer it's pretty tasty. You get some of that lactose sweetness, a touch of milk chocolate, a little bit of roasted malt, and maybe chocolate malt.

This is a mild beer that is not too robust but is light enough to drink in the summer. It's a bit sweet like a soda. It's a fairly complex beer that can be sessioned easily as it's extremely drinkable.

CP

RAINCLOUD ROBUST PORTER

FOOLPROOF BREWING COMPANY

Based in Pawtucket, Rhode Island, Foolproof Brewing is the brainchild of Nick Garrison, president and founder, and brewmaster Damase Olsson. Both started out as homebrewers. Demase is a well-traveled, experienced brewer, and the company is serious about good beer.

Raincloud Robust Porter is the perfect "stay at home" brew, according to the team. Dark, smooth, and rich, this big flavorful porter is brewed with chocolate and crystal malts and a subtle blend of European hops. It's a beautiful, easy-drinking beer.

ROBUST PORTER

BRASSERIE DE LA VALLÉE DU GIFFRE

Vallée de Giffre Robust Porter is made in the Rhóne-Alpes in Sixt Fer à Cheval, France. This 4.6% ABV beer has roasted malt aromas mixed with chicory, roasted nuts, and dried fruit. It pours opaque black with a big khaki-colored head. Roasted malt comes right through, as do cocoa and toffee. The hops are grapefruit and pine. The taste is herbal with a slight hint of cloves and other spices. Dark fruits such as cherry and fig also shine through. A nice bitterness balances this beer. It is almost a black IPA, but with a more intense flavor.

SAMUEL ADAMS HOLIDAY PORTER

SAMUEL ADAMS, THE BOSTON BEER COMPANY

Samuel Adams Holiday Porter is a good example of an average porter that is drinker-friendly. It pours to a seemingly black body that is actually a dark shade of maroon when held up to the light. It forms a generous layer of off-white soapy head that dissolves fairly slowly but almost completely and leaves some lacing on the glass. The aroma has a touch of chocolate and vanilla sweetness as well as a general malty scent. It's neither inviting nor off-putting.

Having thoroughly researched this beer before I drank it, I had some expectations. Porters, much like stouts, tend to have a robust palate with chocolate or roasted malts or both, but Holiday Porter did not have much of either. What I noticed up front was faint sour red grape followed by a burnt chocolate finish and a bitter, dry aftertaste. I've encountered these flavors before in Imperial stouts, but they were much more intense. Here they're quite mild. The palate is surprisingly watery, though I did notice and enjoy a general malty sweetness that does not linger but is replaced with a dry aftertaste.

Considering the target audience for this beer, Sam Adams' Holiday Porter hits its target. Even though it doesn't have a lot in the way of big flavor, its drinkability is commendable. It's not surprising that this beer is so smooth since it's so mild. At 5.8% ABV it's just a tad heavier than the average beer drinker may be used to, but it's nothing Joe or Jane Six-Pack couldn't handle. It would work well with dinner, or one could substitute two bottles for dessert.

CP

SAMUEL SMITH TADDY PORTER

SAMUEL SMITH, THE OLD BREWERY

When I think of porters, Samuel Smith Taddy Porter is the beer that comes to mind. To me it embodies the style as it's distinctly different from a stout; it is sweeter and less bitter yet still plenty flavorful. It is seemingly dark black or brown but is actually a deep ruby red that is beautiful when seen in the right light. It forms a large brown frothy head that retains and laces wonderfully. The smell is a distinct sweet cream or dairy, not unlike chocolate milk, and the body isn't too heavy, though it has the robustness of something stronger.

There is an immediate sweetness as the beer hits the tongue, but in a light way, almost an iced coffee liqueur flavor coupled with a hint of dark chocolate and toasted malt. There is a mild but noticeable bitterness through the middle followed by a slight tangy sensation as the palate begins its descent. On the finish there is more sweetness with a slight chocolate milk or other dairy flavor and sensation. Samuel Smith uses well water for its brews, and that might account for the mineral-like taste and sensation. This is a versatile beer; seasoned veterans will enjoy its nuances, and rookies probably will like its drinker-friendly taste.

It is probably the best of the smaller porters. Not only is it delectable, it's ridiculously easy to drink. The mouthfeel is slightly thick, but with a smooth creamy-velvety texture almost as if it were on nitrogen (like Guinness). It goes down as smooth as water, yet it's not tepid. The aftertaste is mostly clean with just a hint of chocolate or coffee that lingers. At only 5% ABV it's impressive for what it's able to accomplish with its smaller stature. It is an ideal pairing with chocolate desserts or can be enjoyed on its own, though 12 ounces is a bit too small of a serving.

CP

...l holiday porter is made for winter - rich
...ning, the way they like it at the North Pole.
...pired by this famous line from a
... children's storybook:

...nta sat on his great butt,
...ing a hardy brew ..."

...you find that amusing, the brewer hastens
...out that in England "butt" refers to a
...sized barrel customarily used for beer
... large barrel, in fact, holding 108
...al gallons. Back in the day it was
... normal thing for a brewery to put
...r up in a large butt for storage.
...nickering, eh?
...ur mind out
... gutter, or
...u will be skip-
...your house
...rely this year.

...orted By:
...lton Brothers
...chertown, MA

Alc. 6% Vol.

Bottle Conditioned

Santa's Butt
~ Winter Porter ~

1 pt. 9
FL. OZ. U.S.
50 cl ℮

GOVERNMENT WA...
THE SURGEON G...
DRINK ALCOHOL...
NANCY BECAUSE...
(2) CONSUMPTI...
IMPAIRS YOUR AB...
MACHINERY, AN...

SANTA'S BUTT

RIDGEWAY BREWING

"A Christmas beer brewed in Oxfordshire has been banned in parts of the United States because it has a picture of Father Christmas on the label," the BBC reported in December of 2006. The illustration for the Santa's Butt label was painted by Massachusetts artist Gary Lippincott. "Officials in the state of New York told English brewers Ridgeway Brewing that the image on bottles of Santa's Butt could encourage underage drinking. The beer, a 6% ABV winter porter, is brewed in South Stoke for the US market. This is not the first time that Ridgeway Brewing has fallen foul of state authorities in the US. Last Christmas two of its beers—Seriously Bad Elf and Warm Welcome—were banned in Connecticut on the same grounds."

How can you not like this beer already? This English porter pours dark with red highlights and a small beige head that leaves behind decent lacing. Roasty malts, coffee, toffee, and some nice grain overtones come across the palate with a nice sweetness that tastes of brown sugar and molasses. Good bitterings make it balanced and complex. It's a great holiday treat!

SARANAC 4059′ PORTER

MATT BREWING COMPANY

Many people are so used to drinking porters that are flavored, Imperial, experimental, or barrel-aged that they've forgotten about the base porter style. Saranac 4059' Porter is indeed "just a porter." There are no bells and whistles, though a few would be nice.

The opaque black body has no visible carbonation. It forms a large brown, fluffy head that is slow to dissipate and leaves plenty of lacing down the glass. There is a classic pub aroma of dark malts and a hint of dairy sweetness.

When you think of a satisfying, passable porter, the palate to Saranac 4059' Porter is exactly what comes to mind. It's a great representation of the style as it shows there's definitely flavor to be found in a fairly simple recipe and a relatively light body. Mild chocolate and vanilla candy flavors up front have a lactoselike sweetness akin to a milk stout, though there's no lactose in this brew according to the description on the brewery's website. There's a surprisingly sharp, dry, but quick hop bite at the apex before it finishes with the classic malty porter taste. You don't get much in the way of coffee except for the bitterness, though the aftertaste is a tad dry. Overall, it's a decent by-the-numbers palate that's not particularly flawed in any way.

Saranac 4059' Porter would be a fantastic starter porter as the mild palate makes it drinker-friendly in combination with the calm, creamy mouthfeel and smooth finish. It is not quite robust enough to pair with food, but it is a fine stand-alone beverage, and at only 5.2% ABV you won't have any trouble drinking a few back-to-back.

CP

SMUTTYNOSE ROBUST PORTER
SMUTTYNOSE BREWING CO.

I drink so many experimental-style beers so often that I forget how good a beer brewed in a classic style can be. Smuttynose Robust Porter is a to-spec robust porter and would hit every note on a Beer Judge Certification Program taste test. It's tasty and well-balanced with an opaque black body and a a large fluffy frothy dark tan head that retains and laces extremely well. The classic dark malty aroma has hints of dairy and milk chocolate and a faint floral scent.

The palate begins with a sweet taste of dark malts, and according to the recipe on the brewery's website, there are quite a lot of them in this brew. There is an interesting combination of milk chocolate, cola, and

Cirque du François Oeuf

maybe a hint of cherry. It becomes a little bitter through the middle with a slightly toasty flavor. This flavor gets stronger toward the end as the Cascade hops make their presence known and impart a slight citrusy or flowery taste. Additional notes of dark chocolate complement the bitterness well.

The word *robust* in a beer's name tends to imply strong flavor and a huge body, but that's not the case here. Though the palate is plenty flavorful, Smuttynose Robust Porter is not intense or intimidating. The mouthfeel is calm and soft with a smooth texture and finish. It does leave a slightly dry aftertaste akin to burnt toast, but it's easily tolerable. For 6% ABV, this beer has the right amount of taste for its weight and is satisfying one serving at a time.

CP

ST. PETER'S OLD-STYLE PORTER

ST. PETER'S BREWERY CO.

St. Peter's is an independent brewery founded in 1996 by John Murphy in what were once agricultural buildings adjacent to St. Peter's Hall near Bungay, Suffolk, England. The brewery produces cask ales, but they are best known for their cold-filtered bottled, organic beers. The brewery also owns a pub in Clerkenwell, London, called The Jerusalem Tavern. The brewery produces around twelve regular beers plus another six seasonals.

This fine, award-winning 5.1% ABV beer is a blend of a mature old ale and a younger light beer, just as a true porter should be. The marriage produces an extremely characterful brew which is dark in color and complex in taste. It pours black with a brown two-finger head. Sweet malt and coffee come right across on the nose. Figs and raisins come across on the palate after the coffee and dark cocoa. The hops are bright and lend a citrusy note to the end of the beer, which actually make it refreshing. Incredibly flavorful! Robust!

STEELHEAD SCOTCH PORTER

MAD RIVER BREWING CO.

Mad River Brewing Co. is a craft brewery based in Blue Lake, California. Mad River aims to produce English-style ales in an environmentally sound manner. In the late seventies, brewmaster Bob Smith, founder of the Humbrewers Guild, dreamed of opening a small brewery specializing in craft beers. Excursions to buy brewing supplies led Bob to Ken Grossman's Homebrew Shop in Chico, California. After Ken shared his plans to build Sierra Nevada Brewing Co. in Chico, Bob became determined to build a craft brewery in Hum-boldt County and began construction in 1989. Mad River has been in business ever since, winning numerous major awards.

This traditionally styled porter has complex malt characteristics balanced with a mild hop profile. Steelhead Scotch Porter is brewed with 2-row pale malt, crystal 70/80, crystal 135/165, chocolate malt, peated malt, Rauch (German smoked malt), and wheat. They then use Willamette as bittering hops and Tettnanger as their finishing hops. The resulting 6.5% ABV porter has a nose and taste of a Scottish ale, with the smoked and peated malts lending a mild smoky flavor.

Pours a dark, dark brown with a khaki head that's at least two fingers, and lingers for a while. Nice lacing. Chocolate and roasted cof-fee come through. A hint of sweetness. But a nice balance provided by the hops. A nice complexity. Easy to drink, with a nice, unique flavor profile.

STORMAKTS PORTER 2008

NÄRKE KULTURBRYGGERI AB

As dark as an afternoon in northern Sweden in the depths of winter, this beer is spectacular to look at in the glass; it grabs your attention and never lets it go. The thick, impenetrably black, and oily-looking body resides under the most impressive cinnamon head I have seen in years. Watching this beer while you give it a whirl is like watching *Avatar* for the first time: visually overwhelming.

The smell is of chocolate powder sprinkled over licorice, slightly overripe prunes, burnt fruitcake, roasted nuts, tar, a touch of pavement, tobacco leaves, and a splash of caffè macchiato. All the aromas cross over into the taste. What should be pointed out is the mouthfeel, with a simultaneous sensation of oiliness and creaminess that's as baffling as it is amazing. The 9.5% ABV is deftly carried with elegance and lightness. This beer has more than enough flavors to keep you happy. Sip it, savor it, and take your time.

This is the second highest rated beer in Sweden, with only its big brother Kaggen Stormaktsporter ahead of it. If you want to experience true beer artistry, get yourself to one of the few pubs in Sweden that sell it and buy a bottle. You shouldn't care how much it costs because it will be worth every single dollar, pound, or öre.

DP

TOKYO BLACK

YO-HO BREWING COMPANY

Tokyo Black is an American Porter–style beer brewed by the Yo-Ho Brewing Company in Nagano-ken Kitasaga-gun, Japan, who produces the most popular craft beers in Japan. In order to separate themselves from the fizzy, light beer that is ubiquitous in Japan and the US, they decided to make American- and British-style beers in cans. Their ultra-smoky yet smooth porter, Tokyo Black, has made a huge impact on craft beer lovers in the US. Big, intense roasted malts and lovely chocolate dominate this light, well-balanced beer. And at 5% ABV, it's easy to drink more than one!

WALKER'S RESERVE PORTER

FIRESTONE WALKER BREWING COMPANY

Making a standard porter that's really impressive is extremely difficult in the craft beer world; it can be done, but these porters are few and far between. That's not to say that everything else is the same or a waste of time. Firestone's Walker's Reserve Porter has everything I want and expect in a porter. It's even unique in certain ways.

The opaque black body forms a remarkably light-tan frothy head. It retains well but doesn't lace the glass much. There is a classic porter aroma as soon as you pop the cap, with plenty of dark fruit, a slight black licorice scent, and minor syrupy notes as well.

It comes as no surprise that Walker's Reserve Porter is noticeably hoppy for the style; it is made by a California brewery, after all. What's also notable is that it seems to be a little sweeter and fruitier than most beers of the style. There is a distinct Dr Pepper–like flavor to the palate: dark cherry or prune fruitiness combined with a malty sweetness. It doesn't go overboard, though. The palate is still under control; it's not a syrup bomb at all. There's prominent dry bitterness through the middle with a bit of a coffee flavor and bitterness on the finish and momentarily in the aftertaste. There's a residual toffee and black licorice flavor as well, but at no point does it become cloying. It does have the standard porter cough medicine–like component, and the abundance of hops seems a little overdone. Still, it works as a standard porter with a bit of eccentricity.

What makes this beer even more enjoyable is how drink-able it is. The mouthfeel is a little thicker than most, but it's not spastic or sticky, which is impressive considering how sweet the palate is. The texture is creamy and soft, which accounts for the almost ridiculously smooth finish (once it warms up, the hops begin to linger). The aftertaste is somewhat dry but clean and tolerable with no cloying presence. The fact that it is is only 5.2% ABV is amazing, as you usually don't tend to get so much flavor out of something this light.

CP

WASATCH POLYGAMY PORTER

WASATCH BEERS, SCHIRF BREWING COMPANY

Wasatch Beers of the Schirf Brewing Company was formed when Greg Schirf went from Milwaukee, America's beer capital, to Utah only to discover that his newly adopted home state did not have a brewery of its own. In 1986, Schirf opened the first brewery in the resort town of Park City and named his beers after the majestic Wasatch Mountains. Over the next several years, Wasatch found a friendly rival in Squatters (Salt Lake Brewing Company), but soon they joined resources and now share a brewery located in Salt Lake City.

Polygamy Porter is a dark, 4%-ABV, award-winning, medium-bodied ale offering chocolate and malty flavors up front that fade into a slightly dry, silky smooth finish. A lighter-bodied porter style that is easy drinking. Their tagline "Why have just one" is apropos.

BALTIC PORTERS

An unsung also-ran next to the more popular IPA and Russian Imperial stout, Baltic porter is another style that was born from a growing continental thirst for English ale. Originally brewed as a bigger, bolder take on the traditional English porter, the antecedents of Baltic porters were conceived in the late 1700s when there was a need for strong porters that could survive the trip to the countries of the Baltic Rim. However, that's only the prelude. The real story of Baltic porter starts in the nineteenth century, when the imported strong porters proved so popular that enterprising Baltic brewers started making their own. The birth of locally brewed versions of the porter came with an important change: Influenced by German lager brewing, the continental brewers switched from traditional top-fermenting ale yeast to bottom-fermenting lager yeast. In the style, you can expect the chocolate flavors present in many porters to mingle with fruity lager notes and the herbal tang of European hops. It's all backed up by a prominent but not-at-all-unpleasant warming alcohol bite, certainly a welcome aspect for those cold Nordic winters. Sinebrychoff, which opened in Finland in 1819, was the first brewery in the region to specialize in this style. Their porter (still available today), brewed with lager malts and German hops in an attempt to ape an English style, is a great synthesis of the brewing traditions that birthed the Baltic porter.

Like traditional porter, Baltic porter is a style that saw its popularity wane in favor of stouts in the twentieth century. This problem was only exacerbated by the Iron Curtain of the cold war, which locked the style away from many westerners. Nowadays, however, exports of the beer once again flow across national borders, and some enterprising American brewers have taken up brewing the style.

ALASKAN BALTIC PORTER ALE

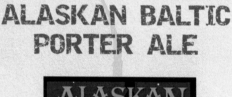

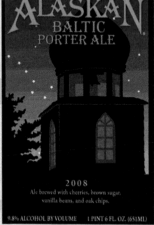

ALASKAN BREWING CO.

Alaskan Brewing is known for its Smoked Porter, and why not? The beer's won more golds than Michael Phelps, impressing so many judges that they've basically made it the standard by which all other smoked porters are judged. However, there is another porter that flows down like oil on a pipeline from the land of Seward's Folly that's bigger, better, bolder, and Baltic.

Baltic porter is a traditional style that was developed by the British in the 1800s for export to their buddies in the Russian court. I hear you can see Russia from Juneau, thus Alaskan is the perfect brewery to lead the way with this style. They make theirs with dark cherries, brown sugar, and hand-scraped vanilla beans before extended aging on chips of toasted French oak.

The Baltic porter is an interesting breed because although it's a porter in name and flavor, it's not technically actually an ale. All Baltic porters are lagers, meaning they're brewed with a strain of yeast that ferments for longer periods at colder temperatures; this contributes a cleaner, crisper flavor to the brew.

Pour Alaskan Baltic Porter Ale into a snifter. From afar, the deep burgundy liquid seems to pulse with darkness, yet holding it to the light reveals surprising clarity. Big, cocoa powder–colored bubbles crackle and pop.

As you take in the aroma, you may picture a large plate precariously balanced on a stick. On one end there are piles of dark chocolate and maraschino cherry syrup; on the other, buttery oak. French vanilla ice cream, cocoa nibs, and high-proof brandy take up whatever space is left at the edges. Alaskan Baltic Porter is that plate. The proportions of the ingredients are perfect, keeping the plate perfectly balanced. It doesn't get better than this.

In the flavor, sugary dark fruits, unmasked alcohol, and vanilla combine to give the beer an almost bourbon-aged quality. Brown sugar, milk chocolate, and dark sweet cherries are also there, and a smooth smokiness permeates the background. A complaint would be that the malts are a little too thin to support the adjuncts and could be kicked up a notch. The body, however, is a silk blanket. Soft carbonation tingles the tongue inside the supple liquid while ethanol heat warms the nostrils and throat.

ZF

BALTIC PORTER

STALLHAGENS BRYGGERI AB

With this beer you can hear the head as it froths into life during the pour and then fizzle like one of those firework sparklers as it vanishes in seconds, leaving nothing behind except an almost pitch-black flat-looking beer that is not particularly pretty.

It tastes of milk chocolate and cling-film, with roasted nuts, brown bread, faint cigar ash, and treacle. It's nice, but like the island it comes from, it's somewhere in between one thing and another.

It is almost flat in the mouth, as though the effort of the pour ripped most of the CO_2 from the beer. There is some coffee-creamer lactic action over milk chocolate and prunes, along with a medium-sweet slightly under-weight body and a mild lightly smoked bitter finish.

A tame Baltic porter like this adds depth to a meat. It also pairs well with boiled ham with mustard.

The name *Stallhagen* comes from the area the brewery occupies in Åland, which was used by the King Gustav Vasa in the beginning of the sixteenth century while he was visiting the island. His residence had stables (*stall*) and an enclosed pasture (*hage*), hence the name. The brewery was founded in 1865 and was active until 1938. Some sixty-six years later, in 2004, it reopened.

DC

BALTIKA #6 PORTER

BALTIKA BREWERIES

As the name of the brewery would lead one to believe, this is a great example of a Baltic porter. It pours black with a tan head. The nutty nose has a lingering aroma of raisins. With spicy hops and a slight burn, the alcohol in this 7% ABV beer is by no means hidden, but it doesn't overpower the flavor. There are also notes of molasses, brown sugar, and pine that balance out the flavor. The carbonation is on the high side, and the body remains smooth.

BLACK BOSS PORTER
BOSS BROWAR WITNICA

Black Boss Porter is a hidden gem. This is an authentic Old World–style Baltic porter that's very flavorful, remarkably drinkable, and dirt-cheap. It's easy to forget or just not know how good obscure beers from out-of-the-way countries can be.

This porter from Poland has a deep mahogany, ruby-red color that is nearly black. It forms a large, tan froth that lasts and leaves a nice lacing. The nose has confectionery notes of toffee and scorched caramel as well as a subtle but noticeable alcohol presence.

Baltic porters have a certain quality that makes them stand out from other strong porters and Imperial stouts. The flavor is akin to a beefy brown ale with a rich toffee and peanut brittle taste. Caramel is also noticeable, though not quite as prominent. Usually, beers this big tend to be quite hoppy for balance, though this one is not noticeably bitter. The alcohol seems to override whatever hop character there may be, imparting some heat but also some sweet, liqueurlike flavors of dark cherry and chocolate. The aftertaste is quite clean and in no way cloying. This is a great example, perhaps the best example, of the style.

As if the taste wasn't good enough, the delivery seals the deal. The mouthfeel is calm, soft, tepid, and thick but in no way sticky. It goes down silky smooth but is difficult to sip, as it probably should be. The 9.4% ABV makes itself known as it imparts gentle warmth throughout the swig. One could call it a tad distracting, but it's in no way annoying.

CARNEGIE PORTER

CARLSBERG GROUP

The Carlsberg Group is a Danish brewing company that was founded in 1847 by J. C. Jacobsen. The company's flagship brand is Carlsberg Beer (named after Jacobson's son Carl), but it also brews Tuborg, Kronen-bourg, Somersby cider, Belgian Grimbergen abbey beers, Russia's best selling Baltika beers, as well more than five hundred local beers. According to Carlsberg, this Baltic porter was first introduced in 1836. It was originally brewed by D. Carnegie & Co. However, strong beers were banned in Sweden from 1923 to 1956, and the beer disappeared. The 5.5% ABV original recipe was reintroduced in 1985 as a beer fermented with both top and bottom yeast. In 1993, the yeast was changed to a single bottom-fermenting strain. In 2009, the label design and name was changed from "Carnegie Stark-Porter" to "Carnegie Porter." Carnegie Porter is the oldest registered trademark still in use in Sweden. Carlsberg, together with Brooklyn Brewery opened the brewery New Carnegie in the Hammarby area of Stockholm. The brewery takes its name from Carnegie Porter, but that beer will continue to be brewed in Falkenberg.

Carnegie Porter is made with pilsner malt 75%, caramel malt 12.5%, and color malt 12.5%. The porter is then aged for two years, where it continues to ferment during storage, much in the same way as wine does. Also like wine, it will continue to improve as it ages. After about two years of storage the beer becomes smoother and more balanced, but the flavor becomes richer and more complex.

This Baltic porter pours dark brown with red tinge. The beige head come up and dissipates quickly while chocolate and coffee come through in the taste with a nice finish. Complex and well-balanced, this beer is sessionable considering the low ABV.

GONZO IMPERIAL PORTER

FLYING DOG BREWERY

Gonzo Imperial Porter is a Baltic porter–style beer brewed by Flying Dog Brewery in Frederick, Maryland. It is big, bold, and beautiful like the man it was brewed in honor of: Dr. Hunter S. Thompson.

In 1990, George Stranahan opened the Flying Dog Brewpub in Aspen, Colorado. In 1994, along with longtime friend Richard McIntyre, Flying Dog opened a 50-barrel brewery in Denver, Colorado, from which its ales were distributed to more than thirty-one states. In May 2006, Flying Dog acquired the Wild Goose brand when it purchased the Frederick Brewing Company in Frederick, Maryland, and in January 2008, all production was moved to the Maryland facility. Although the headquarters remains in Denver, the Maryland location is where close to 70% of Flying Dog Beer is brewed.

This beer was complicated to brew, as its complexity shows. They used special malts such as 120L Caramel, black, and chocolate and included hops such as Warrior, Northern Brewer, and Cascade. They also used two yeast strains. The effort paid off with gold medals at the Great American Beer Festival in 2009 and the World Beer Cup in 2009.

There is no question that this is a web favorite, with hundreds of reviews online. It is one of the holy grails of the beer geek world.

This is a dark, almost black beer with a dark mocha head. The head seems to last a good long time and leaves excellent lace as you drink it down. The nose is incredible, giving off vanilla, caramel, toffee, coffee, licorice, and dark chocolate. Even with a sizable 9.2% ABV, there is not a lot of alcohol on the nose. Some nuttiness also comes across.

Roasted chocolate, coffee, and vanilla malt all come across in a big milky, almost chocolate shake kind of way. There is a nice bite from the hops, but this melds nicely with the body of the beer. It stands up but does not overpower. Some graham cracker comes through. There is a nice hint of bitterness, but again, this is well within the style. There is also a nice hint of sweetness, but within the confines of the overall structure.

This is an excellent example of the style, with great body and flavor.

The brewery also does a limited release of barrel-aged Gonzo Imperial, which though difficult to obtain, is well worth it.

CP

GRAND BALTIC PORTER

GARRISON BREWING COMPANY

At 9% ABV, this is the Baltic porter in this East Coast brewery's arsenal, but along with the power comes plenty of subtlety. The dark auburn chestnut-hued brew pours with a thin off-white head. On the nose, it provides an enticing combination of dried fruit and coffee. On the palate, there's plenty of dark coffee, chocolate, and even a hint of tobacco and leather, along with a bitter finish. Although it's a touch thinner-bodied for some tastes, it's a brew that's well worth seeking out.

JR

GOLD 2011   GOLD 2009

Enjoy this smooth, complex lager brewed coffee-black with a rich molasses & toffee profile balanced by specialty German hops. Luxurious on a cold Baltic night. Skål!

PRESIDENT

INGREDIENTS: Water, Barley Malt, Hops, Molasses & Dates.
INGRÉDIENTS: Eau, Malt d'Orge, Houblon, Melasse & Dattes.

Contains Gluten / Contient du Gluten
OG: 22P IBUs: 31 Colour: 29 L

www.garrisonbrewing.com

6 28432 63159 5

PREMIUM   ☆   SPÉCIALE

Grand

BALTIC

PORTER

Extra Strong Beer   Bière Extra Forte

500 ml
Produced by / Produit par

9.0% alc./vol.
Halifax, NS

Return for Refund where Applicable / Retourner pour Remboursement là où il y a lieu

GRANDE CUVÉE PORTER BALTIQUE

LES TROIS MOUSQUETAIRES

Grand Cuvée Porter Baltique is a Baltic porter beer made by Les Trois Mousquetaires, a brewery in Brossard, Quebec, Canada. This award-winning beer is one of the darlings of the brewing world. Microbrasserie Les Trois Mousquetaires (The Three Musketeers Microbrewery) was founded in 2004, and although it began with a focus on traditional German-style beers, it has applied a North American treatment; they're not afraid to mix tradition with creative interpretation.

Baltic porter is named for its history of being sent to and later brewed in countries bordering the Baltic Sea (Finland, Poland, Sweden, Estonia, and Lithuania). Derived from English porters but influenced by Russian Imperial stouts, the style was produced in the United Kingdom and shipped across the North Sea.

This beer has a complex aroma with prunes, plums, and other dark fruits, leather, tobacco, chocolate, caramel, wood, and a hint smoke. This is a big beer, with molasses, brown sugar, roasted coffee, mocha, chocolate, cherries, and dates all coming across on the palate. There is a nice spicy ending. The rich flavors finish with loads of toffee, fruit, and bitter chocolate, but the taste isn't sticky sweet. This is an exceptional beer.

KAMARADE BALTIC PORTER

SCHILLING BEER CO.

John Lenzini was in graduate school at Purdue University in West Lafayette, Indiana, in 1997, when he first started brewing beer in yellow buckets. He convinced his life-long friend Jeff Cozzens to drink the stuff, and there began their dream of opening a brewery. Lenzi honed his craft for sixteen years, traveling to beer meccas such as Germany and Austria, before teaming up with Jeff, Jeff's brothers Matt and Stuart, and the scion of the Cozzens family, Dr. Bruce. Together, they launched Schilling Beer Co. in Littleton, New Hampshire, naming the brewery in honor Cozzens' grandfather, Dr. Richard J. Schilling.

This is a deep, dark black beer, with a lovely cascading, foamy head, and big flavor. Despite a hefty 9% ABV, this beer has tons of flavor outside the alcohol. It's an incredible example of a Baltic Porter.

KOMES PORTER BALTYCKI

BROWAR FORTUNA

Browar Fortuna still produces beer the way it was brewed in the nineteenth century. It is among the few establishments in Europe that have returned to using traditional open fermentation vats. After the addition of yeast, the beer ferments in a natural way, meaning it is not subjected to artificial acceleration or excessive pressure or temperature. In these conditions, the yeast is happier, as it has ideal conditions to propagate, endowing the beer with a unique, fresh flavor and a rich aroma.

Komes Porter, brewed in Miłosław, Poland, reflects the history of brewing, harking back to the eighteenth-century tradition of brewing porters in the Baltic states. At their prime, Baltic porters accounted for one-third of the market, which is the best evidence of their popularity. Fortuna offers a well-balanced, dark strong beer with a distinct flavor. Slow fermentation at low temperatures in open vats coupled with long (at least three months) maturation results in the beer's character and complete, complex nature. The bouquet matures further in the bottle.

This beer pours black with a small head and only a little lacing. Roasted coffee, roasted malts, caramel, and spices come through. The hint of sweetness is balanced with good bitterness, and it finishes relatively dry. This is definitely a sipping beer: big, rangy, and delicious.

LOST RIVER BALTIC PORTER

BELLWOODS BREWERY

Bellwoods Brewery is a small craft brewpub and retail store in downtown Toronto, Canada. This small-production-capacity brewery opened its doors in April 2012. The brewery impressed when its Baltic porter won a gold medal at the Canadian Brewing Awards in 2012. It's a big, earthy brew. The color is deep brown but not black. Chocolaty, roasty, and slightly sweet rather than bitter, this beer packs huge flavor. The nose has nice dark red fruits, like a slightly sweet dark chocolate. Incredibly well-balanced even at 8.5% ABV and never cloying or overpowering, this is a Baltic porter you may want to sample year-round.

JR

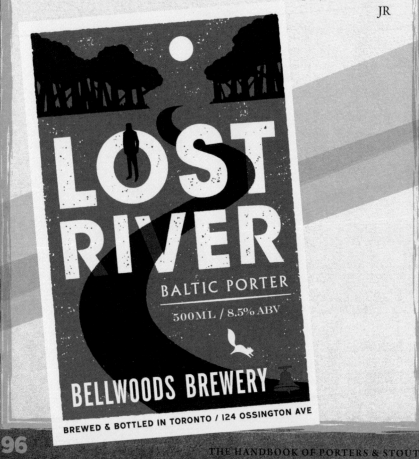

MØRKE PUMPERNICKEL PORTER

BEER HERE

Although the body of this Baltic porter is brown to black like a Coke, the nose is far from sweet. Instead, it is bready, with a spicy tang from rye on the grain bill and slightly earthy hops underneath. The nose doesn't lie; this beer tastes like rye bread. Where one would expect the dark flavors, one gets a spicy rye with bittersweet chocolate and toasted nuts. This is a very interesting and unique member of the porter family that comes in at 7.5% ABV.

JC

OKOCIM PORTER

BROWAR OKOCIM S.A., CARLSBERG GROUP

Okocim Porter is a Baltic porter–style beer brewed by Browar Okocim S.A. in Brzesko, Poland, part of the Carlsberg Group. Okocim Porter is a brew aimed at beer connoisseurs. It has a nice blend of several special malts, including Munich, caramel, and roasted, and two-month maturing process. The simplest way to review it is to say that it reminds one of a sweeter-styled Guinness. A big, beige head develops and then laces nicely. Robust roasted coffee, cocoa, and caramel dominate the palate with a cedary finish. Beautifully balanced and complex, a unique version of a Baltic porter.

PORTER

NØGNE Ø

Nøgne Ø was founded late in 2002 by Gunnar Wiig and Kjetil Jikiun. The brewery name, Nøgne Ø, is old Danish for "Naked Isle." It was selected from a well-known nineteenth century Norwegian poem called "Terje Vigen" by Henrik Ibsen, who worked for a time as an apprentice pharmacist in Grimstad. The brewery creates a range of beers—in all more than thirty-two varieties. In 2009, about 50% of the production was exported around the world to Denmark, Sweden, Finland, Belgium, Netherlands, Italy, Spain, the US, Canada, Australia, and Japan.

Nøgne Ø Porter is made with Maris Otter, Munich, caramel, black malt, and chocolate malt, Centennial, and Northern Brewer hops, and English ale yeast. The resulting beer is a 7% ABV that pours dark brown-black, with big notes of coffee and dried dark fruit.

PORTERIS

ALDARIS

Started by a Bavarian expatriate
in 1865, Aldaris, which is now
owned by the Carlsberg Group,
is one of the largest breweries in
the Baltic states. It now produces
over seventeen different varieties
of beer, mostly incredibly light lagers
that are popular but unadventurous.
More exciting is Porteris, a traditional Baltic porter that does
the region proud. In a market
that's seen increasing growth
from small "craft breweries"
(13% of the market in Latvia is
accounted for by local independent
breweries), Porteris is the only selection in the Aldaris portfolio that holds
a candle to those better-made beers.

If you're used to the deep brown,
nearly black hues of some other Baltic
porters, Porteris will seem surprisingly light.
The porter pours the lighter brown of a
traditional English brown ale, accompanied
by that style's familiar nutty and caramel aroma.
Despite these light forebears, Porteris is satisfy-
ingly potent. The caramel sweetness of the malt
is married with surprising vanilla notes; it's easy-
drinking but definitely shows its nearly 7% ABV.
The burnt bite of roasted barley, so often used to
mask imperfections, peeks in only at the end.

In 2012, Aldaris introduced Porteris Ekskluzīvais,
a version of Porteris that is aged for twelve months.

JC

PORTICUS LEIPZIGER DOPPEL-PORTER

GASTHAUS & GOSEBRAUEREI BAYERISCHER BAHNHOF

Housed in the oldest standing rail station in Germany, the Gasthaus & Gosebrauerei (guesthouse and Gose brewery) Bayerischer Bahnhof is best known for the beer style that's in its name: Gose. The uniquely salty beer is just one of a number of regional German beer styles that nearly disappeared over the last few centuries. Despite the name, the Gosebrauerei isn't a one-trick pony. Bayerischer Bahnhof brews a few curious styles, among them is this unique and strong porter (7% ABV) that fermented with the same yeast early British brewers used to sour their porters.

After an open primary fermentation, *Brettanomyces* is added for a secondary fermentation, and the Porticus's nose has that yeast's slightly sour tang. There's a bit of leather in the aroma and lots of dark fruit. The taste is a bit like an intentionally soured bock. The flavors drinkers expect from a dark German wheat beer—currants, toasted grain, and chocolate—are all present and come out big as the beer warms. Instead of clove and banana wheat flavors, the Porticus has a distinctly Brett, earthy flavor. Traditional porters often have some intentionally soured beer added to give a bit of a tang, and the Porticus brings that funkiness to the foreground.

JC

POTHOLE PORTER

HALF PINTS BREWING CO.

Half Pints Brewing, founded in August 2006 in Winnipeg, Manitoba, Canada, is a small-batch brewer, producing 1,000 liters per batch. Brewmaster David Rudge starts his day by grinding malted barley in a two-roller grain mill. This grist is transported by auger to the brewhouse, where it is mixed with hot brewing liquor (water) to form a mash. The mash looks almost like a 200-kilogram bowl of porridge. For specialty beers in 650-milliliter bottles, they pull out their original hand bottler and fill the bottles one at a time. They take this very seriously.

This Baltic porter is a big, saucy beer that packs a lot of flavor. It is a nearly black beer that has a ring that is almost red where the beer meets the glass. Roasty coffee and burnt bread dominate, and there is a big creamy head. There is bittersweet coffee and red fruit, including dark cherry or chocolate-covered cherries, but none of it is as sweet as one might imagine. The ABV is a robust 7.9%, but it never overpowers.

SINEBRYCHOFF PORTER

OY SINEBRYCHOFF AB, CARLSBERG GROUP

Sinebrychoff Brewery is a Finnish brewery and soft drinks company. It was founded in 1819 in Helsinki, Finland, by Russian merchant Nikolai Sinebrychoff, and is one of the largest breweries in Finland today. It has since become part of the Carlsberg Group.

The Sinebrychoff brewery, now located in Kerava, is the oldest brewery in Northern Europe. Their most notable products are their Koff brand of lager and Sinebrychoff Porter.

Men's Journal wrote of this classic 7.2% ABV Baltic porter, "Mud-black and deeply satisfying, this 53-year-old Finnish recipe sets the international standard by which all other Baltic porters—extra-strong dark ales originally intended for shipment over long sea voyages—are judged." They're 100% right! Pours dark brown-black, with a tan head that settles but leaves decent lacing. A thick, chewy porter brimming with coffee, toffee, raisins, and prunes with sweetness balanced by bitterness for a classic ending. Complex, the taste lingers. A highly acclaimed beer by beer aficionados around the world. Amazing.

TSARINA ESRA IMPERIAL PORTER
BROUWERIJ DE MOLEN

Menno Olivier started Brouwerij de Molen, and after more than a decade of brewing, he is very proud of his company. He started as a homebrewer in his own kitchen years ago. After a year of learning the trade with a Dutch brewer from Westmaas, he started brewing as a professional.

Tsarina Esra Imperial Porter is actually classified as a Baltic porter. It pours dark brown with hints of red. A thick head of cappuccino-colored foam dissipates slowly, leaving a pretty wall of lace. Coffee, fresh baked brown bread, raisins, fig, and cocoa all come through. Plum pudding comes across on the palate with an explosion of dark cherries, prunes, plums, raisins, and brown sugar and a hint of fig. A nice touch of coffee also comes through. An incredible experience.

ŻYWIEC PORTER

ŻYWIEC BREWERY

Żywiec Brewery was founded in 1852 in Żywiec, Poland, which then was part of Austria-Hungary. It was nationalized after World War II. Grupa Żywiec S.A. consists of five main breweries. The Dutch Heineken Group (Heineken International B.V.) owns 61% of the shareholdings and has control over major operations. Production of this porter was moved to Bracki Bowar, a sister brewery, in 2004.

Żywiec Porter, a Baltic porter that is pronounced "je-vi-ets," is a dark, strong beer brewed according to the traditional recipe from 1881, with Munich malt and special malts for caramel and color plus aromatic hops. It's a big beer, coming in at 9.5% ABV, but is very flavorful and complex; the finish is excellent. This is a great example of a Baltic porter.

OTHER PORTERS

Porter was near extinction in the twentieth century, but it has recovered with aplomb. Beyond the tried-and-true English and Baltic (and, to a degree, American) takes on the classic style, a number of cockeyed looks at porter have arisen. Given the longstanding ambiguity that surrounds the definition of porter, it's not a surprise that all kinds of brewers brew all kinds of porters, stretching the term to fit dark brews of all stripes. Many of these apply the stylistic tweaks popular in stouts such as adding adjuncts like chocolate, coffee, and vanilla, or aging the ale in whiskey barrels. The body of a good porter, somewhere between the light sweetness of a brown ale and with the density of a stout, provides a great stage on which to spotlight these flavors. The same goes for smoked porters, where campfire smoke marries perfectly with porter's roast character. There are also "Imperial" porters, a naming trend seen across all styles that basically means "more so"—more hops, more malt, more alcohol, more everything.

ALASKAN SMOKED PORTER

ALASKAN BREWING CO.

When Marcy and Geoff Larson started the Alaskan Brewing Co. in 1986, they were among a handful of small so-called craft breweries in the United States and the first in Alaska since Prohibition. Despite the logistical challenges of brewing in Juneau (surrounded by ice and sea and accessible only by boat and plane), the tiny brewery soon found success with its flagship Alaskan Amber. It has gone on to win multiple awards and a cult following for its brews, especially Alaskan Smoked Porter.

First brewed in 1988, Alaskan Smoked Porter was one of the first smoked porters produced in the United States. The malts used in the brew are dried over Alaskan alder, which gives the porter its distinctive smoky flavor. The beer pours pitch black with a slight head, and the campfire smoke aroma dominates the nose. Woody alder smoke and dark chocolate flavors play across the tongue, with some notes of coffee and dark fruit in the background. Alaskan Brewing suggests that its Smoked Porter is a good beer for cellaring, and it certainly is; in older vintages, the in-your-face smoke fades and plum and cherry come to the fore, making for a different but still satisfying experience with 6.5% ABV.

JC

ALTA GRACIA COFFEE PORTER

OTTER CREEK BREWING/WOLAVER'S

Some of the best coffee beers tend to be Imperial stouts, but a good alternative is a coffee porter. One of the best of that style is Wolaver's Alta Gracia Coffee Porter, a well-balanced, full-flavored coffee porter that's tasty and easy to drink.

This beer has an opaque black body. It forms a small tan soapy head that quickly fizzles away like a soda and doesn't leave much lacing. There is a distinct coffee aroma as soon as the cap on the bottle is popped. Medium roasty notes are quickly evident.

One thing you notice about non-Imperial coffee porters and stouts is that the coffee flavor seems to fade fast. The first swig of Wolaver's Alta Gracia Coffee Porter provides a lot of roasty coffee and roasted barley flavors, but the coffee seems to homogenize with the rest of the palate rather quickly. It's a lovely bittersweet taste of authentic coffee and vanilla creamer (the beer is brewed with vanilla beans). There is more of the same through the middle, with a burst of bitterness on the finish.

Oddly, there is a slight vegetal character in the aftertaste. It's easily overlooked and not distracting unless you concentrate on it. You'll enjoy the coffee and general sweet flavors of this beer. It's got a straightforward palate, but the tastes work quite well in the end.

You'll be surprised by the mouthfeel and body of this beer. It is on the thinner, less carbonated side, but that enables it to be comfortable in the mouth and leads to a smooth finish. You'll also be surprised to find that Alta Gracia Coffee Porter is only 5% ABV, as it seems quite robust for the weight. You could drink two for dessert and not feel guilty about it.

CP

COCONUT PORTER

MAUI BREWING CO.

A brewery operating in Hawaii faces unique benefits and challenges. On the one hand, you're based in a tourist mecca with an audience looking for thirst-quenching beer. On the other hand, you're separated from most brewing resources and supplies by an ocean.

Because of this, or perhaps in reaction to it, Maui Brewing Company founder Garrett Marrero has endeavored to create a local culture for craft beer on Maui. Founded in 2005, the brewery sources as much material as possibly locally and is fiercely proud of its local roots. Marrero often stresses the fact that although other brands (namely Kona) traffic in the "brand" of Hawaii, his actually is brewed there. Maui Brewing has even gone so far as to create Maui Homebrew Club, a homebrew and beer enthusiast's club, with friends of the brewery. Many Maui beers, such as the Lemongrass Saison and Mana Wheat, use local Maui ingredients.

Among all the tropical ingredients that tickle Maui drinkers' palates, my favorite is coconut. It's an ingredient that blends perfectly into the taste of dark beer, particularly the sweetness of porter.

Brewed with six varieties of malted barley, hops, and hand-toasted coconut, Maui's CoCoNut Porter makes the case for dark beer as a dessert in a glass. The porter hits the nose with milk chocolate and coconut as soon as the can is opened and pours a tawny brown with a billowy head. On the palate, it's a silky mix of tropical coconut and sweet, rather than bitter, chocolate. In fact, the brew brings to mind Hershey's "Indescribably Delicious" chocolate-and-coconut Mounds candy bar. There's a touch of hoppy bitterness in the finish, but sweetness rules the day here with a 6% ABV. It would be easy to dismiss a Hawaiian coconut beer as a touristy gimmick, but that's a mistake you'll make only if you haven't tried this beer. This is a well-crafted brew, and the unique inclusion harmonizes rather than clashes with the traditional porter.

JC

FOUR PEAKS PUMPKIN PORTER

FOUR PEAKS BREWING COMPANY

In Arizona, there isn't much indication when the seasons change, but in the fall people know that Pumpkin Porter has arrived.

Pumpkin Porter's eponymous ingredient is added to the brew in the form of pumpkin puree, but this wasn't always the case. Long ago, according to Four Peaks owner-brewer Andy Ingram, the brewery used jack-o'-lanterns that had survived Halloween night. Brewers carved the gourds into manageable slices, roasted them in the restaurant's pizza ovens, and added them to the mash, a task that became nightmarish as they increased batch size to meet demand.

The puree that the brewery uses now, Ingram says, is a godsend, especially since Four Peaks produces more than 400 barrels of Pumpkin Porter a year. A batch that big would require lugging around 70 or 80 large pumpkins.

Ingram says plans were in place to employ Four Peaks' canning line to package a portion of Pumpkin Porter for on-the-go consumption, but the approval process for the labels took too long. Alas, it remains a draft-only beer for now.

The brew darkens its glass in shades of mahogany while a thin yet foamy head the color and consistency of cappuccino froth decorates the container with spatters of lace.

In the decade they've been brewing Pumpkin Porter, Four Peaks has never altered the malt bill. The spices that make their way into the boil—nutmeg, ginger, cinnamon, and allspice—also have remained unchanged for the last several years, but a spice's strength can vary from year to year, producing noticeable changes in a beer's flavor even when the recipe stays the same. In fact, the aroma seems sweeter and spicier than it was in years past. Sugary pumpkin puree takes a backseat to standard pie spices—cinnamon, nutmeg, allspice—and cocoa powder and bubble gum make up the background.

The flavor adds smooth, dark malts to the fall seasonings. Crumbled chocolate mixes with cinnamon and graham cracker in the front, and the swallow brings a sweet blast of pumpkin, bubble gum, and chocolate. Carbonation dances on the tongue, the body is smooth and soft, and lingering notes of toasted pie crust and roasted pumpkin complete the ensemble.

Those looking for a faceful of pumpkin pie will be disappointed. The pumpkin flavor is negligible, which brewers say is what the people asked for. It won't wow you with pumpkin flavor; it'll wow you with subtlety and with the way you'll have downed several glasses without realizing it.

Of course, you could go the obvious route and have Pumpkin Porter alongside an old-fashioned slice of pumpkin pie, but with its sweet malt and interesting array of spices, this brew also would go well with poultry. Try it against some gamy

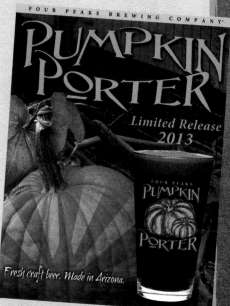

duck, allowing the beer's spice to accent the piquant meat, or get some dark meat turkey for a Thanksgiving-style taste cornucopia.

ZF

LAST SNOW PORTER

FUNKY BUDDHA BREWERY

Funky Buddha Brewery's comes from unexpected beginnings. In 2007, Ryan Sentz purchased R & R Tea Bar in an unassuming stretch of strip malls on Federal Highway in Boca Raton, Florida. What began as a hookah and tea bar, expanded into a lounge serving some of the best craft beers around. He soon outgrew the space and in September 2010, Sentz and his crew raised a glass and toasted the all-new and much bigger Funky Buddha Lounge & Brewery, located farther up Federal Highway.

Last Snow is a beer that Funky Buddha says is near and dear to their hearts. It is a 6.3-%-ABV porter brewed with white chocolate and coconut. With flavors of coconut, coffee, and white chocolate, Last Snow tastes is the incarnation of indulgence in a glass. What an amazing taste treat, with great balance and complexity. It pours a hazy brown and has a beige head, chocolate nose with coffee, cocoa, toffee, and of course coconut across the palate. Nice bitterness keeps the beer honest on the finish. A highly acclaimed beer, and world-class quality. Impressive!!!

LIMFJORD PORTER

THISTED BRYGHUS

Limfjord Porter, commonly referred to LFP, is a beer from Thisted Bryghus in Denmark. This Baltic porter is brewed using a mixture of malts (pilsner malt, smoked malt, caramel malt, and dark malt) and English licorice. It was originally made by a brewery called Urban in Aalborg, Denmark, where the 7.9% ABV recipe was developed during the seventies. When Urban closed in 1986, the Limfjord Porter name was bought by brewmaster Peter Klemmensen at Thisted Bryghus. Production of Limfjord Porter was thus resumed in 1997.

The beer is hazy opaque black-brown that pours a two-finger, tan to beige head that hangs around for a while. Roasted malt, bittersweet dark chocolate, coffee, cocoa, brown bread, raisin, molasses, licorice, and some other spices come across the palate.

MAPLE BACON
COFFEE PORTER

FUNKY BUDDHA BREWERY

There's nothing like a breakfast at a dinner, and that's kind of like what you get in a glass of Maple Bacon Coffee Porter. It's a complex beer with a multitude of flavors at play. It pours opaque black, brown with a frothy, khaki head. Aromas of spicy, grade B maple syrup, coffee, and cream flow out of the glass. It is thinner than you might be expecting given the aromas, but it's still rich and creamy, and the mouthfeel is big and filling. Waves of sweet malt, toffee, and roast waft off the glass, and is that a hint of smoke? The maple syrup flavor pleasantly lingers. This is a fantastic, world-class beer.

MEANTIME CHOCOLATE PORTER

MEANTIME BREWING COMPANY LIMITED

The Meantime Brewing Company based in Greenwich, England, has an excellent reputation around the world. This coffee porter with a 6.5% ABV is a well-respected version of the chocolate porter. They use four roasted malts to get the incredible natural mocha flavors used to brew this rich, dark beer. As the beer is aging, they add real chocolate morsels while it matures. The results are incredible. With great flavor and complexity, this beer is very well-balanced and ends with a wonderful clean finish.

MEANTIME COFFEE PORTER

MEANTIME BREWING COMPANY LIMITED

This award-winning brewery has matched its reputation for authenticity with one for innovation. Its Coffee Porter, which first was released in 2005, was Britain's first fair-trade beer, using coffee from the Maraba Coffee cooperative of Rwanda, and won a gold medal at the 2006 World Beer Cup.

Made with real coffee, it has the expected caffeine punch. Meantime worked with Union Hand Roasted Coffee in London and matched the coffee beans to the roasted barley to create a creamy smooth dark-roasted beer with very distinct flavors of chocolate, bittersweet chocolate, and mocha. There are nice hints of vanilla too, but none of it gets in the way of the balanced finish. This remarkable beer is complex and well-balanced.

MOCHA PORTER

ROGUE ALES

Judging by the name, you'd expect a porter
with significant chocolate and coffee notes.
You don't get much of either in this beer; instead,
there is a little more bitterness and creaminess to
the body than there is in the average porter. Rogue
Brewing in Bend, Oregon, has a way with ales.

    The body is an opaque dark-brown color. It forms
a large tan frothy head that laces and retains fairly well.
The aroma is similar to that of a milk stout with a noticeable
dairy scent, dark malt, and a hint of coffee.

    I was expecting Rogue Mocha Porter to be a liquid dessert, but it's
more of a classic sessionable porter with subtle coffee in the aftertaste.
It begins lightly sweet with the taste of the dairy aisle; this is followed
quickly by dark maltiness, but nothing overtly roasty or bitter as in a
stronger beer. There's a speckled bitterness around the tongue—a slightly

dry sensation that you'd get after drinking coffee—but no actual coffee taste. Chocolate is very light here; you really have to look for it and drink it at room temperature.

Not that this is a bad beer. As a porter it does exactly what you expect a beer of that style to do. It's even missing some of the cough medicine notes you tend to get in other porters. But to label the beer a mocha porter is a misnomer. Rogue's website has the complete ingredients list, and there's nothing indicating that this beer is brewed with real chocolate or coffee (chocolate malts don't count). However, you can appreciate it as a solid porter, and most craft beer enthusiasts will. Those looking for more chocolate may be disappointed.

Since Rogue Mocha Porter is a fairly standard, even light porter by American standards at only 5.1% ABV, it's not a challenge to drink. The body is medium with a low but noticeable level of carbonation. It goes down extremely smoothly, and a coffee aftertaste lingers momentarily but eventually fades. It's not overly sweet, and so it would be easy to drink multiple servings without wearing out the palate.

CP

Lynchburg
NATT
IMPERIAL PORTER
AGED IN BOURBON BARRELS

ÆGIR BRYGGERI

NATT

ÆGIR BRYGGERI

This Norwegian Imperial porter has a mahogany body with ruby highlights that can be spotted on the edge of the glass. It has a roasted malt, dark coffee, and brown sugar nose. Although at first sip it is slightly smoky and almost burnt in flavor, that is quickly followed by a cavalcade of licorice, caramel, and chocolate. As it warms up, the brown sugar and dark fruit notes come out, adding complexity to the flavor. The mouthfeel is thick—almost chewy—and viscous. This complex coffee porter comes in at an intoxicating 10% ABV.

JC

NOCHE DULCE VANILLA PORTER

BORDERLANDS BREWING COMPANY

There's an old joke that says the best thing to ever come out of Tucson is the I-10. While hilarious, it's only mostly true. The craft beer revolution is sweeping over Tucson in a big way, and several new breweries have popped up. Not only is the I-10 coming out of Tucson, so are brews from the Address Brewing Co. (also known as 1702), the Dragoon Brewing Company, and the Borderlands Brewing Company.

Borderlands is in the Tucson Warehouse Arts District in a century-old building that once housed the Tooley and Sons Produce Company. The brewery was founded by Michael Mallozzi and Myles Stone, two friends who came from careers far outside the beer industry. Mallozzi has a PhD in microbiology and researches disease-causing bacteria at the University of Arizona. Myles is a U of A medical student working toward becoming a family physician. The pair started the brewery in 2010 and soon asked Blake Collins, a respected Tucson homebrewer, to helm the mash tuns as head brewer. The conversation, they say, wasn't a long one.

Noche Dulce is the brewery's "Moonlight Vanilla Porter," made with flaked oats as well as vanilla from Mexico. When poured into a snifter, the brew is dead black and completely opaque but thin and topped with an inch of silky, cocoa-colored foam. The nose delivers, in order of the strength of each ingredient, fresh vanilla beans, cola, cocoa, and roasted grains.

Noche Dulce's flavor can be described as Vanilla Dr Pepper with a splash of milk chocolate. In the front, complex vanilla notes blend with oats and the sweetness of brown sugar, cocoa, and maple. It's a fairly saccharine combination, and the mere 15.5 International Bitterness Units

(IBU) contributed by the hops does little to counteract the sugars. Subtle toast rises at the swallow, leaving clean, straightforward toast and cocoa notes lingering after the finish.

Breckenridge Brewery makes a Vanilla Porter that has become something of a standard for the style, but this beats it. As the name suggests, Noche Dulce is a beer for the night. Try it alongside a vanilla-based dessert such as ice cream or vanilla cheesecake, noting the similar notes of vanilla in the contrasting textures.

ZF

OLD LEGHUMPER

THIRSTY DOG BREWING CO.

This beer is seemingly opaque black or brown with maroon highlights. It forms a dark tan foamy frothy head that laces and retains pretty well. There is a very sweet aroma of chocolate milk and a Dr Pepper–like cola.

If there ever was a beer that shows the difference between a porter and a stout, Thirsty Dog Old Leghumper is it. It is a little bigger and notably sweeter than the average porter but lacks the bitter ending of a stout. It does have a lot in common with a standard milk stout, though, with a sweet, creamy, chocolate milk–like taste throughout. There are some earthy, fruity flavors through the middle, especially prune and vanilla bean, which help keep the palate from being alcoholic Yoo-hoo. There's a mild bitterness just as the beer finishes with a very faint coffee taste but hardly anything in terms of roasted and/or toasted malt.

It's a tasty beer to be sure, but the palate is decidedly simple. The sweet and fruity flavors are flavorful, but some drinkers may find it cloying. It's not really chocolaty enough to be a dessert beer but is a tad too sweet and big to be sessionable. It's a good beer to have a six-pack of, though.

What's probably most impressive about Thirsty Dog Old Leghumper is how easy a beer it is to drink. The mouthfeel is thinner and fizzier than you expect, but the texture is soft and velvety, making for a very comfortable mouthfeel. It's surprising that it's 6.7% ABV since it doesn't seem to have the weight or energy of something that big. It's a dangerously drinkable beer.

CP

OLD NEIGHBORHOOD OATMEAL PORTER

MOTHER EARTH BREWING COMPANY

Born in the summer of 2008, Mother Earth was founded by Stephen Hill and Trent Mooring, two guys from Kinston, North Carolina, a small southern town in the heart of the old tobacco belt. They were brought together by a shared love of homegrown vegetables and hand-crafted beer. Family ties made the connection sweeter when Trent married Caroline, Stephen's daughter.

"Expect a huge chocolate malt taste with a semi-sweet finish that graciously blends with a slickness that results from the huge amount of oats," says Mother Earth's brewer, Josh Brewer. Old Neighborhood Oatmeal Porter is a classic dark, rich, and robust ale with a nice balance between the roastiness and the slightest hint of sweetness. The intense flavors are well-balanced, and the beer finishes nicely.

ONCE UPON A TIME.
DECEMBER 6, 1855
EAST INDIA PORTER

PRETTY THINGS BEER & ALE PROJECT

Pretty Things Beer & Ale Project is not a brewery. They made their company a Project, so they aren't tied to bricks and mortar and can be a bit free and quirky. They rent other people's brewhouses and brew all their beer in other people's breweries. The host breweries package their beers for them. It's a unique situation.

The Project is run by Dann and Martha. Dann Paquette is their brewer and an industry veteran with more than twenty-years experience working in more than ten breweries on two continents. Martha is Dann's assistant brewe. She grew up in Yorkshire in the North of England and has a BA and PhD in Virology from the University of Cambridge in the UK. She moved to Boston to work as a research scientist at Harvard Medical School. She attended UC Davis for a short course in brewing science in 2012.

In early 2011, Dan and Martha teamed up with Ron Pattinson (brewing historian) to recreate a beer from history. This was not their first collaboration. But this time, Ron took them back to colonial India in the 1850s. The rum-drinking troops (or "squaddies") were dying at a surprisingly fast clip until a beer sent from London to India saved them, but it isn't what you're thinking. No, apparently, that whole IPA story is a bit of a ruse.

According to Pattinson, "We've all heard the romantic tale of beer being shipped halfway around the world to quench the thirst of the British in India: the birth of IPA. But Pale Ale wasn't the only beer sent to India. In fact, it wasn't even a majority of the beer sent. That honor belongs to beer that's been lost to history: India porter. British military units in India had a big problem. Their men were dying at an alarming rate. Climate and disease played a role, but so did the troops' drink of choice: rum. What was the solution? Give them porter instead."

Pattinson says, "The effect was dramatic. . . . In Bengal soldiers mostly drank rum, in Madras Porter: Porter-drinking troops had a significantly higher life expectancy than their rum-drinking colleagues! The East India Company . . . took notice and began ordering beer. Lots of it. Casks of porter out-numbered the Pale Ale 2:1. Between 1849 and 1857 the East India Company ordered 23,511 hogsheads of pale ale and 46,363 hogsheads of orter."

Once Upon a Time East India Porter is an exotic, historical beer, brewed in Sommerville, Massachusetts. The recipe that Pretty Things used dates back to a brewsheet from Barclay Perkins Brewery in London, from December 6th, 1855. They worked with maltster Thomas Fawcett & Sons in Yorkshire (Fawcett maltings has been around since the 1780s) to source as authentic pale and brown malts as possible. They hopped the beer with massive amounts of Kent Goldings and Spalt (4.5 pounds per barrel! That's a double IPA!)

Their Once Upon a Time 1855 EIP is dry, malty beer with a substantial pipe-tobacco bitterness, dark garnet color and 6% ABV. It pours black, with hints of red here and there. An inch and a half of creamy tan head tops the glass, and settles slowly. There's chocolate and coffee and toffee. And a giant nose full of hops and definitely a floral touch. This highly acclaimed beer has a great balance of sweet and bitter. Beautiful and complex!

PUGSLEY'S SIGNATURE SERIES IMPERIAL PORTER

SHIPYARD BREWING COMPANY

Shipyard Brewing Company is located on the historic waterfront in Portland, Maine, and produces more than a dozen varieties of award-winning English-style ales. Imperial Porter is part of Shipyard's award-winning Pugsley's Signature Series, which is named after Shipyard's master brewer, Alan Pugsley. This 7.1% ABV beer is made with malts like crystal, chocolate, and Black Patent and uses hops such as Warrior, English Fuggles, and East Kent Goldings. It pours black with red highlights and a big tan head that settles relatively quickly with some lacing. This is a full bodied, very dark, malty beer with a good roasted character. Imperial Porter has a slight residual sweetness and is cutting dry at the finish. This beer has won multiple awards and it shows.

SARANAC CARAMEL PORTER

MATT BREWING COMPANY

With a fairly thin body, this beer flows smoothly out of the bottle with a dark amber-brown complexion. It generates an average-size head that is tan and soapy, although it evaporates quickly and leaves only minor lacing on the glass. The aroma is an intense scent of caramel and malts, although it seems more like vinegar (I believe it is actually butterscotch).

Any beer connoisseur knows that the darker the beer, the warmer it should be drunk. Saranac Caramel Porter is a good example of this rule as it has two very distinct tastes based on the temperature at which it is consumed. If drunk at a low temperature, say, right out of the fridge, the beer has a very malty palate with a sweet finish. Caramel is present but is rather mild. In fact, the vinegarlike scent is also prominent in the flavor, giving the beer a dry, bitter taste. If it's actually butterscotch, why isn't it as tasty as those gold hard candies? If it is allowed to warm to about 50 degrees Fahrenheit, the flavor is much different. The palate is a well-balanced mix of roasted malts and a sweet, rich taste of caramel and possibly toffee. It's almost sugary, but not to the point of being gimmicky or overly sweetened. It's like a caramel apple at a summer carnival. Overall, it's delicious and very satisfying.

Saranac Caramel Porter has a soft, gentle mouthfeel, as though it were water. probably because of its low carbonation. The sweet palate finishes smooth, although it does leave a dry aftertaste.

Dark, sweet beers have a reputation of being hefty even though the numbers usually say otherwise. This is true of Saranac Caramel Porter as it is 5.4% ABV and has an original gravity of 13.30. It doesn't drink like anything it isn't; it is a perfect middle-of-the-road brew that works well on its own or accompanying a meal.

Saranac Caramel Porter is impressive because it seems like an authentic example of a niche foreign style. Its attributes might be a liability since this seems to be more of an acquired taste as opposed to something drinker-friendly. Regardless, it is sweet, smooth, and lean, and that's what is good in a beer.

Saranac Caramel Porter walks a fine line between an overt dessert beer and a standard porter with flavoring added. The mouthfeel is slightly thin and a bit tepid, which enables easy drinking. The flavor is seemingly strong, but the palate gets used to it quickly. There's a slightly dry, slightly cloying aftertaste, but it's tolerable. This beer definitely has a lot of body despite being only 5.4% ABV. (This beer is no longer in production.)

CP

SEX PANTHER DOUBLE CHOCOLATE PORTER

SANTAN BREWING COMPANY

Sex Panther debuted on draft at SanTan's Chandler, Arizona, brewpub in early 2011 as a chocolate barley wine, a unique style in the beer world. The reception was mixed, and it worked only 45% of the time as opposed to the preferred 60%, and so in 2012 the brewers switched the style to "double chocolate porter." The current recipe contains Colonial Rosewood Cocoa, white wheat, heaping helpings of chocolate malt, and bits of real panther, so you know it's good.

In a pint glass, the brew's as dusky as a chunk of dark chocolate but gives up lighter amber hues at the edges. Place your nose close if you dare. It's a formidable scent and stings the nostrils with surprisingly tangy notes of raisins, figs, red wine, and Dr Pepper. Hints of toasted sourdough bread can be picked out amid a background of coffee, cocoa, and peanut skins.

The front of the flavor is similar to the front of the nose: prunes, figs, grape skins, and a hint of vanilla. But it isn't until the swallow that this kitty really starts purring. Huge notes of dark chocolate, espresso, truffle, molasses, and cocoa powder meld in mild sweetness before a long roast cacao finish. Summit hops provide some floral bitterness (20 IBU), but most of the astringency comes from heavily roasted malts. When it all comes together, it's almost like a dark chocolate–covered fig. The alcohol content—a saucy 6.9%—is nowhere to be found.

The body's a little thin, and the watery mouthfeel doesn't fit with Sex Panther's chewy, roasty flavors. Maybe SanTan will put the beer on nitro to remedy this. Sex Panther may be illegal in nine countries, but not here.

ZF

SOUTHERN TIER PORTER

SOUTHERN TIER BREWING COMPANY

This beer has an opaque black body with some carbonation visible at the edge of the glass. It forms a small, tan, soapy head that mostly dissipates and leaves a trace of lacing on the glass. The aroma is characterized by roasted malt with hints of coffee and dark chocolate.

If you want a nice dark beer that isn't too heavy, Southern Tier Porter is an ideal choice. It has the classic porter flavor of dark malts, but the palate isn't nearly as bitter and intense as that of a stout. It is moderately sweet, almost reminiscent of a cola but without the overt sugary sensation.

A strong flavor of dark malt is present as soon as the beer hits the tongue. Though black, it has a toasted malt character rather than tasting heavily roasted. There's a gentle sweetness, almost like that found in an oatmeal stout, though it's not nearly as strong. At the apex of the swig there is intense bitterness, a combination of dry bitterness and some astringency akin to burnt toast or baker's chocolate. It quickly transitions back to a sweeter, almost milk chocolaty taste. This may sound complex, but it's actually a bit repetitive and a tad mild overall. It is tasty, though.

Although Southern Tier Porter is far from a session beer, it doesn't drink like anything mammoth. The mouthfeel is not too heavy, with a smooth texture, gentle carbonation, and an easy finish. At 5.8% ABV it's got the right amount of flavor for its midlevel weight class, though it's a challenge to sip and savor it because it's so drinkable.

CP

ST. ERIKS POMPONA PORTER

ST. ERIKS BRYGGERI

This is a delicious-looking, dark-brown porter with a thick, clingy cappuccino-colored head. If you include the embellished and embossed bottle, this is one hell of a sexy-looking beer.

Not surprisingly for a porter named after a type of vanilla, the first thing that registers with your olfactory system is creamy vanilla sauce backed up by dark chocolate, juniper berries, and burnt toast. After a while the vanilla subsides, but the chocolate lingers on.

The intensity of the nose doesn't all transfer to the taste. There's a creamy vanilla sauce up front, and then things suddenly change and the flavors turn dry, bitter, and roasted. The mouthfeel also seems to transform from medium-bodied to a shade thin, making one think of BrewDog's Zeitgeist thinned down with Guinness. There are bags of piquant roasted malt, chocolate, and ink before a dry coffeelike finish. With its distinctive vanilla and chocolate character, this porter screams out to be paired with a rich chocolate cake and other chocolate-based desserts.

Pompona Porter is the latest edition to the revitalized St. Eriks family of beers created by the Swedish brewer Jessica Heidrich and Galatea Spirits. The fact that Jessica has experimented with vanilla with this popular Swedish beer brand demonstrates how exciting and adventurous beer making is in that country. At 5.4% ABV this beer has a lot of the coffee and chocolate flavors you find in more rugged US porters but has a far higher degree of drinkability—if you like vanilla, that is.

DP

TEMPTRESS
CHOCOLATE PORTER
HOLGATE BREWHOUSE

Paul and Natasha met at university when they were nineteen years old, fell in love, got married, traveled the world, and were inspired; they decided to quit their corporate jobs and follow their passion. Paul got his love of baking bread, cakes, and pastries and making jams and ginger beer from his mother. Natasha's Sri Lankan heritage gave her a love of home-style cooking. Growing up in Melbourne gave her a passion for gourmet foods and the dining experience.

At thirty years of age, they cobbled together a brewery in their backyard in Woodend in 1999 and started selling beer. Even after the birth of two boys they were undaunted, and in 2002 they took over a historic Hotel in Woodend that would become the home of their brewing operations and a dedicated outlet and "cellar door" for their beer. The old Commercial Hotel was built in 1896, later became Keatings Hotel, and now is Holgate's.

Holgate Temptress Porter is a luscious, heady porter made in Australia with Dutch cocoa and whole vanilla beans. Rich and even smoky, it has a slightly sweet milkshake feel, but it remains a solid porter that finishes very well; it's a great way to end an evening.

VANILLA JAVA PORTER

ATWATER BREWERY

This chestnut-colored porter is on the lighter end of the spectrum. True to its name, it has a nose like a vanilla latte and the taste of a well-roasted espresso. This porter is simple and light on the palate, and though it may not be a complex brew, its up-front coffee flavor and satisfying vanilla finish make it a light-bodied treat with a nice 6% ABV.

JC

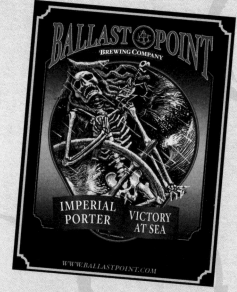

VICTORY AT SEA

BALLAST POINT BREWING COMPANY

For San Diego's Ballast Point Brewing Company, the Yellowtail Pale Ale and Sculpin IPA pay the bills, but it's Victory at Sea, an Imperial porter made with vanilla beans and cold-press coffee, that draws in the beer geeks like a lighthouse in the night.

Victory at Sea's story begins in 1992, when a homebrewer named Jack White, recognizing the dearth of good supply shops nearby with which to enable his hobby, opened Home Brew Mart near Mission Beach in San Diego. Another homebrewer, Yuseff Cherney, soon joined him, and together the two moved the brews they were making in their backyards to the back of the shop. In 1996, Ballast Point was born.

It wasn't until 2007 that Victory at Sea premiered. Visitors to Home Brew Mart went crazy for it, and so White and Cherney decided to bottle the brew in 2009. Was the acclaim the brew continued to gain over the following years due to its rich flavor, or was it because it has perhaps the most epic label art of any bottle out there? Whatever it was, the skeletal captain and his dead parrot sail on in popularity. It got so big that on December 23, 2012, the beer had its own holiday with a dozen different flavor variations.

Victory at Sea looks like breakfast. An abundantly black liquid fills the glass while a powerful-looking head the color of brown sugar and the consistency of pancake batter slowly retreats to a thin but stubborn blanket. Sweet, sticky spatters of lace pepper the glass as it goes. Put your nose above the rim, and the morning meal continues. Aromas of cappuccino gelato and medium-roast coffee with milk meld with subtle background vanilla notes as well as bits of sourdough and brown sugar.

In the flavor, Victory at Sea switches to dessert. An excellent balance of bitter and sweet, the brew tastes almost like tiramisu. Bitter medium-roast coffee flavors play at the sides of the tongue while a sweet vanilla and Irish cream character builds at the front. Toast and molasses make an appearance as well, and alcohol heat rolls down the throat, noticeable but not overpowering. As the drink warms, vanilla becomes more pronounced, lending a sweet finish that counteracts the bitterness of the coffee beans.

ZF

WHISKEY BARREL AGED PORTER

BROWN'S BREWING CO.

The 2008 World Beer Cup silver medal winner, Brown's is based in a 150-year-old warehouse in Troy, New York. Gary and Kelly Brown started the brewery in 1993 and have continued to thrive and change with the times. They have long been a staple of the region. Brown's Brewing also supports the Rensselaer Land Trust, whose mission is to protect watersheds in Rensselaer County in the northern Hudson Valley. This is their amazing porter. Starting out life as a classic English porter, Brown's Whiskey Porter is transferred to a genuine bourbon whiskey barrel for a two-month aging. The barrel imparts the fine characteristics of bourbon and oak into an already complex ale.

It's made using domestic two-row pale and caramel malts and chocolate as well as Willamette hops. It is dark brownish as it pours with a lovely light mocha head that lingers, and there's a nice lace too after you start to drink it.

Oak and dark malt come through right away, as well as some whiskey. Vanilla is also big on the nose. Other aromas come through, such as roasted oats, coffee, and hints of espresso, brown sugar, and caramel. A hint of smoke also dangles. Caramel, salted chocolate, espresso, dark fruit, and whiskey all are present on the palate, with a slight hint of sweetness. Not superthick, it's a good drinking beer. The hops come through slightly, but the lingering aftertaste stays with you a good long time. This delicious rich and dark brew is complex and layered.

If you like big stouts and porters, this is the beer for you with its big chocolate flavors, hints of vanilla and spice, touch of licorice, and big nose full of bourbon. This is a very nice example of a porter aged in whiskey barrels.

30 EXTREME BEERS YOU MUST TRY!

FROM COAL-COLORED IPAS TO INKY SOUR BREWS AND CULINARY PORTERS TO STOUTS AS WHITE AS SNOW, THESE INNOVATIVE BREWS SHOW WHY BLACK IS IN FASHION FOR MODERN BREWERS.

Joshua M. Bernstein

BLACK IPAS

It used to be that you could categorize a brew by its hue. Lagers such as Budweiser are pale yellow, whereas porters and stouts such as Guinness resemble tar. India Pale Ales typically occupy a color spectrum ranging from sunset gold to amber. But as IPAs have taken the throne as craft brewing's king, brewers have applied the bitter template to an array of unlikely pigmentations: white, red, and, most notably, black.

Typically, darker-colored beers flood the palate with intensely roasty flavors that tiptoe from espresso to chocolate—sublime in stouts but overpowering in a bracingly bitter tipple. Black IPAs, though, balance mouth-scrunching bitterness with a kiss of chocolate and roasted-coffee complexity: two great tastes that taste great together.

This chameleonic style has caught on around the world. In San Francisco, 21st Amendment offers the Back in Black IPA, a bitter beauty sold in cans. Utah's Uinta turns out the chocolaty, piney, and highly hopped Dubhe Imperial Black IPA. Pennsylvania's Victory Brewing offers the robust Yakima Glory, and Italy's Birrificio Toccalmatto crafts the fruity B Space Invader with Galaxy hops.

Don't mistake ubiquity for ease of brewing. It's a tricky art to subdue dark malts' astringency so that bitter hops can shine while stout's trademark tint is retained. Some breweries rely on dehusked malt, which is created by a process similar to rice polishing. Much of the scorched grain husk is removed, allowing brewers to impart color without overwhelming roast; it's the secret to Stone's Sublimely Self-Righteous Ale.

When Bend, Oregon's Deschutes Brewery tackled the style, brewers crafted twenty-two batches before locking in the right recipe. The key was borrowing a technique used to concoct *schwarzbiers*, a light-drinking German lager with an obsidian shade. The Deschutes crew steeped the dark-roasted malts in cold water, which dialed back the rough, harsh flavors. (The process is similar to cold brewing coffee.) Deschutes's finished product, Hop in the Dark, has a huge citrusy aroma that's matched with a mellow drinkability, a javalike jolt, and a bitter bolt. However, a close examination of the label reveals that Deschutes does not call the beer a black IPA but rather a CDA—Cascadian Dark Ale.

Fellow Oregonians Oakshire Brewing also use identical phrasing for spring seasonal O'Dark:30, and Portland's Hopworks makes the Secession Cascadian Dark Ale. The practice mostly makes sense. Since black India *pale* ale could be considered an oxymoron, Cascadian dark ale—referencing the Pacific Northwest's Cascades range, which many hop farmers and brewers call home—has been embraced as a substitute moniker.

Thing is, the term *Cascadian* is misleading. The Northwest hardly has a stranglehold on the style. Furthermore, generously hopped dark ales were brewed in the United Kingdom more than a century earlier. As a solution for stylistic confusion, the Beer Judge Certification Program now classifies the dark and bitter beer as American black ale.

No matter whether you call it an American Black Ale (ABA), CDA, or Black India Pale Ale (BIPA), one thing is certain: it's the dawn of a darkly delicious reign.

TEN TO TRY

BACK IN BLACK IPA, 6.8% ABV

21ST AMENDMENT BREWERY

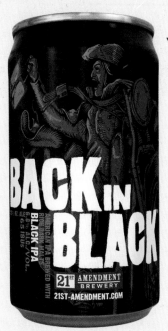

Although you can sip this San Francisco–born brew from the can, pour it into a glass to appraise the handsome mahogany hue. On the nose, there's a floral perfume of pine and citrus that is complemented by flavors of cocoa nibs. It's easy to sip by the six-pack.

#2

BLACK IPA, 8% ABV

BIERBROUWERIJ GRAND-CAFÉ EMELISSE

In recent years, this Dutch brewery has embraced bitter American beers, rolling out a double IPA, a triple IPA, and a drinkable black IPA. The Black IPA blends subtle flavors of chocolate with a smoldering roastiness and, courtesy of Chinook and Cascade hops, plenty of pine tree bitterness.

#3

B SPACE INVADER, 6.5% ABV

BIRRIFICIO TOCCALMATTO

At his brewery in Fidenza, Italy, brewmaster Bruno Carilli specializes in aromatic, hop-driven beers such as the piney Skizoid IPA and the smoothly tropical Zona Cesarini IPA, which contains lemony Japan-bred Sorachi Ace hops. Better yet is B Space Invader, a black IPA brewed with Australia's passion fruit–like Galaxy hops.

#4

BLACK IPA, 6% ABV

OTTER CREEK BREWING

This was originally a one-off batch, but the Vermont brewery's decision to rely on citrusy Centennial and mango- and lychee-like Citra hops helped catapult the IPA into the regular rotation. The creamy beer's tropical profile jibes well with the cocoa notes.

WOOKEY JACK, 8.3% ABV

FIRESTONE WALKER BREWING COMPANY

In both 2012 and 2013, Wookey Jack garnered gold medals at the Great American Beer Festival. The unfiltered black IPA is brewed with a bit of rye, which lends a spicy, peppery touch to the gently charred profile and citrusy charge.

#6
WEEZ,
7.2% ABV

MAINE BEER COMPANY

Pale ales and IPAs that emphasize aroma and flavor, not tongue-torturing bitterness, are Maine Beer's main focus. Named after a brewer's cat, creamy Weez walks a light line between baker's chocolate and coffee while remaining piney, peachy, and resinous in all the right places.

#7
NOONAN
BLACK IPA,
5.7% ABV

SMUTTYNOSE BREWING COMPANY

In honor of New England brewing legend Greg Noonan, who often is credited with creating this hybridized style, Smuttynose dialed up this delightful black IPA. It's plenty piney and citrusy, with a lip-smacking chocolate finish and a low enough ABV to ensure that you can sip several.

SUBLIMELY SELF-RIGHTEOUS ALE, 8.7% ABV

STONE BREWING CO.

Originally released as Stone's eleventh anniversary ale, SSRA proved so popular that the California brewery elevated it to full-time status in 2009. Expect a heady bitterness, a touch of coffee, and a mouthfeel that's downright light considering the elevated ABV.

#9

DUBHE IMPERIAL BLACK IPA, 9.2% ABV

UINTA BREWING COMPANY

Taking its name from Utah's Centennial Star, Dubhe (pronounced "doo-bee") partners an out-of-this-world hop charge with heaps of chocolaty dark malt. The result is an intensely bitter ride to the dark side.

#10

YAKIMA GLORY, 8.7% ABV

VICTORY BREWING COMPANY

Hop lovers' promised land is eastern Washington's Yakima Valley, where new varieties sprout seemingly every year. To celebrate that agricultural cornucopia, Victory utilizes a quartet of Yakima-grown hops in this fruity, full-bodied, and char-licked belly warmer.

SOUR AND FUNKY STOUTS AND PORTERS

Typically, humans associate sour with rotten, like a whiff of expired milk that's destined for the drain. That goes double for beer. You've likely uncapped beers that smell like a skunk's date night, but in the right brewer's hands, sour beer can be transcendent.

Classically, sour beer has encompassed an international collection, from Belgium's tart, spontaneously fermented lambics to Germany's bracing, effervescent Berliner Weisse. Lately, American brewers have embraced the funk, inoculating beers with finicky *Brettanomyces* yeast and bacteria such as *Pediococcus* and *Lactobacillus* (it helps convert milk into yogurt and cheese) and then letting the bugs work their microscopic magic. Over months or even years, they slowly devour beer's sugars and other carbohydrates, tweaking pH levels and creating a mouthwatering tartness and earthy, musty flavors.

Funk was not always brewers' intent. Poor sanitary practices, combined with lengthy maturation in wooden vessels, often provided a welcoming environment for unwanted microbes; dark, wet wood is an ideal home. In fact, many eighteenth-century British porters probably were infected with bacteria and wild yeast, which supplied the dark beers with a lactic tang. With modern brewing sanitation, that tart touch has been banished from stouts and porters. However, in recent years, brewers have begun inoculating these inky brews with *Brettanomyces* (or Brett, as the yeast is also known) and bacteria, creating beers that would have been right at home in bygone London.

Here are several reasons to be sweet on sour stouts and porters.

FIVE TO TRY

#1

SOMETHING LIKE SANDY, 5.5% ABV

CARTON BREWING COMPANY

When Hurricane Sandy pummeled the New Jersey brewery back in 2012, it knocked out Carton's power for eight days. When

the brew crew returned, they discovered that this milk stout, which they'd intended to sour lightly—was *really* sour. You know what? It worked. Something Like Sandy is a tangy tango of dark fruits, coffee, and chocolate.

#2

FUNK METAL SOUR BARREL-AGED STOUT, 8.2% ABV

JESTER KING BREWERY

Situated outside Austin, Texas, Jester King ferments its farmhouse-focused beers with indigenous yeast harvested from the surrounding Hill Country. Aged in oak barrels with a heaping serving of bacteria and wild yeast, the unfiltered Funk Metal stitches a sharp, vinous profile to flavors of chocolate, tart cherries, and dark roast.

#3
BOURBON SOUR PORTER, 6% ABV

ALMANAC BEER COMPANY

To create this lip-tingling treat, the Bay Area brewery fills old bourbon barrels with porter and a yeast medley as well as a sourdough starter. The pitch-black result comes in hard and puckering, with a fudgy undercurrent of dried fruit, bourbon, cocoa, and a touch of vanilla from the oak.

#4

MADRUGADA OBSCURA, 8.1% ABV

JOLLY PUMPKIN

Jolly Pumpkin of Dexter, Michigan, specializes in wild and sour concoctions aged in oak barrels and brewed with French and Belgian yeasts. Madrugada (or "Dark Dawn") is James Brown–level funky, looking like a traditional stout but loaded with aromas of tart cherry and lemon, and flavors of coffee and sour apple.

#5

TART OF DARKNESS, 5.6% ABV

THE BRUERY

Aged in barrels that previously held their famous Black Tuesday stout, The Bruery's Tart of Darkness starts as a low-alcohol stout before being hit by a mix of souring bacteria and wild yeast. The end result marries the roasted flavor of chicory coffee with the sour tang of vinegar—a unique one-two punch that surprisingly succeeds.

WHITE STOUTS

One sun-splashed afternoon I took my taste buds for a test drive at Los Angeles's Angel City, a graffiti-adorned brewery in the downtown Arts District. Glass by glass, I worked my way through the brewery's weird and wonderful offerings, each more head-scratching than the last.

First up was French Sip, an aromatic, beef sandwich–inspired brown ale seasoned with rosemary, peppercorns, sea salt, and umami-rich seaweed. That was chased by the creamy Avocado Ale and the refreshing brine-infused Pickle Weisse. Although those brews could top any oddball scale, the most confounding beer was still to come. White Nite poured out hazy gold with a whipped cream head, a look that screams witbier. I sniffed. Coffee. Chocolate. I tasted. Biscuits. Cream. More java and cocoa. A stout? But stouts can't be light, right?

Wrong. These days, stouts can demonstrate the white stuff. It's not an easy trick. Classically, stouts and porters receive their flavor profile and midnight tint from the addition of well-roasted malts. Subtract dark malts and you lose both the hue and the trademark flavor profile. Mimicking a stout's flavor and aromatic profile requires brewers to utilize a runaround. At Wisconsin's JP's Craft Beer, Casper White Stout is aged for several weeks with coffee beans and cacao nibs, a technique also employed by Angel City. The goal is maximum flavor extraction with minimum color.

"The most common reaction people have when trying White Nite is a look of befuddlement, quickly followed by a big smile," says Angel City brewmaster Dieter Foerstner. "I've long said, 'Don't judge a beer by its color,' and this beer is a great example of why that statement is true."

FOUR TO TRY

#1
SNOW, 4.5% ABV

NIGHT SHIFT BREWING

Instead of in the winter, Massachusetts-based Night Shift Brewing typically releases Snow—flavored with freshly roasted Ethiopian coffee beans—in May, right when the weather starts breaking warm. Loads of wheat and oats ensure that Snow drinks smooth and creamy.

#2
WHITE
STOUT,
7.2% ABV

THE DURHAM BREWERY

Hazy, pale gold, seriously bitter, and perfumed to the hilt, this UK-brewed stout is unlike any you've ever sipped. That's because the brewery interprets stout according to its original meaning: a strong beer with no mention of color.

The

durham

BREWERY

White Stout

Pale Stout

7.2% abv

Premium Bottle-Conditioned Beer

www.durhambrewery.co.uk

#3
NAUGHTY SAUCE, 5.5% ABV

NOBLE ALE WORKS

To devise its golden stout, the Anaheim, California, brewery employs locally roasted Portola Coffee, which gives the golden-orange ale an intoxicating aroma of freshly brewed java. Naughty Sauce drinks as creamy as a full-fat latte.

#4
CASPER WHITE STOUT, 6% ABV

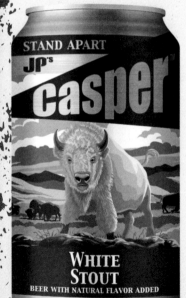

JAMES PAGE BREWING COMPANY

Most white stouts use coffee to get traditional stout flavors into a golden beer. JP's Casper White Stout is aged both on coffee beans and cocoa nibs for two weeks, packing in the traditional chocolate flavors that other takes on the style are missing. Call it a trick of the eyes on the taste buds, but the taste of white chocolate (yes, white chocolate) is the one that dominates this light stout.

CULINARY STOUTS

In a simpler era, brewers relied mainly on hops, grain, water, and yeast to create an endless range of ales and lagers, but for modern brewers, the power of four tends to bore. In search of new flavors, brewers have begun digging into the pantry and refrigerator. Though you can add edibles to nearly any beer style (Ballast Point's Habanero Sculpin IPA, Elysian's Super Fuzz blood orange pale ale, Sam Adams's beef heart–fueled, Oktoberfest-inspired Burke in the Bottle), the most popular platforms are stout and porter. Typically, brewers played up their roasty, cocoalike characteristics by incorporating coffee or chocolate. Now they're turning to bacon, peanut butter, pretzels, and even oysters to devise dark beers as curious as they are delicious.

"Stouts and porters have such a wide range of strong flavors to work with," says Tony Hansen, the head brewer at Michigan's unconventional Short's Brewing. "Whether it's the sweetness of a milk stout or the dark-fruit flavor in a Baltic porter, it's pretty easy to isolate a component to enhance or complement with experimental ingredients."

Many of Short's beers read like an *Iron Chef* episode. The Cornholio porter contains red popcorn, beach plums, and herbal horehound leaf, and S'more Stout stars graham crackers and marshmallows. Then there's the PB&J Stout, a childhood-style adult pleasure inspired by peanut butter and jelly sandwiches, as well as Turtle Stout, which, like the namesake candy, contains chocolate, caramel, and pecans.

When it comes to stout, the snack and dessert paths are well trodden. If you're feeling peckish, start with Martin House's Pretzel Stout before finishing with Rapp Brewing's Chocolate Peanut Butter Stout or Southern Tier's Crème Brûlée Stout. If you favor an entrée, may we suggest a carnivorous stout? Michigan's Right Brain Brewery uses cold-smoked Mangalitsa pig heads and bones to make its smoky Mangalitsa Pig Porter (sublime with a side of Blind Bat's Long Island Potato Stout or Bell's Sweet Potato Stout), and Funky Buddha's Maple Bacon Coffee Porter is a hangover-banishing breakfast in a bottle. For the adventurous carnivore, Wynkoop Brewery's Rocky Mountain Oyster Stout is, fittingly, sold by the pair.

Instead of a turf-based oyster stout, other brewers seek out the surf. Classically, oysters have been an ideal pairing with dry stouts such as Guinness, with their briny profile complementing the full-bodied creamy brew. To underscore the pairing, brewers have begun tossing oysters into brew kettles, creating beguiling ales with one foot in the ocean and the other behind the bar. My recommendation: take a sip of an oyster stout, such as Flying Dog's Pearl Necklace, and then slurp the oyster; it will draw out the beer's inherent brininess.

Although a culinary approach to beer is increasingly popular, it isn't simple. Offbeat fermentables such as bananas and nuts are finicky. For Short's, one notable misfire was the Nutcracker, which was brewed with the nuts typically found on a holiday platter. Furthermore, there's a fine line between doing shtick and creating a complex and engaging brew that people will want to drink twice. "Anyone exploring culinary brewing needs to understand that the key to making your beer delicious is balance," says Jared Rouben, a Culinary Institute of America graduate and former brewmaster at Goose Island's brewpubs. During his nearly three-year stint, Rouben honed his food-focused technique, crafting farmers' market beers such as a baby carrot witbier, a rhubarb saison, and a green-strawberry IPA.

With Chicago's Moody Tongue, Rouben aims to create America's most culinary-focused brewery, relying on seasonal fruits and vegetables as well as spices, teas, and chocolate during the fallow winter months. Using the same technique as a chef constructing a dish with carefully selected ingredients and cooking techniques, Rouben builds a beer with layers of flavor. No single ingredient should overwhelm. "It should make the overall beer better. Nothing frustrates me more than when people sprinkle garnish around a plate. If we incorporate it into the recipe, it's there for a reason."

That means food-driven beers such as a brandied blackberry Belgian dubbel and a gingerbread chocolate milk stout. "We're pushing down the walls of culinary arts and brewing," he says. "People love beer. People love food. Now you don't have to decide between the two."

ELEVEN TO TRY

#1

LONG ISLAND POTATO STOUT, 3.9% ABV

BLIND BAT BREWING

Nearsighted, color-blind brewmaster Paul Dlugokencky specializes in distinctive ales such as the robust Hellsmoke Porter, Long Island Oyster Stout, and Long Island Potato Stout. Locally grown organic taters give the beer an extra-dry edge.

#2

PEARL NECKLACE OYSTER STOUT, 5.5% ABV

FLYING DOG BREWERY

The Maryland brewery uses locally harvested Rappahannock River oysters to concoct Pearl Necklace, a silky indulgence crammed with roasted-malt goodness and a dry, coffeelike finish. Furthermore, drinking a bottle makes you a do–gooder: the proceeds go to the Chesapeake Bay's Oyster Recovery Partnership.

#3

LUGENE CHOCOLATE MILK STOUT, 8.5% ABV

ODELL BREWING

Gobs of milk chocolate and healthy dose of lactose—milk sugar—supply the Colorado stout with an incomparable creaminess. It's a childhood pleasure in an indulgent adult package.

#4

CHOCOLATE PEANUT BUTTER STOUT, 6.8% ABV

RAPP BREWING COMPANY

At his namesake Seminole, Florida, brewery, former IT professional Greg Rapp dabbles in dozens of different beers, from his bracingly acidic Berliner Weisse to this wildly popular stout. The secret ingredient: plenty of cocoa and peanut powders.

#5
ROCKY MOUNTAIN OYSTER STOUT, 7.5% ABV

WYNKOOP BREWING COMPANY

It took balls for the Denver brewery to make this beer. Seriously. The oysters in question are in fact bull testicles. Though this may horrify vegetarians—and a fair share of flesh eaters, too—the rich and inky stout drinks smooth and chocolaty. P.S. The beer originally started as an April Fool's Day joke.

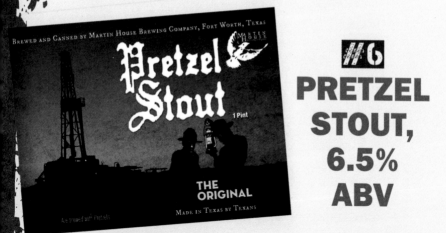

#6
PRETZEL STOUT, 6.5% ABV

MARTIN HOUSE BREWING COMPANY

Like pretzels with your beer? Try pretzels *in* your beer. For each barrel (31 gallons) of stout, the Fort Worth brewers use more than six pounds of crushed sourdough pretzels. The result will hit your salty, sweet, and roasty sweet spot.

#7
MANGALITSA PIG PORTER, 6% ABV

RIGHT BRAIN BREWERY

The Michigan brewery adds cold-smoked Mangalitsa pig heads—brains removed, in case you're curious—and bags of bones to each batch of this porter. The smoky result would go great with BBQ. Seriously.

EXTRACTS ARE FOR SISSIES

Since 2007

#8
JEFFERSON STOUT, 4.65% ABV

LAZY MAGNOLIA

At Mississippi's Lazy Magnolia, husband-wife duo Mark and Leslie Henderson—he handles finances, she brews—rely on the local agricultural bounty for their beers. For Jefferson Stout, a chef's suggestion led Leslie to brew the light and luscious milk stout with sweet potatoes.

#9
AUTUMNAL MOLÉ STOUT, 5.5% ABV

SKA BREWING

Taking its cues from Mexican molé, the Colorado brewery's seasonal fall stout is spiced with cocoa nibs and a trio of peppers, including sweet and smoky ancho, mild mulato, and Hatch chilies—typically harvested in neighboring New Mexico in August. Strong flavors of cocoa keep the peppers' heat in check.

#10

SALTED CARAMEL STOUT, 6.8% ABV

BREAKSIDE BREWERY

To create this dessert-friendly beer, the madly creative Portland, Oregon, brewery collaborated with the ice cream shop Salt & Straw. Made with salted caramel and sea salt, the rich and silky stout tastes, in the best way possible, like boozy melted ice cream.

#11

OYSTER STOUT, 4.6% ABV

PORTERHOUSE BREWING CO.

Porterhouse was founded in 1996 by beer importers Liam LaHart and Oliver Hughes, who aimed to bring indie beer and unique styles to a country dominated by global beer brands. Their oyster stout, made with fresh oysters shucked straight into the conditioning tank, adds sweetness and slight brine notes to a smooth, roasted Irish stout.

Lovely day for a **GUINNESS**

These now-famous toucans made their debut in 1935

THE STORY OF STOUTS

By Greg Clow

Just as we tend to refer to all facial tissues as Kleenex, all cotton swabs as Q-tips, and all fruit gelatin desserts as Jell-O, there's a certain historic brewing company whose name has become inexorably linked with a particular beer style in the minds of many people. Like most companies of its era, this brewery is named for its founder, and the beer it produces is one of the most popular in the world, with sales being especially brisk around a particular day in mid-March each year.

The brewery I'm referring to is Guinness, of course, and the style is that beautiful near-black beverage known as stout. While Guinness hasn't quite reached the point where the name is completely interchangeable with stout, it's still managed to build up the brand and the beer to a level of being so ubiquitous that many beer drinkers aren't aware of any stouts beyond this black stuff from Dublin.

Like most companies, the Guinness Brewery started humbly. In the 1750s, Arthur Guinness took over a family brewing business in the small town of Leixlip in County Kildare, Ireland. He soon moved his operations

Arthur Guinness.

Part of the 9,000-year lease.

to the disused St. James's Gate Brewery in Dublin, where in 1759, he signed the now famous 9,000-year lease with a rent of £45 per year (about $75). In the early years, Guinness produced a number of different ales, but none were the dark and roasty beer that they're known for today. Some of the beers may have been described as "stout," as the term was often used as a descriptor for any strong beer, with "brown stout," "pale stout," and other versions being mentioned in various brewing manuals and other documents of the era. But it wasn't until nearly two decades into business, in 1778, that Arthur Guinness decided to start brewing his own version of porter. By the end of the century, he'd abandoned all other styles to concentrate on porter full-time.

As Guinness and other brewers made porters of varying strengths, it became common to refer to them with names like "plain porter," "stout porter," and "double stout porter." Eventually, the overwhelming popularity of porter led to the descriptors becoming so synonymous with the

The St. James's Gate Brewery.

style that "stout" was rarely used in reference to any other beer, and by the mid-1800s, asking for a "stout beer" in a pub or tavern would inevitably get you a glass of strong porter.

The point where stout became different enough from porter to be considered a completely different beer style is still a point of debate, with some people arguing that they're not different even now, but just two variations on the same beer. But for those who favor a split, one year often used is 1817, when Daniel Wheeler invented a process to kiln barley at a high enough temperature that it carbonizes, producing a malt so dark that using just a small amount will render a beer almost completely black. Known as simply as black malt (or sometimes black patent malt, as Wheeler was awarded a patent on his process), it was used in a number of different dark ale styles, but it was stout that became most known for the remarkably dark color it imparts, as well as the slightly burnt undertone it sometimes adds to the flavor.

Guinness employed
the largest number
of coopers in all of
Ireland to keep their
barrels rolling out
onto the market.

THE HANDBOOK OF PORTERS & STOUTS

Another landmark year for stout was 1820, when Guinness changed the name of their Extra Stout Porter to simply Extra Stout. By 1833, they had overtaken their competitor and fellow stout brewery, Beamish & Crawford in County Cork, to become the largest brewery in Ireland and one of the largest in the United Kingdom.

Most of the stouts being brewed in the late eighteenth and early nineteenth centuries would be what are today considered Irish stouts, also known as dry stouts because of the drying sensation in the finish. This is due primarily to the addition of roasted but unmalted barley as a small percentage (usually 10% or less) of the grain bill, which gives the beer flavors that are reminiscent of dark roasted coffee or bitter chocolate. In addition, these stouts are relatively highly hopped, which also gives the beer a dry and slightly bitter finish.

But while Irish dry stout might be the starting point for the style, a number of variations have been brewed over the years, with some triggering the creation of new stout sub-styles: Oatmeal stout is a fuller and richer version brewed with oatmeal. Milk stout is a variation made sweeter by the addition of lactose sugar. And Imperial stout is a much stronger version (often as high as 10%), which was originally brewed for export to the Russian Imperial Court. And new sub-styles continue to bubble up.

So while Guinness may be the default and only stout available at many bars and pubs around the world, there are dozens and dozens other options out there as well. The fact that they don't have the marketing and distribution might of the multinational alcohol company Diageo behind them means that they'll never be as easy to find as Ireland's gift to the beer world, but on a cool fall evening when you need something rich and roasty and satisfying in your glass, it's well worth taking the time to track down a locally brewed stout. That said, there's certainly nothing wrong with tipping back the occasional pint of Guinness. Cheers and sláinte mhath!

BELHAVEN SCOTTISH STOUT

BELHAVEN BREWERY COMPANY LTD

This English stout has a distinctly Scottish twist with peat and smoke in the nose and flavor. It is an opaque brown beer with a khaki head. The nose has coffee and cocoa powder in addition to the light notes of peat. The nutty body is dominated by coffee and molasses flavors, but it manages to stay light. The dry finish makes it suitable to tip repeatedly, even at 7% ABV.

JC

BELL'S SPECIAL DOUBLE CREAM STOUT

BELL'S BREWERY

One of the best things about drinking beer is having a sweet stout to top off a good dinner. A beer like Bell's Special Double Cream Stout can be even more satisfying than a piece of chocolate cake because it's much more complex. Although this is not a chocolate stout per se, it definitely is one of the sweetest, creamiest stouts you'll encounter. It's also surprisingly lighter in body than you'd expect, which makes it highly drinkable and accessible to beer drinkers of all experience levels.

This beer is completely opaque black (no ruby red highlights at all). It formed a thick creamy brown head that lasted throughout the life of the drink and left some decent lacing on the glass.

The aroma was surprisingly mild, although it did live up to its name as the most noticeable scent was indeed cream. There were faint hints of milk chocolate, but otherwise the nose was rather quiet. The thick creamy head was quite roasty-tasting, and the beer was very sweet, not unlike a cola. In fact, it was so sweet that it dried out my mouth and had me craving a sip of milk or water between swigs.

What's weird is that the beer is actually not quite as rich or intense as it may sound. There is a distinct creamlike and milklike combination of flavors, but the overall palate is rather reserved. There are mild roasted malt flavors in the mouth, although they seem to gain strength in the aftertaste. There is only faint bitterness, which may be attributed to subtle notes of chocolate.

This brew is more reminiscent of an Irish dry stout with a sweeter body than a traditional milk stout. It's actually quite light in body but not watery like a Guinness Draught. Still, the mouthfeel is velvety and smooth, and the aftertaste is strong and pleasing.

At 6.1% ABV, Bell's Special Double Cream Stout is the type of beer you'd rather drink on nonspecial occasions and probably in greater quantities than any kind of Imperial stout. Almost anyone would find this brew very drinkable since it's not too intense and goes down so easily. Special Double Cream Stout is, at the very least, a solid performer. It has everything a good beer should, and it's the type that would appeal to pretty much anyone.

CP

BLACK BEAR STOUT
BERKSHIRE MOUNTAIN BREWERS

We're so used to drinking large Imperial stouts that we sometimes forget what can be done with smaller versions such as Berkshire Mountain Brewers' Black Bear Stout. This is a by-the-book brew in the sweet stout style. It has everything you expect and nothing you don't. It's good, but it's been done before.

This stout is opaque dark black with no highlights. It forms a large dark tan frothy head that laces and retains well. You smell plenty of roasted barley, hints of vanilla, and milk chocolate. There is light, sweet maltiness at the beginning of the palate. There are slight milk chocolate flavors with perhaps a dairy flavor often found in stouts brewed with lactose sugar (not sure if this one is). There's slight tanginess through the middle with hardly any bitterness, and it finishes with a short but noticeable burst of roasted malt or coffeelike bitterness that fades away almost completely cleanly and rather quickly, making this a beer that's satisfying. Not quite robust enough to be a dessert beer, it's a stout for the sake of drinking stout.

The stout's mild palate gives it a drinkability that is quite impressive. The mouthfeel is a bit thin, but it's a deliberately lighter-bodied beer. It's soft and smooth across the tongue and glides down the gullet with ease. At 4.9% ABV it's perhaps a bit too big to be defined as a session beer, though drinking it in large quantities should not be a burden.

CP

CAPTAIN SWAIN'S EXTRA STOUT

CISCO BREWERS INC.

Tiny Nantucket island, thirty miles off the coast of Cape Cod, may seem like an unlikely place for a brewing concern, but it is the home of Cisco Brewers, a triumvirate of brewery, distillery, and winery. Cofounder Wendy Hudson started homebrewing beer in California in the 1990s and introduced her husband and cofounder, Randy Hudson, to the hobby when she returned to Nantucket. Their nanobrewery started in a backyard, with only the air conditioner–cooled cold room indoors. From those humble beginnings as the United States' only outdoor brewery, Cisco has found success and steadily expanded, bringing sister operations Triple Eight Distillery and Nantucket Vineyard under the Cisco Brewers umbrella.

Cisco's Captain Swain's Extra Stout, a bold export stout named after one of Nantucket's seventeenth-century founders, is one of their finest brews. Brewed with a boatload of malts (thirteen different types, to be precise), the big beer has flavors ranging from dark-roast coffee to blackberries and cherry. With significant notes of smoke and hints of pine from dry hopping with Chinook hops, Captain Swain's is pleasantly reminiscent of a crackling New England fireplace. It's a beer fit for a captain and the 8% ABV is surely substantial enough to survive the long journey at sea the style originally was brewed to weather.

JC

DIESEL

SIX POINT BREWERY

This is a good winter stout in a can with great packaging. Diesel looks scrumptious in the glass: it's an eponymous black and pours a nice one-finger head with beautiful lacing. Like many stouts, this beer needs to warm up to cellar temperature before any of its wonderful flavors wake up.

After a few minutes, rich malty aromas of toffee, coffee, and licorice emerge, making for a welcoming, sumptuous nose that suggests a winter ale; the palate, however, shows just a flash of sweet maltiness before the cold shower of a substantial hop profile.

There's a little bitterness from the roast, too, making for more than enough zip to balance that hint of sweetness. Diesel is only 6.3% ABV but feels a little boozier, probably because of the rich malt character.

This is a punchy, interesting winter brew with a deceptively malty nose but a surprisingly hoppy finish. It could be paired with a porterhouse steak, beef stew, or an aged Gouda.

JB

DE DOLLE EXTRA EXPORT STOUT

BROUWERIJ DE DOLLE

De Dolle Brouwers ("The Mad Brewers") is based in Esen in West Flanders, Belgium. The building housing the brewery is believed to date from 1835, when it was founded by the local doctor Louis Nevejan. It became the Costenoble brewery in approximately 1882 and remained in that family for three generations. It was defunct when purchased by De Dolle, which restored it to function as a brewery in 1980.

De Dolle Extra Export Stout is a dark stout with 9% ABV. The beer originally was brewed at the request of the US importer of the brewery's products. It is now brewed several times a year with the same fermentation as De Dolle's Oerbier. The beer starts with a creamy massive head that eventually starts to settle. There is very nice consistent lacing. The nose starts with sweet malt, roasted malt, coffee, and chocolate, along with a hint of sour cherries. It is all chocolate on the palate but is nicely balanced, with a creamy mouthfeel. This is a very good example of a foreign extra stout.

DRAGON STOUT

DESNOES & GEDDES LTD

When it comes to Jamaican beers, most people know only Red Stripe, but the same brewery makes a stout in the "foreign extra" style. It's called Dragon Stout, and it's not bad.

The beer has a jet black hue and is completely opaque. It initially forms a thick frothy brown head, but the head quickly begins to fizzle away and become soapy. It leaves only minor lacing on the glass and almost completely dissipates.

There is a mild nose of anise and/or brown sugar.

When it comes to stouts, even though there are bunch of substyles, there's an expectation of the style overall. It's fine if they're sweet, but there are certain flavors you expect from them, most of which are absent from Dragon Stout. It's closer to alcoholic brown sugar cola than to a true stout. Not that it tastes bad; this taste of brown sugar up front and again on the finish is enjoyable. There is not much in the way of roasty malts and little hop character, but there are no off flavors. The sweet soda taste is a bit simplistic and repetitive, but it doesn't get old or cloying.

With a relatively thin body and a lightly sweet, clean taste, Dragon Stout is highly drinkable. Even though the alcohol is light for an Imperial at 7.5% ABV, it's nowhere to be found in the aroma, taste, or body. Dragon Stout goes down smoothly and has a clean aftertaste. It's an ideal stout for warmer weather (and considering where it's brewed, that's understandable).

CP

ENGLISH DARK STOUT

STENSBOGAARD BRYGHUS

People throw the terms *artisan* and *craft beer* around a lot these days. The boundaries are often stretched by breweries desperate to convey the message that they still roll their sleeves up and get involved in the creation of beer rather than leaving it up to computers, buttons, and valves. Where to draw the line between craft and noncraft beer is an ongoing and hotly debated subject. What isn't open to debate is the fact that beer brewed in an old dairy on a farm in a field near the east coast of Denmark is craft beer with a capital C.

Stensbogaard Bryghus is a family-run brewery that produces batches of only 1,000 liters of beer at a time. Likely there aren't that many computerized processes involved in the making of any of their seven main beers. Two of them, English Dark Stout and an IPA, are currently available in limited numbers at the Systembolaget.

It poured as expected: a deep dark brown with an attractive off-white, beaten egg head so packed with hop aroma that it smelted like a bag of old pennies. This aroma vanished after the head died away.

Considering the beefy 6.8% ABV, the mouthfeel was disappointingly thin, with some mild coffee, dark toffee, cigar box, and an unsettling salty sourness in the finish that lingers. In a way this beer had a real yesteryear taste about it, a little raw, like something people might have drunk in the eighteenth century, but many people like that kind of flavor. Drinking this beer is a unique experience.

DP

GAME OF THRONES
TAKE THE BLACK STOUT

BREWERY OMMEGANG

Ommegang and HBO® announced the fourth beer in their Game of Thrones® collaboration series. Taking its name and inspiration from the brotherhood of the Night's Watch, Take the Black Stout is deep, dark, and complex to reflect the men who defend Westeros against all that lies to the north. On the label is the Weirwood tree under which Jon Snow recited the oath before joining the Night's Watch.

The beer is made using specialty malt, chocolate malt, midnight wheat, and roasted barley, and hopped Northern Brewer and Columbus. Licorice root, star anise, and other spices are added during the brewing process. Take the Black Stout pours pretty much opaque back, with a full mocha-colored head. The nose is big with roasty notes, dark chocolate, caramel, molasses, malt, and a touch of dark fruits like plum, fig, and cherry. Also, there's a smokiness to it. Chocolate, coffee, and roasted malt come across on the palate, and the hoppy bitterness give this stout a nice finish with some much-appreciated spiciness at the end. This beer is big, complex, and well-balanced. (It is no longer in production.)

BREWERY
OMME-GANG
COOPERSTOWN N

GAME OF THRONES

TAKE THE BLACK STOUT

THE HANDBOOK OF PORTERS & STOUTS

GUINNESS FOREIGN EXTRA STOUT

GUINNESS LTD.

Surprisingly, the Guinness in American bars wasn't real Guinness, according to globetrotting beer geeks. No, it was simply a weak imitator. The good stuff was the Extra and Foreign Extra stouts, they said. The basis for those Extra brews is unfermented (but hopped) Guinness wort extract. It's shipped from Dublin and then added to local ingredients and fermented locally. It's a bigger, beefier beer, and it is what many around the globe think of as Guinness; Foreign Extra accounts for around 45% of the company's worldwide sales.

After one takes a sip of the Foreign Extra Stout, it's immediately obvious that Guinness isn't screwing around. The beer is full-bodied and intensely bittersweet. The taste is of dark chocolate backed by coffee and caramel. Basically, the FES tastes the way you remember your first Guinness tasting. The finish is quite dry and quite long, with lingering notes of hazelnut. It's an absolutely drinkable beer, easy to quaff but flavorful enough to work as a dessert beer. *This* is the beer all those "foreign Guinness only" snobs were talking about.

If you're a beer geek who once loved Guinness Draught or never really got what all the fuss was about, this is the St. James Gate beer for you. Guinness nostalgia aside, this is simply a phenomenal stout at 7.5% ABV. The bloom is back on the rose.

JC

HEART OF DARKNESS

MAGIC HAT BREWING COMPANY

Heart of Darkness has an opaque black body with no carbonation visible. It pours to a fairly large dark tan frothy head that laces and retains very well. The nose has light notes of roasted malt, some dairylike scent, and well water.

Heart of Darkness is a straightforward stout in pretty much all aspects. The palate is simple and mild, and the taste is decent. The first half of the swig is slightly sweet, with a thin cola taste. There's only a little bitterness on the second half with some roasted malt that's prominent at first but fades away quickly. It has a taste reminiscent of certain British brews made from hard well water, but without any other British character (it is fermented with English ale yeast). There's a hint of nuttiness right as it finishes, which is nice. Overall, this is a fine stout.

Although this isn't the most robust stout in the world, it's no challenge to drink. The mouthfeel is light, with a wet, watery sensation and no carbonation crispness. This enables a smooth finish and high quaffability. It drinks and feels like a lighter beer than its 5.7% ABV. It is too heavy to session, though.

CP

't Hofbrouwerijke hofblues

Belgian Imperial Stout

75cl/1 PT 9.4 FL OZ   ALE REFERMENTED IN THE BOTTLE   8% ALC/VOL

PRODUCT OF BELGIUM
BREWED & BOTTLED BY
't HOFBROUWERIJKE · BEERZEL, BELGIUM
IMPORTED BY *Sheldon Brothers*

HOFBLUES

'T HOFBROUWERIJKE

This dark-brown, porteresque stout has an off-white head. The nose is dark and fruity with a pleasant estery quality that is due in part to the Belgian yeast used to make the brew. It has a medium body with big, billowy carbonation and a 5.5% ABV. This helps highlight the sweet, dark fruity flavors such as cherry, plum, and currant that give this beer its signature flavor.

JC

HOGGLEYS
SOLSTICE STOUT

HOGGLEYS BREWERY

Hoggleys Brewery officially began in 2003, the dream of homebrewer Roy Crutchley. Their first beer was brewed using the simplest of recipes and was served up at the Alexandra Arms in Kettering, and it's been nothing but press clippings and success ever since. For a while it was regarded as the smallest licensed brewery in Britain, but this is no longer the case. After expanding from the original small batches, the brewery since August 2006 has become a full-time operation running on a regular basis. Hoggleys Solstice Stout (5% ABV) is a rich full-flavored stout made with a wide range of malts. Originally brewed for the frosty dark night of the midwinter solstice, it is now brewed year-round.

This is a classic English stout, jet black with a dark, creamy head, light lacing, and a hint of red on the edges. There is a big nose of roasti-ness with a hint of cocoa and mocha. It is dry and well-balanced.

JOPEN EXTRA STOUT

JOPEN BIER BV

From the Middle Ages to the early twentieth century, Haarlem, Netherlands, was a city with a rich history of beer. In the fifteenth century, Haarlemsche Koytbier was the most consumed beer in Antwerp, and between 1620 and 1640, Haarlem had as many as fifty-two breweries. Even one of their mayors was a brewer! But sadly in 1916, the last brewery in town, Scheepje the Houtmarkt, closed their doors. Then came Jopen Bier to get things back in order and start brewing again in this medieval city. The name Jopen comes from the city's history, as it was the word for the massive 112-litre barrels that were used to ship the beer down the river from the city.

Jopen Extra Stout is a beer style that was brewed in Haarlem until early 1900. It is somewhat heavier than an Irish Stout. Extra Stout contains 5.5% ABV and has the distinctive roasted bitterness for a stout (about 45 EBU). It pours blackish brown with red edges and a small beige head that dissipates about halfway through, leaving behind some lacing. The flavor has a roasted bitter note that is reminiscent of espresso coffee and dark chocolate. There are also burnt grains and dark fruits in there along with nice carbonation, and good complexity and balance. It is easy to drink a few of these!

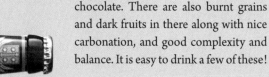

KALAMAZOO STOUT

BELL'S BREWERY

The first thing you'll notice about Bell's Kalamazoo Stout is its impenetrable dark body and thick, rich caramel-colored head. No drinking from the bottle here; pour this into a proper pint glass and appreciate the view.

Next, on the first taste you start off with an initial hoppy bite that quickly transitions into the expected smooth mocha and dominant dark-roast coffee and malt mix with a final reemergence of hoppy bitterness for a dry finish. This stout is well-balanced and has great earthiness from the roasted malts. This beer comes across at 6% ABV and 51 IBU.

The brewer's licorice used here comes across as a natural result of the hops and coffee; it is not just a head-line-catching brewmaster's experiment. The possibly preconceived strange choice successfully marries the bitterness of the hops and the acidity of the coffee so well that you may not think it was the result of the licorice addition but rather inherently derived from the other core ingredients. Overall this is an exceptional American stout with great coffee flavors that is smartly crafted.

KW

LION STOUT

LION BREWERY LIMITED

Lion Stout appears in Michael Jackson's *Great Beer Guide,* and Beer-Tubers have reviewed it with high acclaim. It's brewed in Ceylon at the Lion Brewery Limited.

This stout is as black as spent motor oil and totally opaque. It forms a large frothy and creamy head that retains and laces very well. The aroma is black licorice with a slightly tangy, almost sour dairy scent.

Despite the ominous aroma, the first swig will quickly relieve any apprehensions you may have. The first half is strong with rich sweetness, especially black licorice, and the second half delivers the strong bitterness of deeply roasted malts with a quick burst of dark chocolate. As the beer warms, the palate really begins to develop with even more sweet flavors of toffee and caramel in the beginning. There's a faint sourness on the finish, but it works with the palate, surprisingly enough. The mouthfeel is thick, soft, and tepid with a velvety smoothness.

Weighing in at 8% ABV, Lion Stout doesn't have the overwhelming hubris one might expect. There is no alcohol in the aroma or taste, and drinking one is satisfying, not a challenge. The soft mouthfeel enables the beer to slide across the tongue and down the hatch like water.

Overall, this is a very impressive stout, especially considering that it hails from a country not known for beer. Many American brewers could learn something from this stout.

CP

LUMP OF COAL

RIDGEWAY BREWING

This is a big, foreign export stout with 8% ABV, brewed by Ridgeway Brewing in South Stoke, United Kingdom. It pours dark brown, and has a nice, off-white head that leaves sheets of lovely lacing behind. Roasted coffee, milk chocolate, baker's chocolate, cocoa, chocolate milk, and caramel all come through the nose and palate. Licorice also comes through in the creamy mouth-feel. This one is easy drinking.

ALC 8% VOL

Lump of Coal

Dark Holiday
~ STOUT ~

Much More Than You Deserve for Xmas This Year...

IMPORTED BY
Shelton Brothers
BELCHERTOWN MA

OBSIDIAN STOUT

DESCHUTES BREWERY

Deschutes is brewed in Bend, Oregon. It enjoys a reputation as a top-flight brewery, and this beer is no exception. This is everything you look for in an American stout It's jet black but slightly translucent with a nice dark tan foamy head thatretains well but lacks lacing. There is a light dairy quality to the smell with a touch of roasted malts and dark chocolate. There is a sweet, tasty, milky-oaty flavor up front and deeply roasted, almost burnt malts on the back end. It's not terribly robust or complex; it remains sweet throughout, but the malty notes fade as you drink on. There's a touch of chocolate here, but you may have to reach for it. The mouthfeel is not too thin and not too thick. It's slightly fizzy on the tongue and very belch-inducing for a stout.

Because the palate is flavorful but not too intense and the body is only medium, Deschutes Obsidian Stout is dangerously drinkable. The 6.4% ABV seems a little high as this beer has the drinkability of a more deliberately sessionable stout. Overall, this is a good American stout and definitely a solid performer.

CP

PHANTOM PUNCH WINTER STOUT

BAXTER BREWING CO.

Brewed in Lewiston, Maine, site of the Muhammad Ali (then Cassius Clay)–Sonny Liston heavyweight championship bout, the beer is named for the phantom punch that knocked out the ferocious Liston. Baxter Phantom Punch Winter Stout is technically a traditional foreign extra type of stout that happens to be brewed with vanilla beans and cocoa nibs. That makes it difficult to grade because it doesn't taste like either a typical FES (foreign extra stout) or a typical chocolate stout. What it ends up being is a fairly robust stout that's got plenty of sweetness and bitterness.

This beer is a dark, opaque black. It forms a large dark-brown, frothy head that retains and laces splendidly. There is a fairly typical sweet stout aroma with hints of milk and vanilla, but it is not particularly roasty or spicy.

The head imparts initial bitterness that quickly transitions to bittersweet or dark chocolate. Through the middle the bitterness fades, and in comes a sweet flow of vanilla and hints of milk chocolate. There's a strong bitter bite on the finish, though. It's a mixture of roasted malt, burnt toast, and a hint of spicy hop flavor. It's rather dry and leaves a slightly cloying aftertaste. Still, while it's in the mouth, Phantom Punch Winter Stout is tasty and delectable.

You might prefer a more chocolate-forward stout, but since it's not meant to be a chocolate stout per se, this brew works well for what it is. The prominent vanilla is a nice change of pace and accounts for a lighter, milkier flavor component. You may find the bitterness surprising, interesting, and maybe a tad challenging. All the parts work well together and make for a versatile brew.

Although it is not an Imperial stout, Baxter Phantom Punch Winter Stout is certainly on the full-bodied spectrum. There's plenty of flavor and energy from start to finish, yet the mouthfeel is comfortable and a little thinner than you'd expect. It goes down smooth, but it does dry out the tongue. At 6.8% ABV, it's exactly where it should be in terms of weight and body. You could drink two, but one probably will be satisfying.

CP

SOTHOLMEN EXTRA STOUT

NYNÄSHAMNS ÅNGBRYGGERI

With breweries producing ever more intensely alcoholic beers these days, it's a welcome relief to see that Nynäshamns Ångbyggeri agrees that good things can come in little packages. The brewery recently upgraded its bottling line so that it can handle smaller bottle sizes, and Sotholmen Extra Stout is the first beer in its new, rather cute 25-centiliter bottle format.

Sotholmen is an impressive beer to gaze at. It pours very dark, almost black, and has an appetizing fluffy dark tan head. The aroma promises much, with a hit of filter coffee and port wine. However, in the mouth there isn't really the something "Extra" the beer claims to have. If Nynäshamns is referring to extra alcohol, that's in there, but it fails to give the beer the body and complexity you look for in a strong stout. This is surprising because this beer, like all beers from Nynäshamns, is unpasteurized, and there is normally a full mouthfeel in the "live" beers from this brewery.

The flavor is cold coffee with a dash of milk: There's lots of that and a little bitter chocolate. It feels a little grainy and thin considering the 7% ABV, ending with a dry, slightly boozy finish.

Drinking a small bottle of Sotholmen is a pleasant way to pass the time, but so is watching curling at the Winter Olympics. Still, this is one to try.

DP

ST. PETER'S CREAM STOUT

ST. PETER'S BREWERY CO.

This beer has an opaque black body with traces of red along the edges. It forms a large dark tan foamy head that mostly evaporates and leaves a trace of lacing on the glass. The aroma is that of a classic British stout with a dairylike sweetness and some confectionery scents.

Beers like this remind one of how good a classic, no-frills stout can be. There's no chocolate, coffee, or intense body. You get a pleasantly sweet bouquet of roasted malt, some milky or creamy flavors, and significant peanut brittle in the finish. It's not hugely hopped, though the Fuggle hops, a mainstay of British brewers, come through at the apex of the swig. There's plenty of flavor from start to finish, though you will like the ending the best as there's a significant toffee component to the palate. This is a sweet beer that is not cloying and is well balanced all around.

With a soft, comfortable mouthfeel and smooth, tepid texture, St. Peter's Cream Stout is a stout drinker's ideal beer. The robust flavor lets you know it's not a session beer, yet you'd never figure it for a remotely heavy beer at 6.5% ABV. It's a pleasurable drinking experience.

CP

STOUT

KROSS CERVEZA INDEPENDIENTE

Kross Cerveza Stout is brewed by Kross Brewing (Southern Brewing Company) in Curacaví, a one-hour drive west of Santiago, Chile. When people think about Chile, they think about Pisco and wine; they rarely think about beer. Kross Cerveza was the brainchild of José Tomás Infante, a well seasoned traveler with a penchant for beer, and Asbjorn Gerlach, a journeyman master brewer who came to Chile from Germany. This beer is smooth and well-balanced. It has a deep black color with little lacing. Coffee and caramel come through, as well as a shot of hops. There is a dry aftertaste with a touch of bitterness. This is a classic easy-drinking American stout brewed in Chile.

STOUT

TITANIC BREWERY

Titanic Brewery was founded in Burslem, Stoke-on-Trent, England, in 1985, where many famous men have lived. Burslem was the mother town of the potters Wedgwood, Doulton, and Claris Cliff. They all had their apprentices in Burslem, and then dedicated their lives to bringing the world the finest china. *Titanic* Captain Edward John Smith was born in Etruria just down the road, and the brewery was named in his honor. It is owned by brothers Dave and Keith Bott, who have overseen the continual growth of the brewery.

This is an old-fashioned stout, made from Maris Otter pale malt, wheat malt, roasted barley, and finished with Northdown, Yakima, Galena, and Goldings hops. It pours dark brown with roasted malts, coffee, chocolate, and licorice all coming through on the nose as well as the palate. A hint of sweetness is balanced by the roastiness and hops. This is a pretty much straightforward beer, but that is not at all a criticism; that is a compliment. If you're looking for a robust stout, this is pretty much it—strongly flavored and well-balanced. Despite the name, at 4.5% ABV, you won't get that sinking feeling if you down more than one.

SURVIVAL 7-GRAIN STOUT

HOPWORKS URBAN BREWERY

Hopworks Urban Brewery and Hopworks BikeBar are Portland, Oregon's, first eco-brewpubs. Christian Ettinger, the brewmaster and owner, opened the doors in 2007. They offer handcrafted organic beers made from fresh local ingredients, all served in sustainably built and operated buildings. Hopworks incorporates many aspects of sustainability. From composting to salvaged materials and from pervious pavers to hand dryers, they walk the walk. Hopworks is 100% renewably powered and "cradle to gate" carbon-neutral. This 20-barrel brewery produces 10,500 barrels a year.

The seven grains used in this beer are barley (Egyptian), wheat (Mesopotamian), oats (Egyptian), amaranth (Aztec), quinoa (Incan), spelt (Mesopotamian), and kamut (Egyptian). The brew is finished with 20 pounds of cold-pressed local Stumptown Coffee Roasters Organic Holler Mountain coffee.

This 5.8% ABV beer pours garnet dark brown. With lots of roasty grains and great nuttiness, it has a nice mouthfeel from the oatmeal and other grains. The low ABV helps it go down easy.

TRES BLUEBERRY STOUT

DARK HORSE BREWING COMPANY

Arron and Cally Morse of Dark Horse Brewing Company continue to brew high-end dark beers for their number series. Number three is a full-bodied stout made with malted barley and blueberries. It pours a dark black-brown with a dark tan head that lingers, showing nice lacing. Flavors of chocolate, roast malt, and light blueberry make up the palate, with lots of fruity blueberry aroma. This full-bodied brew is sweet up front with a pronounced blueberry nose and finishes dry. It is an amazing beer.

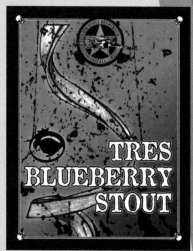

TROUBADOUR OBSCURA

BROUWERIJ THE MUSKETEERS

Troubadour Obscura is a dark red-brown beer with a rich malty body combined with different touches of a stout in a very nice balanced way: roast, chocolate, coffee, and vanilla. A lot of lace is left on the empty glass. Though technically a mild Belgian strong ale, it blurs the line between ales and stouts.

It has a pretty dark color, as one would expect from a stout, though it is slightly more red-brown than Irish stouts. A dense, rich creamy beige head crowns the glass. The beer referments in the bottle. This is deceptive, because the relatively high alcohol content (8.5% ABV) is not felt immediately, except maybe as a slight glowing sensation. There is a complex aftertaste with some licorice undertones, and a pleasant bitterness survives till the end.

JC

COFFEE STOUTS

Perfect for the java junkie, coffee stouts capture the flavor of everyone's favorite caffeinated pick-me-up. Brewers build the telltale flavor of coffee into their beers in a couple different ways, either by using dark roasted malts (like black patent) to add coffee-like notes, or by simply adding ground or brewed coffee into the brew. Coffee stouts tend to have the dry, bitter character of coffee, not to mention mimicking the look and smell of morning joe. Some sweeter examples are brewed with milk sugar (think latte) or chocolate, and oatmeal is sometimes used to provide for a velvety, smoother drinking brew. Coffee stouts drink well on their own but also pair well with dark chocolate desserts or coffee-rubbed meat entrees.

BLACK DAMNATION II—MOCHA BOMB

DE STRUISE BROUWERS

This beer really lives up to its name with an impenetrable black body capped by a huge creamy whipped mocha–colored head. It is menacing, unsettling stuff.

The smell is a coffee junkie's dream behind which lurks rich milk chocolate, charred wood, and hard roasted malts. After smelling this, you know that what's coming your way is going to be huge.

The word *complex* is often used to describe big beers, but in this case that descriptor falls woefully short. There are coffee beans smothered in dark chocolate, some slightly vinous notes (prunes), ash, vanilla, oak, and is that chili? If you took a sip of this beer every day for the rest of the year, you'd probably keep finding a new flavor in it.

The Black Damnation series is a dark twist of Struise brewmaster Urbain Coutteau's mind. His concept is to create a dozen intense beers using the brewery's Black Albert as their base. Black Damnation II is another blend of Hel & Verdoemenis from Brouwerij De Molen in which 50% of Black Albert was used after being matured for a while on whole coffee beans from a Columbian coffee plantation. Then it was blended with 25% of Hel & Verdoemenis that had been aged for six months on Jack Daniels barrels and 25% of Cuvée Delphine.

DP

BLACK MOCHA STOUT

HIGHLAND BREWING COMPANY

Highland Brewing Company rolled out its first kegs in December 1994. Built almost entirely of retrofitted dairy equipment, their original brewery in downtown Asheville, North Carolina, could produce up to 6,500 barrels of beer per year. They now brew more than 50,000 barrels annually after moving their operations to a larger facility in October 2006.

Black Mocha Stout pours dark brown-black with a nice head that lingers, and leaves a very nice lacing around the glass. Brewed with 2-row brewers malt, Munich, roasted barley, caramel 40, caramel 60, chocolate, extra special malt, and malted wheat, and balanced with Chinook and Mount Hood hops, this beer is well balanced and complex. It has a big roasty nose with toffee, coffee, and dark malt. The coffee generally gives way to dark chocolate, and a nice bitterness balances the beer. At 5.6% ABV, this is a nice drinking beer you can have more than one of . . . and you will.

BOURBON SIDAMO

HARDYWOOD PARK CRAFT BREWERY

This Imperial coffee stout aged in bourbon barrels is made at Hardywood Brewery in Richmond, Virginia. An assertive stout aged twelve weeks in bourbon barrels and conditioned on custom roasted Sidamo coffee from Lamplighter Roasting Company, Bourbon Sidamo showcases the signature flavors of whiskey, roasted malt, and Ethiopian coffee. This robust stout displays a midnight hue with a caramel head and offers a dark chocolate character laced with hints of blueberry from this unique coffee bean, rounded out by charred white oak.

BREAKFAST STOUT

LONG IRELAND BEER COMPANY

Long Ireland Beer Company began a little differently than most businesses. Two guys named Greg and Dan wanted to start a brewery, not so different yet. But while setting up the legal aspects of the business, they had a unique opportunity. They became friends with Rob, the owner of New England Brewing Company in Connecticut. Rob is a highly respected brewer with almost twenty years experience in the brewing industry, and he was willing to allow them to work hands-on with him in *his* brewery and begin making *their* beer.

Now they have their own brewery, in Riverhead, Long Island, where they make this wonderful coffee stout. It has a low 3.5% ABV, so maybe you could have it for breakfast. It is sweet and smooth, made with fine roasted Kenyan coffee, which gives the beer a nice roasty flavor, and a big, big boost of coffee flavor. This beer is made with flaked oats and milk sugar ,which imparts that cream and coffee breakfast taste. Easy to down a bunch of these. Very drinkable.

CAPPUCCINO STOUT

LAGUNITAS BREWING COMPANY

Among the dozens and dozens of breweries that were established on the West Coast in the early 1990s, Lagunitas is one of the greatest success stories. Led by outspoken (to a fault) founder Tony Magee and passionately devoted to the craft side of craft brewing, Lagunitas has been one of the fastest growing breweries in the country for much of the last decade. The brewery is known for an irreverent attitude and esoteric beers, and every one of its concoctions is a delight. Alongside a well-crafted Imperial stout, Lagunitas produces the coffee-infused Cappuccino Stout on a seasonal basis.

With the nose on a bottle of Cappuccino Stout—coffee, more coffee, and a touch of vanilla—the drinker might expect the brew to pour the milky tan of its namesake cappuccino, but Cappuccino Stout pours as dark as black coffee, with just the lightest ruby highlights along the edges. The head, a billowing khaki tan, is a bit closer to a cappuccino's foamy cap. Since there's a pound of Sebastopol's Hardcore Espresso in every barrel, it's no surprise that the main flavor isn't far from dark-roast coffee. However, there is plenty of beer here: The malts add some chocolate notes, and a heavy dose of Cascade hops adds citrusy bitterness at 9.2 ABV. Like a good cup of coffee, the Cappuccino Stout pairs well with chocolate desserts or even a breakfast pastry.

JC

CHICORY STOUT

DOGFISH HEAD BREWERY

If you enjoy the subtle nuances of a well-crafted beer, Dogfish Head Chicory Stout is for you. Although coffee stouts generally are thought of as big, heavy beers and Dogfish Head is known for beers of that style, this beer is surprising in many ways. It doesn't have the in-your-face robustness of an Imperial, but it has the great taste, balance, and drinkability of a high-quality beer.

It has an opaque black hue all around and forms a big frothy coffee-colored heard that retains very well and leaves some lacing. There is a strong coffee aroma, but with a distinct herbal or earthy sweetness even though it is not sugary. It has the classic stout flavor at the core, but the edges are rounded out with fine details. Coffee is a strong flavor throughout the palate and is the first thing you taste. It's not sweet, sugary iced coffee, nor is it intense, deeply roasted coffee. The taste is a perfect middle ground that's balanced with something other than sugar and cream. According to the description, the beer is brewed with licorice root, which would account for that taste.

There is some detectable bitterness in the middle, with hints of citrus, though it's a short-lived flavor. The coffee flavor comes back at the end along with a dry, spicy chicory flavor. It's similar to nutmeg or cinnamon but more refined. All these flavors add up to a delectable, delightful palate and make this a good dessert brew without the chutzpah of something Imperial.

CP

ESPRESSO STOUT MALI RESERVE

NASHOBA VALLEY WINERY

Nashoba, long a winery in western Massachusetts, started brewing beer in 2004. Each beer is hand crafted in small batches, employing both traditional brewing methods and American craft-brewing creativity. They mill their grain on site and grow hops used in their operations, and they use no additives. The Special Reserve Series is where Nashoba shines; each of the beers is brewed in small batches of only seven barrels.

Nashoba Espresso Stout Mali Reserve is a high-alcohol ale made with chocolate malt and roasted barley, which gives their beer a deep black-brown color and bitter cocoa flavor. The beer is aged in oak to add complexity to the flavor. Then come the coffee beans and even more complexity. Mali Reserve is 8.5% ABV, so it's a big, robust beer. The taste is big, big espresso and roasted coffee that give way to a nice balance of dark bitterness with hints of licorice. Despite a slight sweetness mid-body, the beer finishes dry.

HITACHINO NEST ESPRESSO STOUT

KIUCHI BREWERY

There plenty of coffee stouts, but few claim to be an espresso stout per se. Unfortunately, Hitachino Nest Espresso Stout didn't deliver much coffee character but instead drank like a decent Russian Imperial stout, which is the base style.

There is a dark opaque black body with no carbonation or sediment visible. It forms a large dark tan foamy-soapy head that retains and laces well. The aroma is reminiscent of that of a foreign extra stout with notes of black licorice and some dairy. There are slight roasty notes but nothing overtly coffee-smelling. It is mild overall.

Much like the nose, there's a foreign extra stout character to the flavor. Black licorice, some currants or dark berries, and maybe a hint of sour grape are prominent through the first half. There's a dry bitterness at the apex that has the bitterness of black coffee but not the taste. In the end you're left with a pretty standard and enjoyable FES-style brew, and that's okay.

Since Hitachino Nest Espresso Stout isn't all that intense, it's easy to drink. The mouthfeel is a little thin, on the calmer end, and it goes down quite smooth. There is a dry bitter aftertaste, which might be attributed to the use of espresso beans in the boil. The 7.5% ABV is not noticeable as it drinks like something much smaller.

CP

IMPERIAL JAVA STOUT

SANTA FE BREWING COMPANY

Beer: it's what's for breakfast, and when a beer is for breakfast, there's only one style that's appropriate: coffee stout. This is why the appearance of Santa Fe's Imperial Java Stout on store shelves makes me so happy.

Pour the beer into a shaker pint and you'll see that the brew resembles java not just in name but in appearance. Pitch-black and watery thin, the liquid is capped by a pillowy head of cascading bubbles the color of brown sugar. Frothy trails of lace coat the sides of the glass like latte foam.

Because their dark, toasty, burnt flavors often overlap, few ingredients work together so well in a beer as roasted malt and coffee beans. For Imperial Java Stout, Santa Fe makes use of organically grown East Timor coffee beans blended with New Guinea coffee beans, both of which are roasted by Ohori's Coffee in Santa Fe. The result is a stout that's huge in coffee aroma and flavor. The scent is akin to burying your nose in a cup of java; it's packed with espresso and sweet cream. Touches of sourdough and a shot of chocolate syrup mingle in the background.

The flavor delivers a similar dose of roasted beans, though it's a little more acidic. A complex blend of American Bravo and English Fuggle hops lends subtle spice and earthy qualities, and touches of burnt toast play off the coffee. It's a bit harsh, like very black coffee, until the the swallow delivers oats and cream, sweetening things and smoothing them out.

If you're not a fan of coffee, you'll probably hate this beer because the flavor is riddled with it, and the coffee actually overpowers the underlying stout. But the beans are high quality, and if you're looking to replace your morning joe with something a little more alcoholic, pour this in your mug. No one will be the wiser.

The text on the can advises that the brew is "not for use with donuts" but doesn't say anything about coffee cake. The roasted malt tones down the cake's sweetness and accents its flavor, and the buttery dessert smoothes out the bitterness of the coffee beans.

ZF

JAVA HEAD STOUT
TRÖEGS BREWING COMPANY

It's not a common notion that a coffee stout could or should be deliberately hoppy (hoppy, not bitter; there's a difference). But this seems to be the idea behind Tröegs Java Head, a coffee stout with a prominent hop character. It has an opaque black to dark-brown body and forms a dark tan frothy head that laces and retains very well. There is a prominent stout aroma of roasted barley and subtle chocolate and coffee notes but also a surprising hop presence of citrus and pine.

Strong citrusy bitterness is the first thing to hit the palate, making this brew very reminiscent of a classic American IPA. Through the middle there is a smooth, silky, slightly sweet stout taste of roasted barley and a quick kick of coffee flavor. As it finishes, there's a dank resiny character that brings the palate back full circle to the original hoppy character, but this time it's piney instead of citrusy. The aftertaste is surprisingly clean even though this beer has both big-time hops (60 IBU) and coffee in it.

What was most surprising was that it had been bottled nine months earlier yet the hops had not faded at all. In fact, the coffee and stronger stout qualities may have succumbed a bit to age. There was a layer of goo on the bottom of the bottle, so perhaps this beer is bottle-conditioned; this could partially explain why it kept so well for so long.

This brew has pretty much the perfect mouthfeel and drinking experience for a beer of this nature. Not thick and viscous and far from watery, Tröegs Java Head has a medium body and a perfect carbonation level. It's not quite velvety but closer to silky, and it goes down extremely smooth. At 7.5% ABV it's not nearly as heavy as that number would indicate. Most drinkers could put away two 12-ounce bottles or a single 22-ounce bomber by themselves without any trouble.

CP

JAVA STOUT

BELL'S BREWERY

You take a stout, add coffee, and it usually tastes really good. Perhaps that's a cynical way of approaching Bell's Java Stout, but what sets it apart from others of the genre is that the coffee flavor never fades and neither does its genuine hefty stout base brew. It has an ink-black body with no visible carbonation that pours into a large dark tan frothy-creamy head that laces and retains wonderfully. It has a huge nose of coffee and roasted malt. Back to the cynicism: It seems that coffee stouts are almost foolproof in a way. In fact, there really isn't much to critique the taste on; it's a beer that's excellent in comparison to others of the style that are just plain good. What it

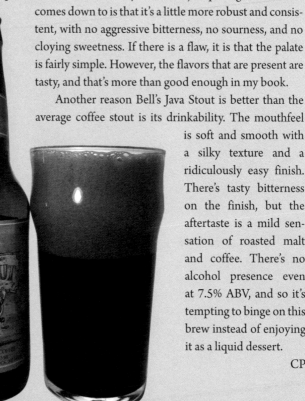

comes down to is that it's a little more robust and consistent, with no aggressive bitterness, no sourness, and no cloying sweetness. If there is a flaw, it is that the palate is fairly simple. However, the flavors that are present are tasty, and that's more than good enough in my book.

Another reason Bell's Java Stout is better than the average coffee stout is its drinkability. The mouthfeel is soft and smooth with a silky texture and a ridiculously easy finish. There's tasty bitterness on the finish, but the aftertaste is a mild sensation of roasted malt and coffee. There's no alcohol presence even at 7.5% ABV, and so it's tempting to binge on this brew instead of enjoying it as a liquid dessert.

CP

MIDNIGHT SUN ESPRESSO STOUT

YUKON BREWING COMPANY

When you live in the land of the midnight sun, drinking plenty of coffee is a way of life (some would say a necessity). So is having the occasional beer. Combining the two makes sense on many levels, including using coffee beans from a local roaster (Midnight Sun) to match the dark, roasted character of the malts in this brew. It's like an espresso with just the right amount of sugar. Although at 6.2% ABV this stout could stand to be a little more potent, it's still a very enjoyable brew.

JR

NEW GLARUS COFFEE STOUT

NEW GLARUS BREWING COMPANY

Dan Carey, a Diploma Master Brewer, is well known in the microbrewery world, having worked in the brewing industry since the age of twenty. He earned a bachelor's degree in food science with an emphasis on malting and brewing science from the University of California at Davis in 1983. Deborah Carey is the founder and president of the New Glarus Brewing Company of New Glarus, Wisconsin. She raised the capital for the start-up as a gift to her husband, becoming the first woman to found and operate a brewery in the United States.

Hearty and satisfying, this coffee stout is a big full-bodied brew made with Wisconsin water, roasted malts, and American hops. Cold-pressed organic coffee from the local roaster the Just Coffee Coop is infused into the brew. The pour is brown-black pour with a big creamy head. The robust malt nose is balanced by an array of exotic flavors.

NILS OSCAR COFFEE STOUT

NILS OSCAR BRYGGERI

This beer pours a clear red mahogany brown with a latte-colored head that collapses pretty quickly to a petri dish finish. It certainly lives up to its name, with a distinct aroma of freshly ground coffee, dark chocolate, and nutmeg and suggestions of berry fruits. There are also smells of stainless steel when it is cold, so let it warm up a bit if you've been keeping it in the fridge.

Initially there is a creamy mouthfeel, almost as though this coffee stout had some steamed milk in it, and a crisp, roasted coffee flavor combined with some subtle medium-sweet red berry flavors and hazelnuts. Toward the end things get a little uncomfortable as the mouthfeel loses a bit of its fullness and finishes slightly sour as the roasted flavor shifts from standard coffee to espresso, leaving a slightly burnt, bitter, and salty aftertaste that lingers for a long time after the glass is empty. It is complex and intriguing.

The obvious fit would be any dessert that has coffee and/or chocolate flavors in it. However, one could take more of a risk and pair it with *älgwallenbergarna* (a kind of posh elkburger) or chicken with a coffee mole sauce.

Nils Oscar turned to the Swedish coffee roastery Johan & Nyström for advice on which coffee to use and opted for an espresso made from coffee from Fazenda Ambiental Fortaleza in Brazil, which is known for its sweetness and fruitiness as the coffee plant fruit is left to ripen fully before being picked and dried in the sun.

DC

SCHLAFLY COFFEE STOUT
THE SCHLAFLY TAP ROOM

People tend to think of coffee stouts as big Imperial brews, and so when you find one with a smaller body, it's an interesting experience. Schlafly Coffee Stout is more of a standard American stout with coffee added and is a drinker-friendly beer in many ways. It's not as mammoth as the imperialized brews, but for something on the smaller end it's impressive.

The body is opaque black and forms a small tan soapy head that almost completely dissipates and leaves little lacing on the glass. The aroma is of medium-roast coffee aroma plus a general sweet scent.

If you want the delectable palate of a coffee stout without the density of an Imperial, Schlafly Coffee Stout is the beer for you. It is remarkably sweet all around with an almost colalike taste and accompanying sweetness yet is not overtly sugary or cloying. A gentle bitterness through the middle imparts some roasted malt taste and a hint of hops. The palate ends with a coffee taste that's on the darker, more robust side, as it should be since the label says it's brewed with French roasted coffee. The coffee taste lingers for a moment or two and can be savored with some effort. It's a somewhat simplistic, repetitive palate, but the net result is enjoyable.

What really makes this beer enjoyable is the fact that its palate is flavorful without needing the raw energy of a bigger beer. The mouthfeel and body are both perfectly medium: neither thick nor thin, neither short nor cloying. It goes down smooth with an aftertaste that's quite clean. At 5.7% ABV, it would be easy to throw back a few of these as dessert without feeling any guilt.

CP

LA SEMEUSE ESPRESSO STOUT

BRASSERIE TROIS DAMES

This stout formerly was known as La Semeuse, it is now labeled simply "Espresso Stout". Brewed at Brasserie Trois Dames in Switzerland, it is made with a coffee blend that contains 90% arabica from Brazil and Ethiopia and 10% robusta from Vietnam. It pours black. In the glass the combination of coffee and beer creates a heady aroma. The head reminds one of cappuccino. Coffee dominates the nose, but there are lovely background notes of molasses, cocoa, and spice. Strong, racy, rounded, velvety, and complex, this beer clocks in at 7.5% ABV. This is a stout that must be treated with respect.

CHOCOLATE STOUTS

Nearly everyone—beer drinkers and non-drinkers alike—is united by a common love of chocolate. While many styles of stout offer hints of cocoa, chocolate stouts bring the flavor of dark chocolate to the fore. As with coffee stouts, brewers create the style's signature taste both through brewing with darker, aromatic malt (which creates a chocolate flavor) and simply by adding chocolate to the final brew. Dark in color, full-bodied, and with an aroma out of Willy Wonka's factory, sweet and decadent chocolate stouts have won over many who claimed not to enjoy beer. Given the purported aphrodisiacal qualities of chocolate, it should come as no surprise that these stouts pair well with similarly salacious foods like oysters, crème brûlée, and chocolate cake.

BRASSERIE
DIEU DU CIEL!
Aphrodite

Stout brewed with real cocoa
and vanilla beans

6.5% ALC/VOL
Unfiltered beer

11.5 fl. oz.

APHRODITE
DIEU DU CIEL!

Chocolate beers are a seemingly foolproof product. What's not to like? In the case of Aphrodite, the Montreal-based microbrewery Dieu du Ciel! has created a beer that lives up its reputation (ranked in the top one-hundreth percentile on RateBeer.com and graded an A overall on BeerAdvocate.

com). It's an outstanding beer for all the right reasons. It is better known as Aprhodisiaque or Aphrodisiac but goes by Aphrodite in the United States because of US Food and Drug Administration regulations.

This beer pours to an opaque black body. Although many stouts appear to be black, they are actually dark ruby red, but Aphrodite does not have the faintest trace of a red outline even when held up to direct light. It forms a large foamy brown head that lasts for the life of the beer and leaves generous lacing on the glass. The aroma is surprisingly mild with a general malty scent, although chocolate is noticeable.

Dieu Du Ciel! describes Aphrodite as a "cocoa and vanilla stout," which is already very intriguing even before one tastes it. There are plenty of stouts that describe themselves as chocolate, but this beer intends to be a little more complex. It is apparent from the first sip that this intention was achieved. The head is rich, sweet, and chocolaty. Immediately the palate is saturated with a rich milk chocolate–like flavor followed by a lightly roasted malt finish. There is a distinct but fairly mild bitterness in the aftertaste. Compared with the baker's chocolate aftertaste in other chocolate stouts, this beer is noticeably sweeter, most likely as a result of the use of vanilla bean in the recipe.

Aphrodite is not to my knowledge oak-aged, but there is a distinct earthiness to the finish. This could be explained by the fact that the brewery lists bourbon among the notable flavors in the palate. This taste becomes more noticeable as the beer warms, and because this is not an Imperial brew, it's quite inviting.

At 6.5% ABV this is a perfectly proportional beer. It's not trying to show off the way a lot of Imperial stouts do, but it's got the gusto that pedestrian session stouts lack. Not only is the palate delicious, the process of drinking it is a pleasure as well. For a carbonated beer, it drinks like a nitrogen-charged brew with a thick creamy texture and a velvety finish. In fact, it's so tasty and so smooth, it was a challenge not to slug it down.

CP

BLACK CHOCOLATE STOUT

BROOKLYN BREWERY

Founded in 1987 by journalist Steve Hindy and banker Tom Potter and helmed by the charismatic brewmaster Garrett Oliver, the Brooklyn Brewery is one of the true standouts in the US craft beer market. The borough of Brooklyn is now a hotbed of brewing and craft beer activity, and much of the credit goes to the neighborhood's original post-Prohibition brewers. As one of the largest independent breweries in the country and the largest exporter of craft beer in the States, Brooklyn's reputation stretches well beyond the five boroughs.

Black Chocolate Stout is one of the brewery's seasonal brews, rolling out every fall for the Northeast's cold winter season. Made from three mashes and aged for four months before release, the beer is a bomb of rich cocoa flavors. Although many chocolate stouts are brewed with some sort of the namesake cacao, either an extract or steeped beans, BCS gains all of its chocolate flavors from its heavily roasted "chocolate" malt. Bittersweet dark chocolate takes center stage in the flavor of this stout, with roasty coffee sneaking in around the edges. It's a thick but velvety-smooth beer, definitely a sipper and a better aperitif than a mealside brew, especially at 10% ABV.

When it first was brewed in the 1990s, Brooklyn's BCS was the first beer brewed in the States to be called a chocolate stout. It's still one of the best.

JC

CHOCOLATE RAIN

THE BRUERY

This a proper dark brown with blood red highlights, though the vintage changes year to year. It pours to a tiny tan soapy head that fizzles away and leaves no lacing. It is not quite as aromatic as expected. It features the barrel character, vanilla, and a strong alcohol presence. The Bruery's Chocolate Rain is a variation of its Black Tuesday Imperial stout. The difference is that this brew is aged on cacao nibs and vanilla beans. Chocolate Rain is actually not too sweet, but it is well-balanced.

The palate here is pretty similar to that of Black Tuesday. A strong presence of vanilla, wood, grape, plum, and cherry are present from start to finish. Ironically, there isn't a lot of chocolate flavor per se, though this is not likely intended to be taken as a chocolate-flavored beer despite the name. The bitterness is low, though the overall sweetness is, too. The alcohol is a major component of the palate, and it works quite well. There is a bit of nutty or earthy character on the back end but not much roasted malt flavor. Overall, this is a tasty, interesting palate, and definitely one of the best extreme beers around.

Chocolate Rain is 18.5% ABV, just a little lighter than Black Tuesday. The alcohol makes up a bigger part of the palate here, imparting warmth throughout, not just on the finish. Regardless, it's tame and not harsh, hot, or slick. The mouthfeel is calm and comfortable with a smooth finish and a relatively clean aftertaste. This is an interesting and impressive beer best enjoyed as a novelty and shared with friends on a special occasion.

CP

CHOCOLATE STOUT

FORT COLLINS BREWERY

Breweries that try their hand at chocolate beers walk a very fine line between genuine craft beer and gimmicks. Sometimes the gimmick is the supposed craftsmanship. This is not true of Fort Collins Chocolate Stout, which has all the makings of a high-quality beer with the addition of a great chocolate taste.

This beer pours extremely smoothly to a dark, seemingly opaque black body that is actually dark ruby red. The body is rather tepid with little to no carbonation noticeable and only a small soapy light brown head. There isn't much chocolate noticeable in the nose, but there is an aroma of roasted malts that is typical of high-end stouts.

Often the first thing one notices about a chocolate beer is, not surprisingly, the chocolate flavor. However, with Fort Collins Chocolate Stout, the first thing one notes is an intense hoppy composition. If you are a fan of hoppy beers such as India Pale Ales, this can be pleasantly surprising. This beer has a strong hop bite and a bitterness to match.

The chocolate is much more noticeable in the finish than in the initial approach. Many chocolate beers tend to have chalky character reminiscent of confectioner's sugar, but Fort Collins has a delicious palate of sweet dark chocolate without any sugary or gimmicky taste. The subtle chocolate taste complements the hop character well, making this a very robust beer. Dark roasted malts are also evident and balance the beer perfectly.

For such a hoppy brew, Fort Collins Chocolate Stout is ridiculously smooth. It has a gentle mouthfeel that's as soft as a pillow, and it finishes just as comfortably. This probably is due to the well-balanced palate and the surprisingly thin body. The only caveat is that it leaves a dry aftertaste, which is a small price to pay for an otherwise outstanding performer.

At only 5.3% ABV, Fort Collins Chocolate Stout isn't close to being an Imperial beer. It's probably a little heavy in calories and carbs, though. From our experience, it certainly doesn't feel like a hefty beer and one could go through many bottles of it quickly and easily.

CP

CHOCOLATE STOUT

ROGUE ALES

This beer is a deep shade of black coming out of the bottle. It pours to a large brown frothy head that retains and laces very well. The aroma is dark chocolate candy with some roasted malt.

When a beer is called a chocolate stout, you go in with an expectation, but although Rogue Chocolate Stout is plenty chocolaty, it's not all chocolate all the time. It's more of a strong stout that happens to have a bitter dark chocolate taste on the finish. It's also quite bitter with significant hop presence throughout.

Big stouts are pretty bitter from the roasted barley. There's a taste akin to burnt toast right away here. It's dry and slightly astringent, but there's an underlying sweetness. It doesn't change much at the apex, though the second half of the swig is the best part because that's when all the chocolate is revealed. It's a bitter dark chocolate, not particularly sweet or milky. A hint of vanilla can be detected as well as some minor citrus flavors from the Cascade hops. At 69 IBU, there's a reason the hops are prominent here. There's a minor oatmeal sweetness on the aftertaste, though it fades quickly. This is a solid, well-balanced stout that may leave you wanting more chocolate. For those who don't like too much chocolate, this may be the perfect beer.

Although Rogue Chocolate Stout is not a session beer, it's not an Imperial beast either. It's a full-bodied beer, though the mouthfeel may seem a touch light for the style. It's comfortable, though, and it goes down smooth. There is a slightly dry residual aftertaste, but it's tolerable. At 6% ABV it's a relatively strong beer, though most drinkers should have no trouble handling the 22-ounce bottle.

CP

HARDYWOOD RASPBERRY STOUT

HARDYWOOD PARK CRAFT BREWERY

This beer is made from chocolate stout brewed with local red raspberries at Hardywood Brewery in Richmond, Virginia. Brewed with heaps of chocolate malt, cacao nibs, and local, late season red raspberries from Agriberry Farm, Hardywood Raspberry Stout captures the essence of a decadent raspberry truffle in liquid form. An intriguing ale, this stout has enticing cocoa aromatics that build nicely to a flavorful high point that resonates with dark chocolate, subsiding with a sweet, tart raspberry jam–laced finish. It is different and delicious.

HARPOON CHOCOLATE STOUT

HARPOON BREWERY

Harpoon Chocolate Stout is very tasty and easy to drink. The only problem is that it's difficult to find. It is exactly what it claims to be, with an opaque black body with only the slightest hint of dark ruby red around the edges. It forms an average-size, dark-tan foamy head that doesn't lace the glass much. The aroma is identical to that of a high-end dark chocolate bar or candy. There is a slight hint of other malts present, but mostly it screams "chocolate!"

There's something really impressive about a beer that is so chocolaty that you're able to taste the palate when the foam hits your lips. That's exactly what happened with Harpoon Chocolate Stout. Once the liquid made it way to my palate, it was even more pleasing.

Up front you get a very intense flavor of dark chocolate, reminiscent of Godiva or Ghirardelli candy. It's quite rich, but not to the point of being gimmicky or overpowering. On the finish there is a dry bitterness like semisweet baker's chocolate. This could be from the hops since this is a fairly hoppy beer at 40 IBU.

As good as the palate is, there's a noticeably thin, almost watery texture to the mouthfeel. You might prefer something more thick and velvety since the flavor does not linger that much in the aftertaste. Harpoon Chocolate Stout's chocolaty flavor is very satisfying and is delivered via a surprisingly thin body. This might seem like a demerit because the beer lends itself to slugging rather than savoring, but it's really a compliment.

At 5.9% ABV this is a pretty robust, full-bodied beer that works very well as an alternative to dessert or paired with something light such as a piece or two of good chocolate or fresh strawberries. One bottle is enough to satisfy the average drinker as the weight is proportional to the flavor and potency. Harpoon Chocolate Stout is available in mixed packs of Harpoon beers or alone in its own six-packs. You'll probably opt for the latter, mostly because it would be difficult to find another beer whose quality can stand up to this one's.

CP

IMPERIAL CHOCOLATE STOUT

SANKT GALLEN BREWING

Sankt Gallen Brewing is made in Atsugi, Kanagawa, Japan. The brewery has an international following for its chocolate beer, which is so popular that in January 2013 Sankt Gallen introduced a new combo set of a 330-milliliter bottle of its Imperial Chocolate Stout with an edible glass made entirely of chocolate. The chocolate cup is safe and specially designed to melt and dissolve in the mouth, not in the hand.

According to Sankt Gallen, the beer style was born in London in the early eighteenth ce ntury and almost vanished in the subsequent one hundred years. With the boom of American beer in the 1990s, there was a stunning revival.

Sankt Gallen's Imperial Chocolate Stout is made using pale ale malt, Myunikku, Crystal 20° L, 60° L, and chocolate malts along with hops such as Chinook and Willamette. The beer pours dark brown in color and has a nose of slightly burnt malt and big chocolate. There's some spiciness from the hops. At 5.5% ABV, the alcohol seems very light, and the beer is very drinkable.

MOO-HOO CHOCOLATE MILK STOUT

TERRAPIN BEER COMPANY

This beer has a dark black hue; it is completely opaque, with no visible carbonation. It forms a small light brown foamy head that disappears almost completely and leaves no lacing. The smell is similar to that of a chocolate candy bar with a hint of dairy.

Terrapin Moo-Hoo Chocolate Milk Stout, brewed in Athens, Georgia, purports to be a classier chocolate stout that uses cocoa nibs and shells, not just chocolate flavoring. It is indeed a good beer, and if you like the flavor of a chocolate candy bar, you'll get it in this beer.

A light sweetness up front is followed by a strong surge of familiar supermarket chocolate candy plus an underlying bitterness. There is a short, dry bitterness at the crest of the palate that is followed by a slight tang or sourness. There's additional chocolate flavor on the finish, but it's quite mild with little aftertaste. Although this beer may not be a mind blower, it's tasty in the mouth and fun to drink.

Sometimes chocolate stouts can be so rich that they're sippers, but Moo-Hoo Chocolate is on the milder side, and so it's easy to drink quickly (maybe a little too quickly). The mouthfeel is on the thinner side, and it goes down easy. At 6% ABV it seems a bit inefficient, as if it didn't take full advantage of its strength, though that makes it much easier to quaff and all the more tempting to drink multiple servings.

CP

240

THE HANDBOOK OF PORTERS & STOUTS

ODD NOTION
(FALL 2009)

MAGIC HAT BREWING COMPANY

In its Night of the Living Dead mix pack for fall 2009, Magic Hat included a Belgian Chocolate Stout as the seasonal Odd Notion. Their Odd Notions change year to year, but this one is worth mentioning. When American breweries market their beers as being Belgian-style, it's often a marketing gimmick, but this case is an exception. You can't say how close this beer is to a real Belgian chocolate stout (technically, it's a Belgian dark ale), but for a beer in and of itself it's impressive. Its mixture of chocolate, roasted malts, and hop bitterness and its smooth finish add up to a great beer.

When you hear the term *chocolate stout*, a certain image comes to mind: A jet black beer with a dark-brown creamy head, and that's a dead-on description of this beer. It looks very inviting and tasty, like dessert in a glass.

Magic Hat's Odd Notion aroma is strong, with roasted malts and chocolate announcing their presence as soon as the bottle is opened. It has all the makings of beers of this style that people love: a complex palate of roasted (but not burnt) malts, milk chocolate, and a bitter hoppy finish.

What distinguishes this beer from other American brews is its use of real Belgian yeast to give it just the slightest Trappist-like taste. There is some spice on top of the chocolate to give it some pep and perhaps a fruity taste of sorts (plum and apple). The flavor is much stronger on the finish and leaves a pleasant aftertaste that's almost as strong as the initial swig.

The roasted malt flavor plays an almost equal role with the chocolate, but this brew is milder than the more intense stouts. Magic Hat seems to be targeting a wider audience with Odd Notion. It is impressive how well the bitterness is balanced against the malt sweetness. At 50 IBU, this is at the level of a pale ale or IPA, but without any dryness.

Chocolate beers are some of the most drinker-friendly brews on the market. This chocolate stout is surprisingly mild and a bit thin on the initial sip, but all the flavor comes out in spades on the finish. The mouth-feel is quite soft but noticeably weighty, and this beer is very drinkable overall. At 6.2% ABV it sounds much heavier than it feels, and should likely be had instead of, rather than in addition to, dessert.

This was the most impressive of Magic Hat's Odd Notion seasonal beers. It's a totally worthy choice. It would be great if it was brewed year-round and sold on its own. (This beer is no longer in production.)

CP

ORGANIC CHOCOLATE STOUT

BISON BREWING

Bison's Organic Chocolate Stout is nearly opaque black with ruby red edges and forms a large, frothy dark tan head that sticks around and laces very well. Its aroma is of roasted malts with a light chocolate, almost candy-like scent.

The first thing you taste is roasted malt, light bitterness, and a quick flavor of chocolate just as it finishes. The chocolate is from the cocoa powder used in the mash, not a refined chocolate candy. This gives the beer an almost chocolate cereal–like taste in the finish. It's similar to the way the milk tastes after a bowl of Cocoa Krispies or Cocoa Pebbles. Those looking for the intense richness of a Southern Tier Choklat shouldn't have that kind of expectation here. The sweetness is low, but the bitterness is low, too. It's one of those rare beers that have a mild palate that is still delectable. The mouthfeel is medium, soft, and tepid with a slightly creamy texture.

With a tasty palate and a silky mouthfeel, Bison Organic Chocolate Stout is an extremely quaffable beer. At only 5% ABV, it's quite session-able, too. Although not extremely robust, it's tasty enough to work as a stand-alone dessert beer or paired with a vanilla or chocolate dessert (cookies, cake, ice cream, pie, etc.). Overall, this is a very impressive stout in more ways than one.

CP

PEANUT BUTTER CHOCOLATE STOUT

BANDWAGON BREWPUB

BandWagon Brewpub in Ithaca, New York, has an unusual history. There are five owners, all of whom worked at the defunct Lost Dog Cafe on South Cayuga Street. They found a space that had housed a restaurant and leased it on December 1, 2008, deciding to open their own brewpub on the site. Asked why a brewpub, co-owner Alex Johnson told the *Ithaca Times*, "We wanted to create an alternative to the many downtown bars that have a dance club or pool hall feel and cater to undergrads. And we definitely didn't want to serve mainstream beers."

They try to be as local as it gets, sourcing local products from local producers. Their Red Rooster Espresso Stout, a malty American stout, is brewed using Red Rooster Espresso from the neighboring Ithaca Coffee Company.

According to the folks at Band-Wagon, "Brewing beer is an art based on a science. It combines age-old practices with modern technologies and liberties. . . . Historically always brewed on a local scale, beer was a craft that was as individual and unique as the person that crafted it and the ingredients available to them. Only at specific pubs could certain tastes be enjoyed. The brewpub served as a meeting place where laughs, ideas, and thoughts have been shared and sometimes where revolutions have originated. They served as the hub of the social and political structures of their surrounding areas, and moreover, as a place where inspirations manifest."

The brewers go on to say, "At the BandWagon Brewery we honor the many facets of brewing as it's evolved over the millennia by taking pride in both the products we put into our beer and the ones we put out. We pay homage to classical brewing through practicing some traditional brewing styles while experimenting with new techniques and ingredients, nurturing our craft to create unique and individual beers."

This beer pours beautifully, with a dark-brown body and a lovely creamy dark tan head. The nose is just like a Reese's Peanut Butter Cup or a box of chocolate and Nutter Butter cookies with big notes of roasted peanuts and deep malted chocolate. The taste isn't the same as what you smell, though, and that's not a bad thing. The peanut so prominent on the nose gives way to a slightly sweet but easy-drinking stout. The mouthfeel is creamy with lots of chocolate, cocoa, and coffee, and there's a hint of raspberry. It is medium bodied and possibly a tad light for a stout. This is more of a drinking beer than one would suspect; chewy as it is, it goes down surprisingly easy. The peanut butter does come back on the aftertaste, but in a nice way. Hints of malt come through at the end as well. This beer is very smooth and silky, making for easy drinking.

SAMUEL SMITH'S ORGANIC CHOCOLATE STOUT

SAMUEL SMITH, THE OLD BREWERY

There are many different ways to brew a chocolate beer: with chocolate malt and/or wheat, cocoa beans, cocoa powder, or even actual chocolate candy. Samuel Smith's Organic Chocolate Stout is made with the first two, and it shows. Although it has the classic chocolate flavor, it's a bit more spicy and zesty while remaining an otherwise mild-mannered traditional stout.

This beer has a seemingly opaque black color. It forms a large tan frothy head that leaves plenty of lacing and retains well. The aroma features distinct cocoa powder or another chocolate-like flavoring. There is a traditional stout aroma at the base.

The first thing you notice about Samuel Smith's Organic Chocolate Stout is the presence of cocoa bean spice. Usually a chocolate beer tends to taste like liquid candy, and although this beer definitely is sweet, it uses the cocoa beans for their liveliness. There's a gentle vibration on the tongue as roasted malt slithers across it. There seems to be added sugar or vanilla flavoring to balance out the cocoa

and impart a bit of candylike flavor. A gentle bitterness through the middle is followed by a somewhat strange taste of perfume or soap. There's more classic chocolate on the finish, followed by a moderately dry but mostly clean aftertaste.

Although this is a good dessert beer, it's not one you're going to get used to. That's okay, because you'll really appreciate the originality.

The body is exactly what you expect in a British stout: full-flavored but still restrained and nuanced. There is a good level of carbonation with a relatively soft texture and a comfortable mouthfeel that makes it go down smooth. At only 5% ABV this beer is extremely efficient but still light enough for to be enjoyed in multiple servings.

CP

SEXUAL CHOCOLATE

FOOTHILLS BREWING

Jamie Bartholomausis is the president and brewmaster of Foothills Brewing, in Winston-Salem, North Carolina. With his wife Sarah and co-owner Matt Masten, he has watched over the brewery as it grew from an 800-barrel production in 2005 into a multimillion-dollar regional brewery approaching 30,000 barrels a year in production.

Sexual Chocolate is a cocoa infused Imperial Stout with a 9.75% ABV. It is opaque black in color with a dark-brown head and a big chocolate aroma with notes of espresso, dark molasses, toffee, and dark fruit such as plum and fig. This beer is one of the most popular made by Foothills. Police have been on hand on release days each February to control the large and enthusiastic crowds. The brewery opens at 8 a.m. on those days, and the first spaces in line are usually auctioned off on eBay. This is a highly-acclaimed, big, impressive beer.

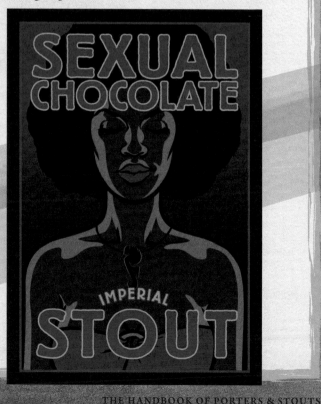

SOUTHERN TIER
CHOKLAT STOUT

SOUTHERN TIER BREWING COMPANY

The Popol Vuh, the sacred book of the Maya, unfolds a complex web of mystery around a beverage known as xocoatl ("ch-co-atle"). At Southern Tier, they're not surprised that hieroglyphs of the ancient Maya depict chocolate being poured for rulers and gods. Moving through the centuries, the circular journey of cacao has been realized in Southern Tier's brewing house, encompassing the complexity of the darkest bittersweet candy together with the original frothy cold beverage of the ancient Maya in the form of the Blackwater Series Choklat Stout.

Even if you're not a fan of big beers, you can appreciate the intense taste that often accompanies a beer of the Imperial style. More often than not you may find the overt alcoholic presence distracting, if not off-putting, but the brewers at Southern Tier seem to have the magic touch when it comes to making truly tasty and highly drinkable Imperial beers, as shown in Choklat, their Imperial chocolate stout.

This is not a Russian Imperial, that is, a big, bold roasty beer that happens to have a chocolaty taste. Instead, this is a chocolate stout first and foremost with the boldness that comes with an Imperial-type beer. It's absolutely delicious.

As soon as the cap was popped off the 22-ounce bomber, the rich chocolate malts came bursting out. As it poured, the chocolate announced itself with a rich presence of high-end milk chocolate similar to Godiva or Ghirardelli candy. The alcohol is not noticeable in the least, although there is a touch of heat to the nose.

The beer pours to a shade of opaque black. Although this is a common appearance for stouts, there are no hints of ruby red around the edges. It forms a fairly small light brown frothy head that dissolves slowly and leaves minor lacing on the glass. The head re-forms itself quite thick if the glass is swirled with enough vigor.

There are many chocolate stouts, most of them enjoyable, but none blow your hair back quite as far as Southern Tier Choklat does on the first sip. As soon as the foam hits your lips, you receive the same taste sensation you get from eating a piece of gourmet chocolate candy. That shouldn't be surprising because this beer is made with real "bittersweet

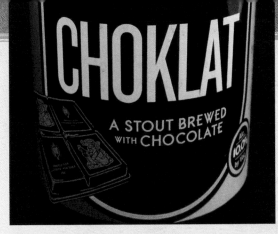

Belgian chocolate," as is indicated on the bottle.

This may be the richest, creamiest, smoothest chocolate taste in a chocolate stout. It's a very bold flavor with a bit of warmth to the finish that does not upstage or overshadow the chocolate. This is as close as a beer can get to liquid chocolate.

Choklat is brewed with Chinook and Willamette hops in the kettle, which gives the beer a touch of a bitter presence up front, but it finishes extremely smooth and rich thanks to the caramel and chocolate malts. Unlike a Russian Imperial, there is no presence of deeply roasted or even burned malts, just slightly toasted ones. The sweetness is similar to that found in many oatmeal or milk stouts, but the chocolate presence is so strong that you may forget you're drinking beer.

If you drank this beer not knowing it was 11% ABV, you would not be able to guess it. How can a beer with such a creamy, velvety mouthfeel and only a slightly warming sensation as it finishes be so potent?

Drinking this beer is similar to taking a bite of slightly melted high-end milk chocolate candy. The chocolate seems to coat the tongue in rich sweetness and leaves a very pleasing aftertaste. It's not sugary or gimmicky as the high alcohol content seems to complement the sweetness, avoiding the artificial sweetener–like taste of many gimmicky beers.

If there is a flaw in Southern Tier Choklat, it would be that it's sold only in 22-ounce bombers and is not inexpensive. The first serving goes down easy, but after the second serving you might have a buzz going. Also, Southern Tier is still a growing brewery, and its beers are not available everywhere. If you're able to find a bottle, pick it up regardless of the price.

CP

IRISH (DRY) STOUTS

For many drinkers, the word "stout" brings the Irish stout, also called "dry" stout, immediately to mind. Many of the world's best-known stouts, such as Guinness and Beamish, are brewed in this style. An evolution of the porters brewed in the UK in the eighteenth century, dry stouts are distinguished from their forebears by being brewed with roasted barley instead of black roasted malt. The use of barley was driven by economics more than anything else (it was taxed less than malt), though it was also a diversification born from the popularity of porter and stout. First brewed by Guinness in the 1820s, the style has come to be emblematic of Irish beer for many drinkers.

The use of roasted barley rather than roasted malt gives dry stout its unique taste. Dark roast coffee is the flavor that dominates the style, even down to the slightly acidic tinge that creeps in at the edges. The dry stout is no one-trick pony, though. Chocolate and a slight roasted smokiness can sneak in as well. Subtle hopping of these beers means that while hops aren't present in much of the aroma or flavor, they offer a pleasantly bitter bite at the end for a crisp finish. Despite a reputation among neophytes for being heavy and boozy, traditional Irish stouts are actually fairly light in both body and alcohol. They are, in fact, perfect (and even refreshing) session beers for a night at the pub—an excellent explanation for their enduring popularity.

BEAMISH IRISH STOUT

BEAMISH & CRAWFORD

The Beemish & Crawford brewery cans this brew with a widget, the little ball you also find in Guinness cans that has nitrogen and beer in it. When you pop it open, the pressure is released, agitating the beer and creating a head that is meant to mimic what happens when it's poured from a tap. This nitro-charged pour makes a white head on the dark black beer and a reverse cascade of carbonation. This beer is sweet with a toasted malt nose that is a bit bready. There is also some slight coffee in the aroma, though it is not overpowering. The flavor, however, is distinctly coffee with a chocolate background. The creamy, velvet body is a bit on the thin side, making it easy to quaff. It is nearly a session beer at 4.1% ABV.

JC

BLACK HAWK STOUT

MENDOCINO BREWING COMPANY

Certain beers and certain breweries have a reputation for being "gateway" or "beginner class" in that they are or produce mild, easy-drinking brews that are appealing to newbies. Mendocino Brewing Company is such a brewery, and its Black Hawk Stout is such a beer, at least in theory.

The opaque, dark-brown body initially forms a huge spongelike tan head. It never completely evaporates and leaves some lacing on the glass. The beer has a mild American stout aroma. There is a touch of milk chocolate notes, but it is all very subtle. This is basically the American version of Guinness. It has a mild palate. If you really concentrate, you get some roasted malt in the first half and candylike milk chocolate in the second half, along with a slightly dry bitterness in the aftertaste. The mouthfeel is light- to medium-bodied with decent carbonation. It feels like chocolate soda.

Mild beers are technically easy to drink because they just slide across the tongue and down the throat with no resistance by the taste buds. Overall, Black Hawk Stout is an easy beer to drink.

BLACK PLAGUE STOUT

STORM BREWING

Storm Brewing is a local craft brewery situated on gritty East Vancouver's Commercial Drive. It thundered onto the market in June 1995, quickly establishing the reputation of brewmaster and owner James Walton. For over seventeen years Walton has been bringing Vancouverites innovative and unpretentious craft beers made in small batches that are unfiltered and additive-free.

During the Middle Ages millions died of what became known as the Black Plague, yet brewers and beer drinkers seemed largely immune. We've since solved the mystery: The plague spread rapidly because of unsanitary conditions such as stagnant water, making beer one of the only safe things to drink. In honor of those pioneering plague fighters, Walton brews his mighty Black Plague Stout. This popular Irish dry–style stout is classic in style. Walton starts with Canadian two-row barley followed by loads of roast barley and oats and a light addition of Pacific Northwest Columbus hops and finishes it off with some fresh licorice root and decadent dark cocoa for a slightly chocolaty mouthfeel. Brewed in small batches even by microbrewing standards, the resulting beer is smooth, rich, and roasty. It is a robust beer at 8.5% ABV.

BLACK
SUN STOUT

THREE FLOYDS
BREWING COMPANY

This dry stout from Three Floyds is made
in that brewery's own way with a lot of hops and chutzpah.

This beer has an opaque, seemingly black body that is actually very
dark ruby red. It forms a very large, fluffy, tightly compacted dark-tan
head that retains and laces extremely well. Piney, resiny hops are the most
prominent aroma, with an underlying subtle, typical stout scent.

Three Floyds is known for experimenting with styles, and Black Sun
Stout is definitely not your average beer. Supposedly it's a dry stout, but a
swig or two makes that difficult to believe. It's by far one of the hoppiest
and most bitter dry stouts you're likely to encounter. It has sweet black
licorice up front with a fairly generic and rather mild stout palate. It
changes on a dime as all the piney hops come rushing in with a strong
burst of sappy, resiny earthiness. The hops fade away quickly as the beer
reverts to the opening salvo of standard stout. There's not much in the
way of roasted malts, although there is a discernible coffeelike taste that
doesn't last long. The beer finishes fairly clean, although the hops add
up by the end. Overall, it provides a very interesting tasting experience.

Although this beer may be too complex and robust to be considered a
dry stout, it definitely has the drinkability of one. The mouthfeel is on the
thinner side with a low amount of carbonation. It goes down so smoothly
that it's easy to drink in big gulps. Not that it's refreshing or as delicious
as a dessert beer; it's just a fun, original take on an otherwise pub-style
brew. The company website indicates that it's 6.5% ABV, but that seems a
little high as it has the weight of something slightly smaller. You could see
the average drinker enjoying multiple servings of this beer without being
overwhelmed or bored.

CP

CADILLAC
MOUNTAIN STOUT

BAR HARBOR BREWING COMPANY

When you pour this Irish stout from New England, you get an inky body with cherry highlights. The bittersweet chocolate on the nose smells a bit like Halloween candy. There is not much in terms of hop aromas, but that comes later. The first flavors are caramel and chocolate on the tongue, with astringent roast malt on the edges, and then come the hops. Floral and citrus flavors round out the brew, and the dry finish with a lingering coffee flavor on the tongue makes it nicely complex at 6.7% ABV.

JC

COBBLESTONE STOUT
MILL STREET BREWERY

The Mill Street Brewery opened its doors in Toronto in 2002 at the old Gooderham and Worts Distillery in what is today known as the Distillery Historic District. It was founded by Steve Abrams, Jeff Cooper, and Michael Duggan. Joel Manning is currently the head brewer. They produce a traditionally styled Irish stout that is served using beer gas to produce a creamy pour. Their black stout has a roasted malt flavor and a hint of toasted walnuts and chocolate in the finish. Select imported hops are used to dry out the finish. This is a classic Irish stout, one of the best known and most popular in Toronto.

GUINNESS DRAUGHT

GUINNESS LTD.

There isn't another stout that inspires the fervent following of Guinness. In fact, there probably isn't another beer that inspires the following of Guinness's most famous creation. Arthur Guinness brewed a variety of ales and porters in the late 1700s and had shifted his brewery's production completely to the popular porter style by the turn of the eighteenth century. It's Guinness's progeny, Arthur Guinness II, we have to thank for the brew now known as Guinness Draught. In the early 1800s, the second Arthur used the newly available patent malt (highly kilned "black" malt) and pale malt to create a stout porter that was dry and bitter without any of the cloying sweetness of browner malt. With this brew, a new beer style—the Irish dry stout—was born.

As with any recipe, Guinness's signature stout has changed over time. In the 1930s, Guinness swapped patent malt for roasted unmalted barley, and it started using flaked barley in the 1950s. In the 1960s, Guinness stopped racking its brews into wooden casks, which were replaced with aluminum kegs. It's impossible to know how the taste of today's Guinness Draught differs from the Guinness of the 1930s, but it's a damn fine Irish dry stout.

Guinness Draught is served exclusively on nitrogen (provided by a nitro tap or a nitrogen widget in bottles), and the small bubbles provide the familiar smooth, creamy texture. It's a subtle stout compared with many others, fairly thin-bodied with a pleasant coffee flavor. It's also got a 4.2% ABV and a sour tang that harks back to the sour notes of its porter predecessors. Rumor is that the bite comes from sour ale from old oak vats that's added to Guinness Draught, but the brewery won't confirm or deny that.

JC

MCGRATH'S IRISH BLACK STOUT

CLANCONNEL BREWING COMPANY

Clanconnel Brewing Company is one of Northern Ireland's most dynamic and innovative craft breweries. The McGrath series is named for a famed Irish racing greyhound, the "immortal black"' Master McGrath. This beer, weighing in at 4.3% ABV, is a handcrafted traditional Irish dry stout that combines rich roasted malts with hints of chocolate, coffee, and dark fruit and is balanced carefully by earthy hops. It is smooth on the palate with a lingering, classic dry finish and a long aftertaste. It is very drinkable.

O'HARA'S LEANN FOLLÁIN

CARLOW BREWING COMPANY

Despite a history spanning centuries and styles known around the world, Ireland's beer scene saw a precipitous decline in the twentieth century. Large multinational corporations moved into Ireland's brewing business, driving the number of locally owned and operated breweries down from over two hundred to only about a dozen. Looking to turn the tide, Seamus and Eamonn O'Hara founded Carlow Brewing Company in the mid-1990s. Originally established primarily as an export brand—craft beer already had a growing market beyond Ireland's borders—the brewery eventually kicked off a revolution in locally owned, operated, and consumed beer. Ireland is now home to more than twenty craft breweries, brewing both traditional and modern styles.

Although Guinness continues to be the standard-bearer worldwide for the Irish stout, Carlow's has a great take on the style that many drinkers will appreciate. The brewery's flagship ale, O'Hara's Irish Stout, is described by the brewers as "how Irish stouts used to taste," a dig at the mass-produced Guinness, no doubt. A deep black beer with a fluffy head and espresso and licorice notes, it's a worthy example of the style. Leann Folláin, the brewery's extra Irish stout, is even better. A pitch-black pour is followed by a delightful mocha aroma. The flavor follows, mixing chocolate and coffee with a vinous tang and a bitter bite from European hops.

The name *Leann Folláin* is Gaelic for "wholesome stout." Though it's unclear exactly how wholesome it is, it's certainly a substantial brew with 6% ABV. It's a good reminder of why many Irish people still describe stout as a meal in a glass.

JC

SARANAC IRISH STOUT

MATT BREWING COMPANY

The Matt Brewery in Utica, New York, has brewed beers of just about every style under the sun, so it's no surprise that it brews Saranac Irish Stout. This brew is much closer in style to a traditional American stout than to something from Ireland; the result is a decent beer, so one can let the market-driven name slide.

There is a black colalike appearance with a two-finger beige foamy head. The head retains surprisingly well and leaves impressive lacing on the glass. The smell is typical of the style with notes of coffee and dark chocolate with toasted malts but is mild overall.

This is the taste people tend to associate with any basic stout, only a little sweeter. Saranac Irish Stout begins with a sodalike sweetness and finishes with a lightly bitter taste of toasted malts; the flavor is more akin to breakfast toast than to the deeply roasted, kiln-fired flavor found in stronger stouts. There's a light coffee flavor through the middle combined with very mild dark chocolate. It's surprising how sweet this stout is, especially considering that Saranac wants us to believe it's an Irish dry stout.

You do notice a certain tang or sourness in the palate like a dairy product on the verge of expiration. This is a trait often found in oatmeal and milk stouts, but it is unexpected here. It also is a little distracting at first, but you'll be able to tolerate it.

The mouthfeel is very fizzy for a stout. The body is medium bordering on thin, or at least thinner than you might expect or want in a stout like this. The 5.5% ABV seems a little high, though, as this beer drinks like the sessionable European stouts that inspired it.

Overall, Saranac Irish Stout is a pretty tasty beer. Its sweetness and low bitterness make it a good alternative for those who don't like Guinness.

CP

ST. JOHN'S STOUT

YELLOWBELLY BREWERY & PUBLIC HOUSE

St. John's Stout is an Irish stout–style beer brewed by Yellowbelly Brewery & Public House in St. John's, Newfoundland, Canada. Sitting where George Street intercepts Water Street in downtown St. John's (the oldest city in North America), YellowBelly Brewery & Public House is set in a building reconstructed after the fire of 1892. It is one of the few remaining after the Great St. John's Fire. The "colorful" name is a nod to the Irish immigrants who entered Newfoundland between 1750 and 1830; the Yellowbellies were an Irish faction hailing from County Wexford who once famously tied strips of yellow cloth around their middles in a hurling match against the Cornish champions. Following their victory, King George III was heard to remark, "Well done the Yellowbellies!"

This traditional Irish stout is very dark, heavy, and complex with an extremely long, dry finish. The recipe calls for shovelfuls of hops in the kettle, which are also buoyed by the bitterness from the roast barley. A creamy head eventually laces the glass nicely. Notes of burnt and roasty flavors, licorice, and bittersweet chocolate come through. But there are also hints of cedar, berry, pear, walnut, and citrus. It's meant to be a beer enjoyed with meal, particularly, steak, ribs, or oysters. At 4.8% ABV, you can have a few and enjoy!

STOUT

4 PINES BREWING COMPANY

The 4 Pines Brewing Company is not your normal brewery. In 1774, Captain James Cook discovered and named Norfolk Island in Australia and its pine trees. By the 1850s Norfolk pines begin to be planted extensively around the Manly area. For more than a century those trees have been one of the best attractions in Manly. However, in the 1960s many pines died from pollution, and the forests were reconstituted beginning in 1991, when new plantings commenced. In 2008, 4 Pines Brewing Company was established.

They wanted to offer "handcrafted beer brewed naturally." Each brew is made in a 500-liter batch. Brewed to the German purity laws, 4 Pines beers have only four ingredients—hops, water, yeast, and malt—but include the odd bit of mandarin, ginger, and other natural stuff from time to time to keep the taste buds tingling.

The malts include ale, Golden Promise, Munich, crystal, Carapis, roasted barley, and Carafa, balanced by a generous helping of Fuggles hops. An Irish-style stout with 5.1% ABV, this stout pours almost black and bears a generous tan head. The nose is a big wafting of coffee, chocolate, and caramel malts. 4 Pines Vostok is being tested to become the first certified "space beer" in the world. Vostok was formed with the ambition of creating the world's first beer designed for consumption in space!

IMPERIAL STOUTS

As black as a winter night and loaded with roasted character, Imperial stouts are the goliaths of the beer world. The style lends itself well to layered flavors, barrel conditioning, adjunct additions like vanilla and chocolate, and even to aging in a cellar for years or decades. Given the complex nature and wide variety of options for brewers playing with Imperial stouts, it's little surprise that the style often dominates "Best Beer in the World" lists in print and online.

The original style was the Russian Imperial stout, which came into being at the end of the seventeenth century when Peter the Great opened Russia to the Western world. Peter found himself enamored with porter when he visited England and quickly requested that the dark brew be exported to Russia. While early attempts to send traditional porter east and overland from London failed (it went bad before getting to Russia), later attempts amped up the hops, malt, and alcohol to a degree that it would survive the journey. Combine the fact that strong porters were then called stouts with the beer's destination in the imperial court of Russia, and voilà, you get the Russian Imperial stout. And, as the first "Imperial" brew, the strong stout is to blame for every extra-strength version of a traditional style being saddled with the term—Imperial Porter, Imperial IPA, Imperial Pilsner . . .

Like a handful of other English exports, the style nearly went extinct in the twentieth century. American craft brewers are largely responsible for reviving it in the '90s when they were looking to distinguish themselves with big, bold (some would say extreme) beers. Since then, the style has exploded in popularity in the US, and brewers worldwide, such as Scotland's BrewDog and Italy's Birrificio Del Ducato, are also getting in on the action. Sometimes pushing north of 20% ABV, these potent neo-Imperial stouts are even stronger than the originals.

THE ABYSS

DESCHUTES BREWERY

This Deschutes brew has everything a barrel-aged Russian Imperial stout should have and is one of the best examples of the style. As its name promises, the Abyss is absolutely pitch black. It forms a small, dark-brown, foamy and frothy head that laces and retains well considering how heavy the beer is. The sweet aroma has black licorice, vanilla, and cherry in it.

There's a lot going on in this beer, though that's not surprising since it's brewed with licorice and molasses, with one-third of it aged in oak and bourbon barrels. Imperial stouts of this caliber tend to be rare and expensive, but this one deserves all the acclaim it receives. It begins with a luscious, sweet flavor of dark cherry. It's almost tart in a way, like raspberry, but without getting to the point of tartness. Some chocolate syrup flavors come through toward the middle, and then the palate changes to something more bitter on the back end. Big Imperial stouts like this tend to be highly hopped for balance, but the Abyss is only 65 IBU, giving it balance but keeping the hops in check. There's a delicious woody vanilla flavor on the finish, which is nice to let linger on the tongue. The alcohol mellows nicely and fades into the background, which probably accounts for the vanilla and woody character.

Although the Abyss is a big beer at 11% ABV, it ages remarkably well. The body is pretty full, though the mouthfeel is a little thinner and cleaner than expected. It's calm and soft and goes down smooth with no burning or warming sensation, leaving a lovely aftertaste of licorice and roasted malt. However, it's not drying or cloying.

DESCHUTES BREWERY®
BEND, OREGON

THE ABYSS
2013 RESERVE

THE ABYSS: MALT BEVERAGE BREWED WITH BLACK STRAP MOLASSES, LICORICE, WITH CHERRY BARK AND VANILLA ADDED WITH 6% AGED IN OAK BOURBON BARRELS, 11% AGED IN OAK BARRELS, AND 11% AGED IN OAK WINE BARRELS.

CP

BARREL AGED IMPERIAL STOUT

MOO BREW (MOORILLA ESTATE)

The Moo Brew brewery was installed at MONA, then Moorilla Estate, in 2005. In June of that year the first keg was sold and went on tap at T42° on Hobart's waterfront. In 2010, Moo Brew opened a second brewery site ten minutes up the road in Bridgewater, Tasmania. All the brewery operations are now carried out at the secondary site.

Moo Brew's label designs display the works of the Australian artist John Kelly. In response to Kelly's sculpture series based on William Dobell's camouflaged cows, Moo Brew commissioned him to produce a series of paintings for the beer labels. Kelly suggested that the connection between his sculptures and Moo Brew was a little trite and that he wasn't working with cows anymore. Kelly now lives in Ireland.

Locally referred to as the Velvet Sledgehammer, Moo Brew Imperial Stout is intense and deceptively smooth considering its 8.5% ABV. They use a mixture of specialty malts to create a huge flavor. It pours an opaque black color with a rich brown head. The rich dense palate is a complex matrix of high residual sugar, bitterness, and an active alcohol vector. There is a big caramel nose, but the hops give it a nice balance to finish in a refreshing way for such a big beer.

BARREL ROLL PUGACHEV'S COBRA

HANGAR 24 CRAFT BREWERY

The creation tale of many leaders of the craft beer industry begins with a hobby: homebrewing. In need of a downtime activity, today's master brewers started cooking up and bottling beers. They soon found they were so good at it that they could brew for a living. Their hobby became their passion, and their passion became their profession.

But after the mountaintop is reached, what replaces the hobby? What does a brewer do with his or her spare time? Jeff Brown, the president of Boulder Beer Co., is a master cyclist who has competed in several bicycle racing events. Adam Avery of Avery Brewing Co. loves to go rock climbing. But Ben Cook, founder and master brewer at Hangar 24 Craft Brewery, may have the coolest hobby of all: he flies.

The story of Hangar 24 began in hangar 24 at the Redlands Municipal Airport, where Cook and his friends often would meet after a day of flying to talk planes and drink beer. Eventually, the more earthbound hobby won Cook's interest, and he followed it from the Anheuser-Busch Brewery in Van Nuys, California, where he worked quality control, to the Master Brewers Program at the University of California, Davis. After graduation, Cook picked up some brewing equipment and opened Hangar 24 Craft Brewery right across the street from his favorite airfield.

The brewery is known mainly for two things. The first is its popular flagship, Orange Wheat, a refreshing dram brewed with California-grown oranges. The second is its Barrel Roll Series, a group of strong barrel-aged brews that first saw distribution in 2010 with the release of Immelmann, a bourbon-aged porter. Some of the beers in the series were one-time deals, whereas others come out every year. So far, there have been seven unique Barrel Rolls, but the most popular is Pugachev's Cobra.

To make this substantial Imperial stout, the brewers combine three different roasted malts and maple syrup throughout the brewing process and then place the fermented beer in freshly emptied bourbon barrels for eight months. Variations in the aging process have toned down Pugachev since the beer's first release in December 2011. The brew that year came out at a brain-melting 16.5% ABV; the December 2013 version was only 13.8%.

Each of the beers in the Barrel Roll Series is named for an aerobatic maneuver, and Pugachev's Cobra refers to a move that is pulled off when a pilot suddenly raises the aircraft nose to near vertical while the plane is moving forward and then drops back into attack mode. It's a dangerous and breathtaking maneuver much in the same way that taking on a bottle of Hangar 24's Pugachev's Cobra is dangerous and breathtaking.

When poured into a snifter, the brew is fairly thin and unimposing in appearance. It's dark but watery, and the head is nearly nonexistent, with bubbles as fizzy as those in a soda popping away in no time at all. A whiff, however, provides the first inkling of sharp, woody whiskey. The bourbon character is strong, though notes of sweet vanilla, brown sugar, butterscotch, and marshmallow can be discerned beneath it.

Tangy bittersweet dark chocolate coats the tongue as the beer is sipped. The whiskey flavor is again wood-soaked; it's like sucking on a oak chip. The alcohol flavor is also impressive—this is almost more whiskey than beer—but the sharp stuff is smoothed out in the midpalate by tones of vanilla and buttery toffee.

Though the body is smooth and soft, there is a similar layer of heat from the substantial alcohol. This is a brew we'd call hot, which means it could stand a few months of aging. If you can find a bottle, put it in the cellar to settle.

ZF

BELGO ANISE IMPERIAL RUSSIAN STOUT

STONE BREWING CO.

This beer has an opaque ink-black body with no visible carbonation. It pours to a fairly large brown soapy-foamy head that laces and retains well. There are huge black licorice notes along with toffee and some chocolate but no roasted malt or alcohol.

You don't tend to associate Belgian character with American-style Imperial stouts, and so it's interesting that Stone chose to use a Belgian yeast strain plus anise in its standard Imperial Russian stout base recipe. The result is a stout that's only slightly different from the usual brew, though it's sweeter and less bitter.

Up front one gets a strong fruity flavor of black cherry and blackberry. This is followed quickly by the strong sweetness of black licorice and a Tootsie Roll–like chocolate flavor. There is not much in the way of bitterness and no hop taste. There may be some coffeelike bitterness hiding in the background that shows up in the aftertaste, but for the most part there's not a lot of bitter flavor. The big wallop of roasted maltiness one might expect seems to have faded. It's difficult to pick up on the Belgian quality since the base brew is so strongly flavored. A hint of alcohol at the end imparts some rum and vanilla flavor. Overall, it's a sweet brew that's tasty and satisfying.

The first thing you notice about Stone Belgo Anise Imperial Russian Stout is its light, slightly fizzy mouthfeel. That's probably due to the yeast strain, though it is a nice change of pace from the stick-to-your-teeth viscous mouthfeel of most stouts of this type. It's no challenge to drink as it goes down smoothly with a surprisingly light aftertaste. There's almost no alcohol warmth, which is surprising considering that the beer is quite hefty at 10.5% ABV.

CP

BIERLAND IMPERIAL STOUT

CERVEJARIA BIERLAND

Brewed by Cervejaria Bierland, Bierland Imperial Stout is a Russian Imperial stout–style beer brewed in Blumenau, Brazil. Founded in 2003, this brewery has specialized in the Germanic brewing tradition and has been impressing palates since it opened its doors. In this brew, chocolate punches you in the nose, with hints of burnt caramel as well. The creamy mocha head lingers a long time. A nice balance of bitterness and dark unsweetened chocolate keeps this beer honest and big.

BIG DADDY VLADY'S RUSSIAN IMPERIAL STOUT

TERRAPIN BEER COMPANY

This beer is as black as night although seemingly thinner than most Russian Imperial stouts. There is only the slightest hint of ruby red; otherwise it is pitch-black. The one-finger tan creamy head sticks around for a while and leaves minor lacing on the glass. The aroma features espresso and semisweet chocolate, along with deeply roasted coffee and barley. There is some alcohol, which later gives way to a sour, solventlike smell. The distinct sour red grape scent is not too strong.

Up front it's a strong palate of espresso and bitter dark chocolate followed by a red wine taste. It is very robust at first but quickly mellows out. This brew drinks more like a coffee stout than a Russian Imperial, but without the dry bitterness that usually comes with a coffee beer. There's a slight dairy quality, too. The beer becomes a little sourer as it warms but remains tasty throughout.

The mouthfeel is surprisingly creamy for a beer of this style. It is only medium-bodied for such a statistically big brew. Bitterness lingers on the tongue momentarily. This beer definitely does not taste or drink like a 10.25% ABV brew. There is little to no alcohol burn even as it warms. Overall, it is a very good dessert beer, but it is difficult to enjoy more than a single serving. (This beer is no longer in production.)

CP

BLACK ALBERT
DE STRUISE BROUWERS

De Struise Brouwers is a microbrewery located in Oostvleteren, Belgium. It began when Urbain Coutteau and Philippe Driessens developed an interest in making distinctive regional beers to serve guests visiting their farm. In 2001, they began making beer with the help of local wine maker Carlo Grootaert, and the project was so successful it eventually grew into its own business. The company takes its name from the historic Flemish word for ostrich, which also is a contemporary slang term meaning "tough." In English, their name loosely translates to "The Sturdy Brewers." In 2008, RateBeer's annual members' poll declared Struise to be the best brewer in the world!

They have collaborated with other European artisan brewers such as Denmark's Mikkeller, fellow Belgians Picobrouwerij Alvinne, and Brouwerij De Molen of the Netherlands, as well as American brewers. Point in fact, Black Albert was originally conceived when Chris Lively, the De Struise's good friend and owner of Ebenezer's Pub in Lovell, Maine,

asked the brewery to create a special beer for Ebenezer Pub's third annual Belgian Beer Festival. The result was a Russian Imperial stout that they christened a Belgian Royal Stout named Black Albert, referring to the beer style (blacker than black stout). This beer is a tribute to Albert II, sixth king of the Belgians, who was nicknamed the "laughing king." This big mother of an RIS is often considered one of their true classics.

The brewery claims that "this is not as much a beer as it is an experience," and they are right! It pours a deep, opaque black, with a dark, foamy head that quickly dissipates but leaves a nice lacing down the length of the glass. It has a thick, tar-like body with big chocolate notes and slight hints of coffee and some nice creaminess. Roasty bitterness and the unique sweetness of real Belgian candy sugar make for a complex ale. Yes it may be 13% ABV, but you won't really taste it. An amazing beer. One of the best around.

BLACK JACK STOUT

DUCLAW BREWING COMPANY

Dave Benfield, the owner of DuClaw Brewing Company, began home-brewing in college. In 1995, he began construction of the DuClaw Brewing Company of Bel Air, Maryland. Today, Dave and brewmaster Jim Wagner are the masterminds behind an amazing array of craft brewed beers. Brewed with grains such as pale malt, roasted barley, flaked oats, Caramunich, and chocolate malt and topped off with hops such as Galena and Golding, this award-winning classic Russian Imperial stout pours jet black with a small tan head and a full body. Black Jack boasts a swirl of dark chocolate, coffee, smoky malt, and fruit flavors and a lingering, warming 8.3% ABV well concealed by its big bold flavors. It is engineered for an original gravity of 21 Plato so that every glass—and every drinker—is a winner.

BLACKOUT STOUT

GREAT LAKES BREWING CO.

When it comes to stouts, there are many different substyles, especially flavored styles (coffee, chocolate, milk, etc.). Sometimes it's nice to enjoy a plain old Imperial stout, and Great Lakes Blackout Stout is just that. It's a robust, complex, and delectable beer that reminds you how tasty a strong stout can be without added flavor.

This stout has an absolutely pitch-black body with no other colors visible and forms a small dark tan frothy head that dissipates mostly but not completely and leaves some lacing (it regenerates easily with a good swirl). There is a strong nose of black licorice, vanilla, and a hint of whiskey or wood.

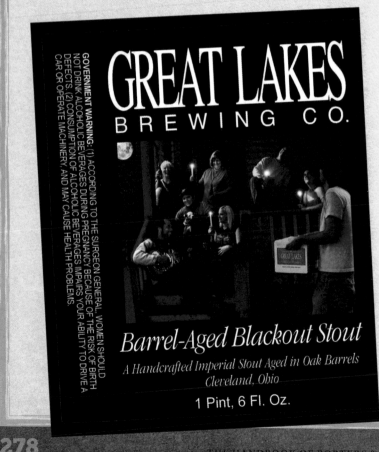

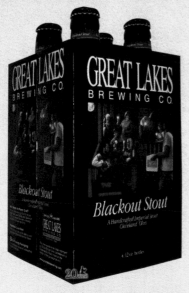

There are two very distinct but quite enjoyable halves to the palate. It begins with a sweet side in which black cherry, rum-soaked raisin, vanilla, and a colalike taste are all prominent. For a moment it reminds you of a short-lived Dr Pepper flavor. Through the middle the tastes becomes drier as the alcohol makes itself known. It's similar to whiskey but without any smokiness or to rum without the spice. It's a bit like black licorice–flavored vodka.

The second half features a warming sensation as the alcohol dominates the profile. It's not distracting from the initial flavors and in fact complements them and transitions to the bitter finish very well. Deeply roasted malts, burnt coffee beans, and dark chocolate appear fairly briefly just as the beer finishes. The aftertaste is a very nice combination of sticky vanilla extract, cough syrup, and bitter dark chocolate. It is delectable but borders on cloying.

Great Lakes Blackout Stout weighs in at 9% ABV, which is on the cusp between "a little big" and "proceed with caution." Its alcoholic characteristics are no secret, so there's a lot of sheer energy in the mouthfeel. Although the aftertaste is sticky, the liquid is not that thick; it is full-bodied but with a moist, smooth velvety texture. There's noticeable heat even for experienced drinkers. Start with a cold bottle and sip it over an hour. The complexity and intense mouthfeel justify each other.

CP

BOURBON BARREL STOUT

BLUEGRASS BREWING COMPANY

Bluegrass Brewing Company started its life as a single brewpub in Louisville, Kentucky, the product of a partnership between a father and a son, Monte and Pat Hagan. Growing from the pub founded in 1993, the operation expanded to retail and bottle sales in 2002, followed by second and third locations in 2006 and 2010. Along with a full complement of self-described "hoppy beers" (brews that were loved by Pat but certainly were a gamble in 1993), BBC brews specialty beers ranging from spiced ales to a raspberry mead. With the popularity of bourbon in Kentucky, it should come as no surprise that Bluegrass ages a number of its beers in bourbon barrels.

There's no beer style that harmonizes with bourbon as well as a stout. The oak and vanilla (and, yes, whiskey) flavors from the bourbon barrel meld with the chocolate and coffee notes of a good stout to make a whole truly greater than its parts with 8.6% ABV. Bluegrass's Bourbon Barrel Stout is light on the bourbon, with the stout itself doing most of the heavy lifting. Brown sugar and coffee flavors dominate, but they're nicely rounded out by tasty hints of vanilla and bourbon. It may not be the most extreme version of a bourbon barrel–aged stout, but it's one case in subtlety is definitely a virtue.

JC

BOURBON COUNTY STOUT

GOOSE ISLAND BEER COMPANY

This Imperial stout is the color of opaque ink and black all around. Perhaps there are some dark maroon highlights on the edge, but this is definitely one of the darker beers you'll see. Initially, it forms a small coating of brown foam, but that fizzles away quickly and leaves no lacing. It is highly aromatic and the massive black licorice, dark cherry, and bourbon notes can be smelled from an arm's length away.

County Brand Stout is a monster of a beer. Even after three and a half years of aging, it can still pack a punch. There is massive sweetness where

the first half followed by overt boozy character on the second half. Black licorice, chocolate syrup, black cherry, vanilla, and a hint of plum or grape can all be detected throughout the palate (in that order). To call it sweet would be an understatement, but to call it sickly or cloying would be a lie.

What's so impressive about this beer is the fact it's so well balanced. While there isn't a hop character per se as far as citrus, pine, flowers, etc., there definitely is a prominent bitterness to the palate. This makes the beer drink like the imperial stout it is, rather than any kind of borderline spirit or what other "extreme" beers tend to be like. The bourbon character is quite pronounced as well, leaving a slightly woody aftertaste along with hints of scorched sugar or vanilla. Sure there's a raw alcohol component as well, but it complements the taste well.

This is not exactly the type of beer you drink on a whim. At 13% ABV and a high price tag, Goose Island's Bourbon County Brand Stout is a special brew. That being said, savoring the experience is the drinker's responsibility. It's not simply syrup plus alcohol; it's a genuine stout body. Thick and viscous in the mouth for sure, but with no sticky or chewy sensation. The finish would be clean if it weren't for the alcohol, which dries out the tongue. A fantastic liquid dessert by itself—there's no reason to distract your palate by attempting to pair this with anything other than serenity.

CP

BROOKLYN BLACK OPS

BROOKLYN BREWERY

According to the Brooklyn Brewery's website, "Brooklyn Black Ops does not exist. However, if it did exist, it would be a robust stout originally concocted by the Brooklyn brewing team under cover of secrecy. . . . Supposedly 'Black Ops' was aged for four months in bourbon barrels, bottled flat, and re-fermented with champagne yeast."

This Imperial stout is a limited-production vintage beer that is fervently sought after by Brooklyn Brewery enthusiasts. Its short supply and known aging potential create a demand that evaporates Black Ops before it hits the shelves. Years of bottle aging allow the complexity and softness this beer develops with time.

The beer pours a dark brown to black with some brown persisting around the glass rim. There is a cappuccino-colored wispy head that dissipates but leaves a bit floating. On the nose, bubble gum, maple syrup, and peanut brittle are a bit overpowered by the prominent fusel alcohols. As the beer warms and the alcohol blows off, sweet toffee, bourbon, and orange "circus peanuts" start to show.

The palate is preceded on the nose but also incorporates more vanilla and whiskey flavors. The impression of drinking homemade Irish cream whiskey comes to mind. Chocolate and roasted

malt in the mouth are a bit more typical of this style, but the medium-high carbonation from the Champagne yeast brings a surprising lightness to the midpalate. The bitterness of the beer is soft and is subdued by a faint sweetness to round out the long but mellow finish.

The Black Ops 2013 would benefit from a few years of cellaring. Bottle aging would help round some of the harsh barrel notes and integrating the 11.5% alcohol. This beer was great with a spicy puttanesca sauce, but it might pair better with dry-aged beef or a decadent dessert course. But of course, none of this really matters because "Black Ops does not exist."

GC

COURAGE IMPERIAL RUSSIAN STOUT

As brewed for Catherine II Empress of Russia since 1795
Best savoured after 13 years of maturing

IMPERIAL RUSSIAN STOUT

275ml ℮   ALC. by VOL. 10%   9.3 US fl.oz

WELLS & YOUNG'S LTD

Courage Imperial Russian Stout is one of the classic English versions of the Russian Imperial stout and has become an iconic and sought after brew. In 2011, the beer was brewed in London for the first time in decades, and it was officially relaunched at the Great American Beer Festival in Denver of that year.

Wells & Young's master brewer Jim Robertson said at the time, "I was one of the last brewers to produce this beer in London and it has been an honor, a privilege and, I must admit, a labor of love for me. This beer is a real test of my abilities as a brewer—it uses a large amount of raw ingredients."

Courage Russian Imperial Stout (10% ABV) is a strong, dark stout dating back to the eighteenth century, when it was produced at Thrale's Brewery in London to export to the court of Catherine II of Russia. The high alcoholic content was necessary to prevent the beer from freezing in the low temperatures of the Baltic Sea on its voyage to Russia, and along with a high degree of hops it has the keeping quality of a fine wine. In 1791, the brewery changed hands and the beer became known as Barclay Perkins Imperial Stout. When the brewery was taken over by local rivals Courage, the beer was renamed Courage Imperial Russian Stout. Wells & Young's acquired the Courage brands in 2007.

Courage Imperial Russian Stout has a rich espresso body with pear overtones and an intriguing fresh, smoky, fruity finish. Dark-red fruits of cherry and red cassis come through. The beer is brewed with chocolate, amber, and pale ale malts Hersbrucker and Styrian Goldings hops are used to provide balance. It is one of the classics of the style.

CRUISING WITH RUBEN & THE JETS

LAGUNITAS BREWING COMPANY

This beer pours like a typical jet black stout. It initially forms a generous fluffy tan head that evaporates and leaves little lacing. From the nose, you won't be sure this is a Russian Imperial stout. It smells like sour red grape and Hershey's chocolate milk syrup. There is a noticeable booze aroma too. The taste, just like the aroma, is sour red grapes and chocolate syrup. It has a surprisingly mild palate without much bitterness or aftertaste. It will dry your mouth out with sourness, though. It doesn't have the roasty notes of a good Imperial stout, and the alcohol is very prominent for an 8.6% ABV beer. Overall, it's a good drinkable stout.

THE CZAR

AVERY BREWING CO.

The name of Avery's rich, strong Imperial stout is a big nod to the style's history. Russian Imperial stouts came into being at the end of the seventeenth century, when Peter the Great opened Russia to the Western world. On a trip to England the czar fell in love with the then-in-vogue porter and demanded that the dark brew be sent to his court in Russia. The first attempt was an abject failure; the cold weather and the long trip east caused the porter to go bad by the time it arrived. The solution was a more alcoholic, more hopped brew that could survive the journey. At the time, *stout* was a term for stronger porters, and so the strong porters headed for imperial Russia were termed Russian Imperial stouts. Although Avery's label portrays a later czar (Nicholas II), it's a worthy successor to those earlier brews.

The Czar is brewed with German hops, English yeast, and American water, a fitting fusion of the style's Old World roots and New World popularity. In the glass, the inky brew lets just the slightest hint of light through, giving the black stout a ruby edge. Spicy, floral Hallertau hops are strong in the nose, backed with molasses and more than a little alcohol. The taste is heavy on roasted malt and mocha, pleasantly balanced by the bitter bite of hops. Avery suggests cellaring this 10.5% ABV RIS, and a bit of age mellows the alcohol while amping up the dark fruit and chocolate flavors.

The Czar is the first in a series of decadent Imperial beers from Avery in the appropriately named Dictator Series. The others, The Kaiser and The Maharaja, are amped-up takes on an Oktoberfest and an IPA, respectively.

JC

DARK HOLLOW
ARTISANAL ALE

BLUE MOUNTAIN BREWERY

This self-proclaimed artisanal ale pours a deep, dark brown with a lighter, slighter head. Coffee may be in the background in the nose, but the bourbon is right up front. Bourbon, vanilla, and oak just dominate the nose. It's the same thing with the flavor, with bourbon up front—fresh, delicious bourbon—followed closely by the associated vanilla and oak notes. The flavor rounds out with a lingering chocolate finish. Light on carbonation and with a body that is heavy on the tongue, this is absolutely a sipper at 10% ABV.

JC

DARK HORIZON, THIRD EDITION

NØGNE Ø

This beer looks like a pool of melted licorice with an Alka-Seltzer dropped into it. It is slightly hazy with a tan head that violently fizzles into thin air; this is not surprising given the high alcohol content.

The nose has slightly burnt cocoa beans, rich dark chocolate cake, ground coffee, and figs, with an intense rummy alcohol vibe. It's the beer's way of telling you it's going to be sweet and sugary. An almost ridiculous amount of sugar is left in this beer, dominating the cold coffee and figgy pudding flavors and unfortunately reducing the complexity of the experience of drinking it. There's little suggestion of the heavyweight ABV (the sweetness smothers it). It's a solid Imperial stout but one for people who like a sweeter version.

This is a beer that benefits from pairing with food because on its own, even in its slimmed-down 25-centiliter bottle, it's too rich to finish on its own. This is the third edition of Dark Horizon, which is turning into something of a beery happening every time it is launched. Nøgne's cofounder and brewer Kjetil Jikiun says the idea behind every edition comes from people working at the brewery in Grimstad and can take weeks or months to evolve. You can be sure is that it will be different from the last Dark Horizon, as Nøgne has promised never to reproduce any versions of Dark Horizon.

DC

DARK LORD

THREE FLOYDS BREWING COMPANY

Three Floyds Dark Lord is like the Westvleteren 12 of the United States. It's brewed only once a year, and the only way to get it is to go to the brewery and wait in line on a certain Saturday in April.

This beer is as dark as night, with just a hint of ruby red at the edges and a small brown frothy head that regenerates with a vigorous swirl of the glass.

The aroma is similar to red wine with sour grape notes as well as some dark chocolate–rich syruplike scents (honey and molasses). The

taste is two flavors in one: red wine up front and bittersweet dark chocolate on the finish. It's very rich, and as it warms, more fruity flavors open up: cherry, plum, molasses. An alcohol presence is noticeable and distracts somewhat from the palate. It has typical stout consistency but was not as thick as expected. The chocolate bitterness lingers, as does the sour grapeness.

For a 15% ABV beer, it drinks like something with half the potency. There's definitely an alcoholic presence, but it's a gentle warmth, not a burn. It's a really good Russian Imperial stout and a really good (great, actually) beer.

CP

DARKNESS

SURLY BREWING COMPANY

The Surly Brewing Company is in Brooklyn Center, Minnesota. In 1994, its owner, Omar Ansari, received a homebrew kit as a gift. Purchased from St. Paul's Northern Brewer, and it became the gift that keeps on giving. In 2002, Omar and his wife, Rebecca, had their first child, Max. Instead of traditional birth announcements, Omar created a beer announcement, and the idea for a brewery was born. A building was procured, and Omar enrolled at the American Brewers Guild and then spent a week at Otter Creek Brewing in Vermont. His education was completed with an apprenticeship at New Holland Brewing in Michigan. At the spring 2004 Craft Brewers Conference in San Diego, Omar met Todd Haug, an experienced head brewer at the Minneapolis, Minnesota, Rock Bottom Brewery, and Surly became Minnesota's first new brewery west of the Mississippi since 1987—and one of the best in the region.

They use English Ale yeast and make the beer with pale ale yeast and Golden Promise, crystal, dark crystal, oat, black, chocolate, and roast malts, along with Belgian dark candi sugar and Columbus, Amarillo, and Simcoe hops. This massive Russian Imperial stout (9.8% ABV) brings waves of flavors: chocolate, cherries, raisins, coffee, and toffee. They add a bunch of hops to make it massively delicious. Each year when they release this beer, thousands descend on the brewery. It is a major event.

DEATH

BACKLASH BEER COMPANY

Backlash is a funky little brewery. Founded in July 2011, they contract brew at Paper City Brewery in Holyoke. But, day-to-day, you'll find them at their headquarters in Boston. You gotta love their viewpoint: "We brew beer the way it was intended to be brewed—flavorful, gimmick free, and not produced in ridiculous quantities. We know you're not impressed by spiral necked bottles or labels that change colors when they're so cold you can no longer taste their contents. You have hands (probably). You're familiar with how temperature works (…right?)" How can you not love these guys?

Death is the fourth and final installment in their Apocalypse Series. This Russian Imperial stout pours black as night with a big (count 'em, almost four fingers) rich khaki head. The nose is chocolate, coffee, and roasted barley with a nice hint of bitterness at the end. This is not a small beer, weighing in with a hefty 9.5% ABV, but it goes down pretty easy. A very good example of the style.

DOGFISH HEAD WORLD WIDE STOUT

DOGFISH HEAD BREWERY

This beer is opaque black with no visible carbonation. It initially forms a small dark tan foamy head that lingers for a while but eventually disappears. There is a vinous aroma of black grape, licorice, and mineral spirits. It's sweet, though.

It's always interesting coming back to certain beers after a long interval. I tasted the same vintage four years apart. The first time, the beer was intense and boozy, but I still liked it. With nearly four years of age under its belt, it's a lot different yet the same. It's smoother and sweeter and drinks like a liqueur rather than an Imperial stout.

A fresh bottle tends to be very bitter to balance out the large amount of barley with which it's brewed. There isn't much hop presence in this vintage four years later, though. The hops have faded, giving way to the malty base, with toffee as the most prominent flavor. It is rich and sweet like a candy bar, with a strong presence of black grape concentrate. Black licorice and dark chocolate are also present but not nearly as strongly, and there isn't much roasted barley flavor. Alcohol is of course a major player, imparting a strong but gentle warmth that complements the base brew perfectly. You can't imagine one without the other. This is a great-tasting beer.

When you're about to crack open an 18% ABV beer, you tend to have some apprehension, but all fears will be erased after just a few swigs. The alcohol was prominent but not distracting or abrasive. The texture is amazingly smooth—almost creamy—with a soft, calm, comfortable presence in the mouth. It leaves an aftertaste of toffee and cola, though there's no dry sensation and it is not cloying. This is a sipping beer but not an intimidating one.

CP

DOUBLE STOUT

GREEN FLASH BREWING CO.

Mike and Lisa Hinkley established Green Flash Brewing Co. in 2002 in San Diego, California. Their highly respected brewmaster, Chuck Silva, and his talented brewing team explored nineteenth-century British stout recipes and then charted a fresh course to come up with a modern American version of the Old World classic. Their 8.8% ABV Double Stout, they feel, encompasses the best of both worlds. Made with golden naked oats, dark crystal, and roasted malts, the beer is a robust but balanced beverage with the right amount of bittersweet chocolate and hints of coffee and other spices.

DRAGON'S MILK

NEW HOLLAND BREWING CO.

Some people call barrel-aged beers a cliché, but if the beer tastes great, who cares? This beer certainly isn't a cliché, since it's an Imperial stout that's been barrel-aged.

Its appearance is extremely dark brown to black, completely opaque. When poured, it forms a small, dark-tan, soapy head that dissipates quickly but leaves some lacing on the glass. The aroma is milky and dairylike with a slight farmhouse funk and a typical stout aroma backbone. Vanilla flower, wood, and spiced rum are quite prominent as well.

Barrel-aged Imperial stouts tend to be monsters on the palate, but Dragon's Milk is much closer to a soda pop with lots of chutzpah. Up front i's very sweet, almost sugary. There's a colalike flavor with accompanying sweetness, almost as if it contained aspartame. Light vanilla crème and woody, earthy flavors develop through the middle of the palate. It has a thin and fizzy mouthfeel like a soda with some life left in it before it goes flat. The end is all alcohol with plenty of warmth but amplifies and complements the vanilla character, creating a taste not unlike crème brûlée. The only problem is that the palate doesn't really develop even at warmer temperatures. A vintage with a year or two under its belt would be amazing.

Dragon's Milk might win the award for the most drinkable beer. The thinner mouthfeel and sweet but not cloying palate enable it to be drunk like flat cola. The alcohol is certainly prominent but never distracts from the genuine stout palate, and the aftertaste is remarkably clean. In fact, the beer is borderline refreshing in the mouth. Overall, New Holland's Dragon's Milk is an amazing beer in many respects. All stout lovers need to try this beer.

CP

ELLEZELLOISE HERCULE STOUT

BRASSERIE ELLEZELLOISE

Hercule Stout is a Russian Imperial stout–style beer brewed by Brasserie Ellezelloise in Ellezelles, Belgium. Hercule Poirot, the famous fictional detective, was born on April 1, 1850, in Ellezelles. This is the only self-proclaimed "Belgian stout"; it is 9% ABV and is considered a world classic. Made in small batches and then aged for ten days in German oak casks, Hercule is considered by many to be a classic in the European beer canon. It pours black and is big and very malty but dry, with a hint of sweetness in the finish, and is perfectly hopped. There are creamy aromas, a taste of mocha, and chocolate with a strong and mellow flavor. It has a very distinctive and intoxicating spicy aroma of fresh spruce. This unique house character probably derives from the strains of yeast used by the brewery and possibly from the fermentation in oak. This was voted best Belgian stout at the Best Belgian Beer of Wallonia competition in 2012.

EXPEDITION STOUT

BELL'S BREWERY

This stout pours as dark as motor oil with a very small head that also looks like motor oil. It has dark chocolate notes with a very slight hint of vanilla and oak. The body is thick and chewy. The flavor is dark, tasting of roasted malt and coffee in the front with dark fruit in the back. And with 10.5% ABV this is definitely one serious stout.

JC

FIRESTONE PARABOLA

FIRESTONE WALKER BREWING COMPANY

This is a brew that has been generating major buzz the last few years, but Firestone Walker beers can be difficult to get, and Parabola in particular is rare.

Parabola has a midnight black color; it is completely opaque with no carbonation visible. It forms a good-size brown frothy head that laces and retains very well for such a big beer. There is a potent nose of whiskey, sour grape, black licorice, and roasted malt. There are also sweet, oaky vanilla qualities with a hint of smokiness.

Barrel-aged Imperial stouts are all the rage these days, and for good reason: They're delicious. Usually these beers are aged in one barrel for a year or more, but Firestone Parabola is aged in multiple barrels, including those used for spirits, wines, and previous beers. This creates a unique and complex palate. Of course, the base brew has a lot to do with that.

Parabola hits the tongue with a massive amount of pure taste. Red grape, black licorice, and toffee and caramel syrups are the most prominent flavors up front. It's sweet

and rich, but in an authentic, all-natural way, with nothing candylike or artificial. The second half transitions to more traditional stout qualities with deeply roasted malt and a strong bitterness to balance the palate. On the finish there is a rush of wood, vanilla, and more whiskey. The after-taste, however, is remarkably clean with no lingering bitterness or cloying or sticky sweetness. Interestingly, there's little to no chocolate or coffee flavors in the palate but instead more vinous and licorice qualities.

The mouthfeel is full-bodied, with a thick, soft comfortable texture. There is noticeable warmth and whiskey sweetness across the tongue and a warming effect in the throat.

This beer is big at 12.5% ABV, but there are smaller beers that feel and drink much more potently. The palate is amazing in that it's so robust yet not intimidating. It's amazingly smooth, with a gentle presence of alcohol. This is a fine dessert beer or something for a special occasion. Drinking an entire bottle by itself would be challenging, though.

CP

FOUNDERS IMPERIAL STOUT

FOUNDERS BREWING COMPANY

Founders Imperial Stout is extremely dark black with an almost purple hue. It is completely opaque and pours to a very large, dark-brown, frothy head that laces and retains excellently. There is a distinct vinous aroma of black grape and alcohol. There is some roasted malt, though it is surprisingly mild for such a big beer.

Founders Brewing Company makes many great beers. The first thing you notice about this one is its intense bitterness. The bottle indicates 90 IBU, though that's not surprising since huge stouts need a lot of hops to balance out their supersweet maltiness. This Imperial stout might be a tad overhopped, though. There's a strong taste of classic Imperial stout through the middle. It imparts flavors of chocolate, red wine, coffee, and roasted malt. There's a consistent alcohol character in the background that gives it a bit of vanilla or rumlike character, but at the same time it is noticeably dry and warm. Although tasty, it is very simple and straightforward, though the flavors are enjoyable despite their repetitiveness.

Founders Imperial Stout drinks exactly like a 10.5% ABV beer of this style should. The mouthfeel is thick and viscous, though soft. There's a strong intensity to the mouthfeel as a result of the bitterness. This is a sipper if ever there was one. The alcohol creates a warmth that's difficult to overlook, though it's not cloying or distracting. It finishes surprisingly clean with just a trace of dry bitterness on the aftertaste.

CP

FROST MONSTER IMPERIAL STOUT

CAPTAIN LAWRENCE BREWING COMPANY

Scott Vaccaro was a student at Villanova when he decided to become a brewer. His parents objected when he opted to quit college and open a brewery. Luckily, Scott was as hardheaded about opening the brewery as he is about quality and innovation. Captain Lawrence Brewing Company is one of the best in the valley. The top four executives are all named Vaccaro, but what matters is the beer, from classic bottled beers to extravagant, cutting-edge brews that wine experts collect.

This beer is brewed with a huge amount of malt to give it a big roasty and smoky flavor. They say it's as big and deep as a cold winter's night, and the 15% ABV says they probably aren't far from wrong. Frost Monster is brewed with two-row black malt, roasted barley, oats, crystal malt, and chocolate malt. That's a lot of malt, and they use Columbus hops as well.

The beer pours with a big latte-colored head but without an extreme amount of lacing, which is surprising given the body. There's no question what the backbone of this big, brawny beer is: malt. It's big and roasty, and chocolate and dark stewed fruits such as dark cherry (like in a Bavarian Black Forrest Cake), come across on the nose. But don't be fooled; this is all about the malt despite the aromas of coffe, mocha, bitter chocolate, baking cocoa, and a hint of sweet chocolate.

This beer provides silky smooth drinking with a big mouthfeel. However, despite the high alcohol content, it is easy to drink. It's not the heaviest Imperial you've ever had, but there's plenty of taste and a nice long-lingering finish.

The beer would be incredible poured not just into a pint glass but into a snifter, because there are lots of good smells. It would go beautifully next to a cheese plate, just as it might stand up to a chocolate brownie sundae. This is a very impressive Imperial-style beer.

CAPTAIN LAWRENCE
BREWING COMPANY

FROST MONSTER
IMPERIAL STOUT

FULL SAIL IMPERIAL STOUT

FULL SAIL BREWERY & TASTING ROOM

The Imperial stout style has a reputation for being big and bold. It's rare to find a beer of this style that's just good, but Full Sail Imperial Stout is one of them. It has plenty of flavor and is highly drinkable but is missing a certain wow factor.

The beer pours with an opaque blood red–black color with no carbonation visible. It forms a small tan frothy head that mostly dissipates and leaves some decent lacing on the glass. All the usual notes of the style are in the aroma, but they are milder than in others of this style.

Full Sail Imperial Stout's aroma carries through to the palate and to the beer as a whole. Imperial stouts tend to be roasty and bitter with coffee flavors, but this one is remarkably sweet for the style. It imparts a taste akin to Diet Dr Pepper Cherry since the first flavor you notice is a cola-like taste.

There is definite bitterness to balance it, though. Significant hoppiness can be felt at the beginning and middle of the palate. There's almost a hint of citrus, but mostly it's just dry. You wait for a taste of black licorice and/or coffee but never get much of either. It ends with an even stronger rush of colalike sweetness before finishing quite clean.

The ABV is only 7.2%, and that probably explains the lightness, though it makes the beer all the more drinkable. The mouthfeel is thin and a bit flat, but it goes down extremely smooth with no cloying aftertaste. This would be a great introductory Imperial stout because it is so drinker-friendly.

CP

GUANABARA
IMPERIAL STOUT

CERVEJARIA COLORADO

This impressive Russian Imperial stout is brewed by Cervejaria Colorado in Sao Paulo, Brazil. This beer is known as Ithaca in Brazil, but Guanabara in the US. Guanabara gets its name from the awe-inspiring Sugarloaf Mountain in Rio de Janeiro.

Colorado was established in 1995, and was one of the first craft brewers in Brazil. Instead of making copies of American or European beers, they decided to involve the rich traditions and food of Brazil to their brewing. They combine traditional malts and hops with ingredients like local coffee, brown sugar (Brazilian unrefined cane sugar), manioc (cassava flour), honey, and Brazil nuts. They are located in the sugar cane growing region a few hours drive north of São Paulo, in the city of Riberão Black. This city was an important brew center in years past because of the extremely high quality of the water, which comes from the Guarany aquifer.

This RIS has a hint of Brazil's Northeast tucked inside. The beer is made from malt, hops, and burnt rapadura (a traditional Brazilian candy). When poured, it is dark, dark black, with more than two fingers of khaki-colored head forming at the top of the glass, which leaves a very nice sheet of lacing. Roasted coffee, molasses, brown bread, raisins, and

figs come wafting out of the glass. These flavors also come across on the palate. The body has medium carbonation that is very creamy and full. The 10.5% ABV is not obvious, as the beer is slightly sweet with just enough bitter hops to keep it in balance. It's sweet but refreshing and a very easy beer to drink despite its alcohol. Well done!

HAPPY ENDING

SWEETWATER BREWING COMPANY

This beer has a jet black opaque body and forms a large brown frothy head that laces and retains very well. The aroma includes pine, flowers, citrus, and some candy. That's odd considering that it's an Imperial stout; in fact, there isn't much of the stout in the aroma.

SweetWater Happy Ending is marketed as an Imperial stout, so it is included here, but really it is a double black IPA that's all about the hops rather than having the typical beefy stout body. Though only 51 IBU, it drinks like a California-style hop bomb with intense piney bitterness from beginning to end. It only grows stronger and drier as it reaches the apex and then gives way to some milk chocolate and black licorice and leaves a slightly dry aftertaste. If you let it linger on the tongue, the pine character grows a little stronger, as does a chocolate candy taste. These are two flavors you wouldn't think would work well together, but they do here mostly because it's not a 50–50 ratio (more like 90 hops–10 malts).

As it warms, the classic Imperial stout character becomes a little bit stronger, but not all that much. You could easily give this beer to people under the guise of an Imperial black IPA and they would have no trouble believing you. In fact, there could be more of the base stout character such as roasted malt and a stronger chocolate and coffee presence.

SweetWater Happy Ending doesn't taste like an Imperial stout and doesn't drink like one, either. Though it is potent at 9% ABV, there is no alcohol presence. The body is crisper than the average Imperial stout; it's more on the medium side rather than being viscous and sticky. It's easy to sip or drink in big gulps, and the palate makes it rather versatile as it can stand up to a strong meal or be enjoyed as a liquid dessert.

CP

HARVEY'S IMPERIAL EXTRA DOUBLE STOUT

HARVEY & SON

Usually available only bottle-conditioned as Imperial extra double stout, this beer occasionally has appeared in casks as Harvey's Imperial Russian Stout. It also is known as A le Coq Imperial Stout.

This is a historic Russian Imperial stout. Legend has it that Belgian Albert Le Coq was invited to tsarist Russia to brew the beer there to avoid import tariffs. In 1912, Le Coq released the first Imperial extra double stout from his brewery in Tartu, but the Russian Revolution and World War I brought it all to an end. This beer adheres to the original recipe, paying homage to the father of Imperial extra double stout.

Harvey & Son in the United Kingdom makes this beer from pale, amber, brown, and black malts and large amounts of Fuggles and Goldings hops. This stout is regarded as one of the world's most unusual and prestigious beers. The recipe contains a dense concentration of varied malts and hops to produce a bottle-conditioned stout. This brew will improve over six months to a year its complexity develops. It has an intense flavor that is intricate and distinctive. Big notes of roasted malts and exotic spices combine to make this unusual sweet-and-sour beer brew one of the best-known high-end beers in the world.

HUNAHPU'S
IMPERIAL STOUT

CIGAR CITY BREWING

Cigar City Brewing's Hunahpu's Imperial Stout has gained astronomically high marks from beer-rating websites, publications, and the beer community since it was released in 2008. According to the *Tampa Bay Times*, "more than 9,000 people attended [the release party], which is held at the Tampa brewery every March." In Mayan mythology, Hun Hunahpu was the father of the Mayan hero twins Hunahpu and Xbalanque. Hun Hunahpu, along with his brother Vucub Hunahpu, was tricked by the Dark Lords of the underworld and slain. Hun Hunahpu's corpse morphed into a cacao tree, with his head becoming a cacao pod, which in typically mythology fashion spit on the hand of a young maiden named Xquic, who promptly became pregnant with the hero twins. The twins ultimately grew up to avenge their father and uncle and defeat the Dark Lords and ascend to the heavens to become the moon and the sun.

This beer is 11% ABV. It pours an opaque brown-black and has a roasted malty aroma. Huge flavors of chocolate, coffee, spices, and vanilla dominate. The sweet beginning evolves into balanced bitterness. This is a beer that lives up to its immense hype.

IMPERIAL BROWN STOUT LONDON 1856

THE KERNEL BREWERY

The Kernel Brewery in London states, "The brewery springs from the need to have more good beer. Beer deserving of a certain attention. Beer that forces you to confront and consider what you are drinking. Upfront hops, lingering bitternesses, warming alcohols, bodies of malt. Lengths and depths of flavour. We make Pale Ales, India Pale Ales and old school London Porters and Stouts towards these ends. Bottled alive, to give them time to grow."

How can you not like a brewer who writes like that? In 2010, Evin O'Riordain, a home-brewer and cheese salesman, founded the brewery. It is tucked away in London within the arches under the railway that leads out of London Bridge. O'Riordain and his crew are beer enthusiasts and make everything, including American-style hoppy IPAs, saisons, and classic London porters and stouts.

This is a huge stout that is complete with cocoa, mocha, cassis and cherry, figs, and exotic spice. It's got grip and body and heft. It is as good a handcrafted stout as one can find in London. Beer geeks who make geek beers for beer geeks; that's The Kernel, and that is why you should try this beer.

The beer is an opaque black with a tan head. The body is rich and thick and unctuous, with lovely lacing. It tastes like coffee smoothed out with chocolate and cocoa. It is a big, gorgeous beer.

IMPERIAL STOUT

CHATHAM BREWING

Jake Cunningham and Tom Crowell have been making beer since 2007. Like most craft brewers, they started brewing to sooth their own palates and enjoy the camaraderie of brewing quality beer. As they've grown, they have developed a dedicated following. In April 2012, Chatham Brewing won the 2012 Matthew Vassar Brewers' Cup for the best craft beer brewery in the Hudson Valley at TAP New York, the state's largest craft beer festival and competition, which is held every year at Hunter Mountain in the Catskills.

"Credit for this really goes to our Brewer, Matt Perry," said Crowell. "Matt takes traditional styles and puts a unique twist on them, making some of the most drinkable beers you will find anywhere. And if you can't find them at your favorite pub, be sure to ask for them!"

Cunningham and Crowell own and operate Chatham Brewing on Main Street in Chatham, New York. The brewery is one of the most popular stops along the Hudson Berkshire Beverage Trail. Their handcrafted beers can be found in dozens of restaurants in New York City and upstate New York. In the summer of 2012, they began making some of their premium styles in 22-ounce bottles, including their Imperial stout.

Chatham Brewing's goal was to offer a big chocolaty Imperial stout of superior quality. The pour proves very promising, with a deep black body and a frothy tan head that lasts for a decent interval. Chocolate assaults the nose. There is almost a chocolate croissant aroma, with deep chocolate and hints of baked bread. The beer has a smooth texture, soft and chewy. The flavor is like a big, deep dark chocolate malted. Hints of fig and other fruit also come through, with a nice hint of hops. This beer is nicely balanced and very refreshing, a good example of the style.

IMPERIAL STOUT
MIDTFYNS BRYGHUS

Midtfyns Bryghus Imperial Stout is a heavyweight 9.5% ABV beer from Denmark that pours as black as the volcanic rocks of Mount Teide.

We don't know much about this quirky brewery, though we have tried their IPA and found it pleasant. Regardless, microbreweries don't need to look pretty as long as they deliver in the bottle. MB's Imperial Stout was voted the best new beer of 2007 by the Danish Beer Enthusiasts, and so our expectations were high.

The beer pours a coal black color with an impressive and firm O'boy-colored head. It smells initially of milk chocolate, cereal husks, and burnt coffee beans, but there's something odd in there that is a bit like sour cream.

In the mouth the beer starts with salty, stingy bitterness and raw burnt flavors of *rågbröd* (rye bread), licorice, and ash, making it a little uncomfortable to drink. Considering the high ABV, this Imperial stout doesn't have the flavor muscle expected. There are lots of burnt tones, but you're left searching for something to add contrast. However, it is still drinkable.

DP

IMPERIAL STOUT

MINOH BEER (A.J.I. BEER INC.)

Minoh Imperial Stout is brewed by A.J.I. Beer Inc. in Osaka, Japan. A.J.I. Beer Inc is the name of the brewing corporation that runs Minoh Beer similarly to the way Boston Beer Company runs Samuel Adams and other subsidiaries.

The beer pours black with hints of red and reddish-brown. An eggshell off-white head foams up nicely. This is a thinner style of stout and is meant to go with food. However, the aromatic notes are still there: coffee, milk chocolate, roasted mocha, hints of sweet chocolate, and maple, all balanced with just the right amount of hops bitterness. There is nice carbonation, and it finishes dry.

IMPERIAL STOUT TROOPER

NEW ENGLAND BREWING CO.

This beer is dark brown out of the bottle with an inklike, ultra-black hue in the glass. It forms a large brown frothy head that laces and retains wonderfully well. The smell is a bit on the mild side, but with a standard Imperial stout aroma of black licorice, roasted malt, and dark chocolate.

Imperial Stout Trooper has a delicious palate that's as robust and complex as some of the highest-ranked chocolate, coffee, oatmeal, milk, cream, and Russian stouts but isn't one of those niche styles. It shows that you don't have to be an obese brew to have a big taste.

There is intense rich sweet-ness as soon as it hits the tongue: black licorice, chocolate-covered cherry, and a hint of vanilla or wood. Though it is not strongly

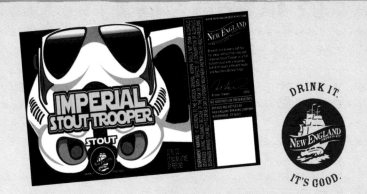

bitter, there is a significant hop presence from beginning to end, complemented by roasted malt, though it's never dry per se. It has a strong bitter bite at the crest of the swig that quickly recedes and gives way to the rich sweetness of milk chocolate, molasses, and a hint of citrus. The aftertaste is akin to Kahlúa with a slightly milky character plus liqueur flavor and sweetness, yet at no point is it boozy or cloying.

Imperial Stout Trooper is full-bodied but very drinkable. Though not a mammoth beer at 8.5% ABV, it's definitely on the heavier side, though it never feels like it. The mouthfeel is thick but soft and smooth with no oily or syrupy texture. It goes down so easy that you have to concentrate to sip it slowly instead of slugging it back. This would make a great dessert brew and is best enjoyed alone; the 500-milliliter bottle is the perfect serving size.

CP

KATE THE GREAT

PORTSMOUTH BREWERY

The year 1991 saw the birth of New Hampshire's first brewpub and craft brewery, the Portsmouth Brewery. Founded by siblings Janet and Peter Egelston, who previously had started the Northampton Brewery in Massachusetts, the brewery has become a staple of Portsmouth's busy downtown. The brewpub soon was joined by Smuttynose, its sister brewery (founded by Peter Egelston), which brews beer for distribution throughout the Northeast. Brewer Tod Mott, previously of Catamount, Harpoon, and Commonwealth, joined the breweries in 2003. He quickly distinguished himself with excellent beers, including the modern classic Kate the Great.

Kate the Great is a rare American beer in that it basically has its own holiday. Dubbed the "best beer in America" by *Beer Advocate* and earning perfect scores from RateBeer.com and BeerAdvocate.com, Kate has a devoted cult following. Upon its release every year, customers line up for hours at the brewery to taste the sweet ambrosia. The future of the beer is a bit up in the air. Kate's creator, Tod Mott, left the Portsmouth Brewery in 2012. Mott retained the recipe for the beer, and Portsmouth kept the name and the branding. It remains to be seen what Portsmouth's new head brewer will do with the name and what kind of Imperial stout Mott will brew at his new brewery, Maine's Tributary Brewing Company.

Kate pours exactly the way you'd expect for the style: black and thick as motor oil, with a healthy toffee-colored head that eventually fades to a ring that lasts till the end of the glass. The nose consists of dark chocolate, coffee, roasted malt, and a touch of vanilla. If the 10%+ alcohol is hidden in there somewhere, it's hard to detect. The taste is complex with so many flavors. From the start to the finish there's molasses, chocolate, citrus hops, coffee, smoky-sweet tobacco, and sweet brown sugar. The flavors don't drown out or clash with one another but create a magical mystery tour of taste. Again, the alcohol, which clocks in at 12% ABV, is astoundingly well hidden. It's a velvety smooth brew with a dry finish and is not too thick or cloying. The hidden alcohol, smoothness, and complex flavors make Kate the Great absurdly drinkable.

JC

KENTUCKY BOURBON BARREL STOUT

ALLTECH'S LEXINGTON BREWING AND DISTILLING COMPANY

Alltech's Lexington Brewing and Distilling Company is a passion for Dr. Pearse Lyons, who spent his early years as an intern at both the Guinness and Harp breweries and was the first Irishman to earn a formal degree in brewing and distilling from the British School of Malting and Brewing. Five generations of Lyons's family worked as coopers, supplying barrels to distilleries in Ireland, and for a quarter of a century Lyons's alcohol school was synonymous with brewing and distilling. In 1999, when the Lexington Brewing Company closed its doors, Lyons resurrected the brewing and distilling tradition of Lexington that dates back to the 1790s.

Barrels that once contained world-famous Kentucky bourbon lend a sweet hint of caramel and vanilla to the 8% ABV Kentucky Bourbon Barrel Stout's dark-roasted malts, and the brew finishes with the essence of lightly roasted coffee. The barrel-aged flavors native to Kentucky complement this complex stout brewed and aged with Haitian coffee. This brew is a great treat.

LIL' B

EVIL TWIN BREWING

Lil' B is a an Imperial stout–style beer brewed by Evil Twin Brewing in Copenhagen, Denmark, in association with Two Roads Brewing Company in Connecticut. Weighing in at a hefty 11.5% ABV, this is a big brew, a real heavyweight. You better bring you're A game, because this packs a heck of a punch in the alcohol department as well as the taste department. It is a fantastic beer that lives up to all the hype.

There are notes of cream, caramel, dark cocoa, roasty coffee, dark molasses, whipped cream, freshly cut vanilla beans, burnt toast, black cherries, cassis, raisins, and figs. Hints of tobacco and black leather come through. The hops that are present at the end balance this stout beautifully.

MARBLE IMPERIAL STOUT

MARBLE BREWERY

Marble Imperial Stout comes from Marble Brewery, a beer maker with one of the most underrated portfolios in the state. Though the brewery gets its name from Marble Avenue, a street in the warehouse district of northern Albuquerque, it could just as well allude to its penchant for making rock-solid beer; both the brewery's citrusy IPA and its superhopped Red Ale are worth seeking out.

Both booze and bourbon can be found in Marble's Imperial Stout. In a snifter, the brew is impenetrably black. One finger of creamy cocoa-colored froth grips the sides of the glass in sheets. The aroma exhibits pronounced molasses notes along with roasted peanuts, dark chocolate, maple syrup, prune juice, and a hint of licorice. Each of these ingredients is easily picked out, which is impressive given the aroma's gentle nature. It's a subtle, gently sloping aroma rather than the sharpness you'd expect to find in a beer of this might.

The flavor begins similarly with dry, smoky molasses, but it's followed swiftly by barrel notes: oak, vanilla, and brown sugar. After all, this brew is aged for a whole year in bourbon barrels. Dark chocolate–covered raisins with a touch of smoke and a splash of pure alcohol round things out. Things get fruitier as it warms, but when cold it has a more pronounced bourbon flavor. The real standout, however, is the body. It's glorious; thick and rich, it coats the tongue like candle wax, transforming the beer into a hefty, creamy treat.

Marble Imperial Stout is a dark beer, perfect for when you're in your dark place, but it probably works just as well for celebrating.

ZF

MARSHAL ZHUKOV'S IMPERIAL STOUT

CIGAR CITY BREWING

This is among the blackest beers you'll ever see; it's darker than spent motor oil with the darkest head ever and a dark-brown, soapy texture. There is not much lacing on the glass, but the head never completely dissipates.

The nose reveals black licorice flavoring concentrate with strong anise and subtle but noticeable sour grape or cherry. There is no raw alcohol presence.

The general notion with Imperial stouts is the rarer, the better. Marshal Zhukov's Imperial Stout is quite rare and expensive. It's definitely comparable to other beers of this ilk. It has a strong, complex, robust body with strong syrupy sweetness up front and black licorice flavor with spice. There is dark chocolate sweetness through the middle with mild bitterness at the apogee and then a slightly sour grape and cherry flavor on the back end. There's a hint of sharp bitterness on the aftertaste, but it fades quickly.

If this is the epitome of a well-made Russian Imperial stout, why isn't it a perfect beer? Only because it doesn't have any features that you haven't already had in easier-to-acquire beers of this style. You'll appreciate the fact that it hides its alcohol extremely well, and the palate is plenty complex.

Despite a huge 11% ABV, Marshal Zhukov's Imperial Stout is amazingly easy to drink. The mouthfeel is thick but not sticky, though the texture is soft and the finish is relatively clean considering how big the beer is. It doesn't feel as heavy as the statistics would predict, though I don't recommend drinking an entire bottle by oneself.

CP

MEXICAN IMPERIAL STOUT

MICROCERVECERIA GOURMET CALAVERA

This is an American double Imperial stout brewed by Microcerveceria Gourmet Calavera in Mexico City, Mexico. It is a strong (9% ABV) top-fermented ale with a high content of toasted malt. The taste has hints of chocolate and coffee and an aroma of caramel, raisins, and dried fruits. Chilies are added to give this stout its characteristic flavor and strength.

This is a big, bold, strong, dark, highly fermented beer that, with its high content of roasted malts, has very recognizable tastes of chocolate and coffee and aromas of caramel, raisins, and dried fruit. Abundant amounts of British hops provide a stylish counterweight to the strong caramel and fruity character. Select chilies add a personal touch that gives this beer even more intensity. This beer was created especially to accompany dishes with mole, a delicacy worthy of any generation, past, present, or future.

Caramel and raisins are big on this beer, with hints of cola, coffee, and licorice making it earthy and chewy. Although there are chilies in the brew, they do not dominate, and the beer is not spicy or hot. Rather, the peppers add complexity. One of the two best beers of this type made in Mexico, Calavera Mexican Imperial Stout stands up to international competition as well.

MILES DAVIS' BITCHES BREW

DOGFISH HEAD BREWERY

The body this Imperial stout, which was inspired by a forty-year-old jazz album is black and forms a large frothy and creamy dark tan head that leaves plenty of lacing and retains very well. The aroma is rich milk chocolate and black licorice. For an unflavored Imperial stout it is surprisingly sweet-smelling with little to no bitterness scents.

This is definitely not your average Imperial stout, but Dogfish Head rarely does anything by the book. The label indicates that it is brewed with honey and gesho, although there's no mention of anise despite the fact that black licorice is prevalent throughout the palate. The first half is very rich and sweet with a mix of semisweet chocolate, a candylike sweetness of black licorice, and a distinct honey component.

The second half becomes much bitterer with a slight coffee flavor and a slightly dry, almost sandy texture and sensation. The aftertaste is a mixture of all the flavor components with rich, sticky syrupy sweetness and dry bitterness. This beer may be brewed with gesho instead of hops or in addition to hops. Either way it is not an extremely bitter brew but is bitter enough to balance the sweetness. The black licorice smell and flavor seem to grow stronger with each swig. The flavor is powerful, and this beer is not for the faint of heart.

The mouthfeel shows only medium thickness with a noticeable fizzy sensation on the tongue. It took quite a few servings to taste and feel the 9% ABV of this beer. It starts out very light drinking and tasting, similar to most other stouts, but on the second serving it starts to throw its weight around. As a single-serving beer it would be great with a hearty beef meal or as a complement to a light dessert. Overall, this is an impressive and very satisfying beer.

MILES DAVIS' BITCHES BREW

Ale brewed with honey and gesho.

1 Pint 9.4 fl. oz. · 9% alc. by vol.

GOVERNMENT WARNING: (1) ACCORDING TO THE SURGEON GENERAL, WOMEN SHOULD NOT DRINK ALCOHOLIC BEVERAGES DURING PREGNANCY BECAUSE OF THE RISK OF BIRTH DEFECTS. (2) CONSUMPTION OF ALCOHOLIC BEVERAGES IMPAIRS YOUR ABILITY TO DRIVE A CAR OR OPERATE MACHINERY, AND MAY CAUSE HEALTH PROBLEMS.

Miles Davis' seminal Bitches Brew album was a game changer — a bold fusion of rock, funk, and jazz. To honor the 40th anniversary release, Dogfish Head has created a bold, dark beer that's a fusion of three threads imperial stout and one thread honey beer with gesho root. Like the album, this beer will age with the best of 'em. To hear the music and the story that inspired this beer, go to www.milesdavis.com/brew.

LEGACY

BREWED BY DOGFISH HEAD CRAFT BREWERY, INC. WWW.DOGFISH.COM

38489 00106 7

NARWHAL
IMPERIAL STOUT

SIERRA NEVADA BREWING CO.

This beer has an opaque black hue with no visible carbonation. It pours to a surprisingly large dark-brown, frothy head that laces and retains quite well. The aroma is black licorice with minor notes of coffee, though the alcohol is quite prominent.

Sierra Nevada is known for hoppy beers, though Narwhal is probably its most notable stout. It gets a lot of acclaim from craft beer enthusiasts, though it might or might not be equated with some of the world-class examples of the style. It's a great example of an Imperial stout brewed to spec.

The flavor profile is familiar, but in a good way. The palate is significantly sweet with notes of caramel, milk chocolate, and black licorice. It's also quite bitter with a strong presence of roasted malt and astringent hops. The alcohol is a major component of the taste, imparting dryness and maybe a hint of smoke. It is satisfying and enjoyable, though it doesn't break new ground in the Imperial stout field. This is a beer that could be enjoyed by newcomers and connoisseurs alike.

It was a little intimidating to see the 10.2% ABV on the label. Be prepared for a heavy, intense body in a beer that must be sipped. You'll be relieved by how smooth and comfortable it is in the mouth. Although there is a significant alcohol component, it's a gentle warmth that works with the palate rather than against it. The mouthfeel is actually thinner than you might expect, and the aftertaste is a bit cleaner than it is in most beers of this style.

CP

NIGHT TRIPPER IMPERIAL STOUT

NEW HOLLAND BREWING CO.

New Holland's Night Tripper Imperial Stout is brewed with American ale yeast and uses 2-row, munich, caramel, crystal, black, chocolate, flaked barley, and melanoldan malts. They hop it with East Kent Golding, nugget, and magnum. The result is an impressive beer that comes in at a muscular 10.8% ABV. It pours opaque black with a small but solid dark tan head. A big dose of roasted malts and flaked barley helps give this beer a rich, roasty complexity with coffee, vanilla, and dark chocolate coming through. Nicely balanced. An exceptional example of the style.

OAK AGED
BLACK JACK STOUT

DUCLAW BREWING COMPANY

Owner Dave Benfield and brewmaster Jim Wagner decided that instead of kegging the entire 2010 batch of Black Jack Stout, one of their most popular seasonal beers since it first was brewed in 1998, they would age a small quantity for two months in charred American oak whiskey barrels before bottling it. The result is a smoky, sophisticated Russian Imperial stout that pours jet black with a full body, a small tan head, and warm aromas of smoky malt and charred oak. Barrel aging also adds accents of charred oak, vanilla, and caramelized sugar to Black Jack's bold swirl of dark chocolate, coffee, smoky malt, and fruit flavors, such as fig and cherry, that balance its big, warming 8% ABV. This is an exceptional beer.

OLD RASPUTIN RUSSIAN IMPERIAL STOUT

NORTH COAST BREWING COMPANY

North Coast Brewing Company's Old Rasputin Russian Imperial Stout is a pretty famous beer and is consistently ranked among the best Russian Imperial stouts and beers overall.

The body is black and forms a surprisingly huge frothy head for such a strong beer. There is very good retention and lacing. The aroma is typical of an Imperial stout with roasted malts, a hint of chocolate, and noticeable alcohol that grows stronger and more fusel-like as it warms.

The palate starts off very strong with a robust flavor of deeply roasted malts. It is so roasty, it's akin to a straight-up burnt flavor, especially burnt popcorn. There's a strong coffeelike bitterness as well that borders on salty. The beer seems to foam up in the mouth. The second half is quite pleasing with a baker's chocolate taste. This helps accentuate the bitterness while imparting a rich, syrupy sweetness. The chocolate seems to fade quickly as the beer's palate becomes drier and bitterer as it warms. Though not terribly complex, this beer is still satisfying.

The mouthfeel is not as thick or sticky as you'd expect. It feels like a much smaller beer than it is, almost to the point of being medium-bodied. There is a significant bitter aftertaste, though.

For a 9% ABV, Old Rasputin wears its alcohol well. Although you do notice a boozy smell, there is little warmth in the palate and it goes down very smooth. It is not a sipper and not quite a special occasion beer, but it is not something you'd want multiple servings of, either.

Overall, this is one of the most reliable Imperial stouts on the major craft beer market. You can see why it has the reputation it does. You might not consider it an elite beer, but it is a highly commendable one.

CP

PÉCHÉ MORTEL

DIEU DU CIEL!

Since its origins as a Montreal brewpub in 1998, Dieu du Ciel! has been turning out a wide variety of impressive beers. Péché Mortel, however, remains the brewery's flagship, and with good reason.

The sinfully rich dark-brown Imperial stout is filled with flavors and aromas of bitter chocolate and strong espresso. At 9.5% ABV it's plenty potent, but the alcohol is fairly well hidden by some residual sweetness. It's best paired with dark chocolate but also goes very well with venison. (If you're wondering about the name, it doesn't mean "deadly peach": *Péché mortel* is French for "mortal sin.")

JR

PEG LEG
IMPERIAL STOUT

HEAVY SEAS BEER

Heavy Seas Peg Leg Imperial Stout has an opaque black body with no visible carbonation. It forms a small, light-brown, foamy head that mostly dissipates but leaves a trace of lacing on the glass. The aroma features plenty of dark roasted malt with a general confectionery sweetness. The alcohol is noticeable.

Some people think of the Imperial stout as a foolproof style of beer—even when it's not that good, it's still pretty good. Heavy Seas Peg Leg is a good example of this. It is essentially a by-the-book, no-frills Imperial stout that's a pretty good beer but only okay for the style.

The taste is quite sweet from start to finish, with a mélange of toffee, molasses, and chocolate syrup throughout the first half. There is not much in the way of roasted malt or hop character. Alcohol warmth is present, and it imparts a slightly sweet rumlike character, but with no overt vanilla or woody flavors. The aftertaste is remarkably clean, which is a bit unusual for an Imperial stout. Overall, the flavors are good and solid, and most drinkers will find this brew satisfying.

On the one hand, the mouthfeel is comfortable with a soft texture, smooth finish, and clean aftertaste. On the other hand, there is a slightly distracting alcohol warmth. This is understandable because the beer is rather hefty at 8% ABV, but it feels like a slightly bigger beer than it is. It probably is best enjoyed as a stand-alone nightcap.

CP

PITCH BLACK
IMPERIAL STOUT

INVERCARGILL BREWERY

Invercargill began as a father-and-son team of Gerry and Steve Nally. Steve graduated from Canterbury University with a degree in chemistry but ended up playing rugby for Epernay in France. On returning to Invercargill in the mid-1990s, he briefly landed a job in a laboratory. On weekends he toured abandoned orchards to fill a trailer with ground-bruised fruit to try his hand at making cider. In 1999, Steve and Gerry leased a dairy shed in Oteramika Road on the outskirts of the city and set up business. In 2005, the brewery outgrew the old blue shed and moved to downtown Invercargill. Soon after that Gerry retired. By 2011, the brewery was feeling the pinch again, and, in 2013, it moved to its current home at 72 Leet Street, where the story continues.

According to the brewery, Pitch Black Imperial Stout was five years in the conceptual stage and six months brewing. Pitch Black Imperial is the brewery's award-winning 4.5% ABV stout on steroids. Since head brewer Steve Nally believes the style is all about malt, he decided to see what would happen if he doubled the recipe. What happened first was that the mash got stuck. What happened next was the transfer to Central Otago Pinot Noir barrels, where the brew spent three months on oak after fermentation.

This stout is made for beer geeks. Its high alcohol level and concentration of flavor make this Imperial offering most unusual. Nally has a reputation for experimental brews, continually breaking new ground with his interpretations of traditional European beer styles. He uses malts such as Gladfield Ale, Gladfield Wheat, flaked barley, pale crystal, Caramalt, chocolate, and black roasted barley to give this beer a strong backbone of Pacific Gem hops. This is an excellent example of the style.

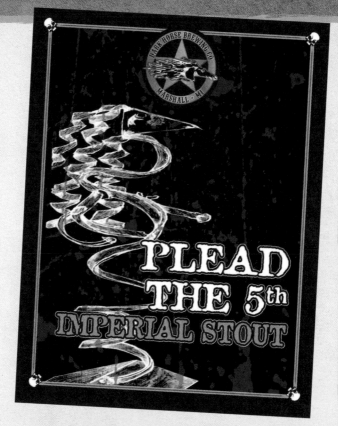

PLEAD THE 5TH
IMPERIAL STOUT

DARK HORSE BREWING COMPANY

Plead the 5th Imperial Stout is number five in the dark beer series from Dark Horse Brewing Company in Michigan. This entry comes only in 750-millliter bottles. It is a big and full-bodied stout. Lots of roasted malts balanced with heavy hops make this Imperial a big player to contend with. The dark beer has a dark head that is only transient with brief lacing, but the body is thick and rich and creamy. Chocolate, fig, dried cherries, hints of marshmallow, soy sauce, something woodsy, and spices make this a complex stout. It is a world-class beer.

POTHOLE FILLER IMPERIAL STOUT

HOWE SOUND INN & BREWING COMPANY

More than a century ago breweries dotted British Columbia's landscape. Hop farming flourished, and the Squamish Valley Hop Company Ranch supplied hops to the British Empire. With the advent of Prohibition, the number of breweries and hop farms dwindled. In 1980, John Mitchell and Frank Appleton pioneered North America's first modern craft brewery at Horseshoe Bay on British Columbia's Howe Sound. Mitchell, long considered one of the fathers of Canadian micro-brewing, designed the current brewery in 1996. The winery still has a relationship with him.

This beer is a strong inky-dark ale brewed with blackstrap molasses and six malts. It is a thick beer with an intense roasted barley flavor, with notes of chocolate and licorice.

REVERY RUSSIAN IMPERIAL STOUT

FOOLPROOF BREWING COMPANY

Revery is Foolproof Brewing Company's Russian Imperial stout. Master brewer Demase Olsson put together a big, brawny string of malts to create a powerful, rich base. He included two-row, Maris Otter, Crystal 40, Carafa, as well as roasted barley, chocolate, and flaked oats. The resulting beer is creamy and rich despite the high alcohol content. A delicate blend of Northern Brewer, Tettnanger, and Hallertau hops rounds out this masterpiece so that it finishes with complexity and balance instead of being cloying.

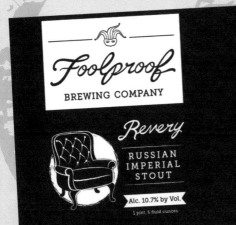

Revery is a daydream in a glass — a dark, malty escape. We put together an insane malt bill for this Russian Imperial Stout — two row, Crystal 40, Carafa, roasted barley, chocolate malt, and flaked oats combine to make Revery incredibly smooth and rich. A delicate blend of Northern Brewer, Tettnanger, and Hallertau hops round out this masterpiece.

November **2013**

Your Life Your Beer

EXPERIENCE RESPONSIBLY

www.foolproofbrewing.com

Brewed and Bottled by
Foolproof Brewing Company
Pawtucket, RI

BARREL AGED IN VERMONT

RUSSIAN IMPERIAL STOUT

ENJOY WITH COMRADES.

Aged in maple whiskey oak barrels, this stout has a rich roasted flavor with overtones of sweet vanilla coming from the American Oak and a velvety smooth hint of whiskey.

SMALL BATCH ★ LIMITED EDITION

STYLE *Russian Imperial Stout* | ALC. BY VOL. *10%* | IBU *65 units* | 12 FL. OZ.

RUSSIAN IMPERIAL STOUT

OTTER CREEK BREWING/WOLAVER'S

This beer looks thick and viscous flowing out the bottle. The body is extremely dark with a brown frothy head. It mostly dissipates but does leave some lacing, which is impressive in such a big beer. There is a strong aroma of dark malt, espresso, and milk chocolate candy, with no alcohol presence.

Otter Creek is a brewery known for making mainstream stuff that you can find fairly easily. That's a good thing in this case. This beer comes with a lot of recommendations, and it's obvious why everyone's raving. This is a quality Russian Imperial stout that can hang with the big boys as it's robust, complex, and highly drinkable.

The first taste you notice is sweet milk chocolate. It almost seems sugary, though it's doubtful that this beer is brewed with any chocolate or other additives. Beers of this style tend to have a strong red grape flavor, and though that taste is present here, it takes a backseat to deeply roasted but not burnt) malt and iced coffee flavor balanced by a strong hop presence. The label indicates that the beer is 65 IBU, which seems a bit low since big Imperial stouts tend to be high in bitterness to balance out the intense malty sweetness. It's possible that a lot of balance is provided by the malt's inherent coffee and roasty flavors. There's some alcohol warmth and flavor as it finishes, but it complements the palate quite well.

A delicious Imperial stout is a lot less enjoyable if it's hard to drink. Thankfully, Otter Creek Russian Imperial Stout doesn't have that problem as it has a soft, comfortable mouthfeel with a velvety texture. It goes down smooth with a slight hoppy bite on the finish but leaves no lingering aftertaste other than some chocolate notes. It does not nearly feel as heavy its 10% ABV. Though there is alcohol warmth, it's not distracting. That seems to be what separates a great Russian Imperial stout from an average one. This one is very good.

CP

SEA MONSTER IMPERIAL STOUT

BALLAST POINT BREWING COMPANY

Ballast Point Sea Monster Imperial Stout is brewed in San Diego, California, which has a good reputation for brewing. This beer has a jet-black opaque body with no other colors visible. It forms a large, dark khaki–colored, frothy head that retains and laces very well. The aroma is surprisingly mild with more of a traditional pub-style stout aroma of sweet malts and some black licorice. There is no alcohol presence, though.

You've had plenty of "big deal" Imperial stouts by now, so you're familiar with what can be done with the style, and Sea Monster Imperial Stout leans heavily in one direction. It begins with a mild sweetness, closer to a foreign extra stout than to an American-style or Russian Imperial brew. Licorice, a caramel syrup sweetness, and a sharp dryness all come through in the middle. The finish features a strong presence of pure booze with rubbing alcohol–like flavor and warmth that becomes more tolerable the more you drink but never fades away completely. The aftertaste is surprisingly clean with

a subtle dry combination of roasted malts, sugary residue, and alcohol. It is tasty and quite enjoyable, but perhaps it might it have been more.

Ballast Point Sea Monster Imperial Stout weighs in at 10% ABV, and you definitely can feel the overt alcohol presence. The mouthfeel is thinner and more carbonated than you'd expect. Although there is noticeable sweetness, it's not sticky and cloying and does not have the texture of carbonated molasses. However, it's a hefty, dense brew and you definitely feel the alcohol, so you'll be glad to split the bottle with a friend. This beer almost demands to be paired with a rich dessert to take some of the edge off. As a stand-alone dessert or sipper it satisfies but is a little challenging. It is recommended for experienced Imperial stout drinkers only.

CP

SERPENT'S STOUT
(IMPERIAL STOUT)

LOST ABBEY

The Lost Abbey and Port Brewing are both brands of Port Brewing Company, from San Marcos, California. Like Chevrolet and Cadillac, both are produced by the same company but targeted at different markets. Lost Abbey produces Belgian-inspired ales packaged in 375ml or 750ml corked bottles. Contrary to popular opinion, they are not owned or connected to Pizza Port. There also seems to be a belief that they are somehow affiliated with Stone Brewing. Also not so. They took over Stone Brewing's old brewhouse when Stone moved to their new digs in Escondido, California, back in 2006.

The sign above the barrel room tells you a lot about how they brew the Lost Abbey beers. It reads, "In Illa Brettanomyces Nos Fides"; a Latin phrase meaning "in this place we have faith in British fungus." In specific, Brettanomyces. Brett, as it is commonly referred to, is a

very strong yeast strain that changes the flavor and aromas of beer and wine. Lovers of this yeast agree with the beer geeks at Lost Abbey, who say it "is a wild yeast prized for the complex flavors and sensory compounds it produces."

The Lost Abbey relies heavily on the practices of the Trappist tradition. Many of those beers and styles were born in abbeys. Thus, Lost Abbey liberally blends the use of beer and religion, but in an inoffensive manner. According to Lost Abbey, "The history of the bible and religion is indeed the struggle of good vs. evil. Our Serpent's Stout recognizes the evil of the dark side that we all struggle with." The Serpent's Stout is a massive, 11% ABV Imperial stout. It is easily one of the most highly rated Imperial stouts on the Internet and by beer writers around the world.

If you can, pour it into a snifter. It deserves it. It pours a thick, opaque black. The dark, medium head is almost an inch deep and lasts a good, long while. Burnt malt, toffee, mocha, molasses, and bittersweet chocolate all come across the nose. Mocha, cocoa, and raisin all come across on the palate. A massively thick beer. Chewy. Overall, it's a brawny, classic, well-constructed Imperial stout of exceptional quality, taste, and experience.

SLOTTSKÄLLANS 2012 BARREL AGED IMPERIAL STOUT

SLOTTSKÄLLANS BRYGGERI

This beer pours a mild murky dark chestnut brown with hints of red under an egg-white head that fails to gather any sort of momentum and collapses quickly into a faint ring

The beer's barrel-aged background immediately makes itself known with distinctive fruity rumlike notes of raisins, dried prunes, and figs. There's some nice vanilla and caramel over a vein of milk chocolate. From the smell you know this is going to be powerful stuff, complex and inviting.

Barrel aging can add exciting complexity to beer but also can transform it into an alcoholic mess. Fortunately, Slottskällans has played this one well, with soft oaklike flavors of vanilla and toast complementing a rather sweet fruity beer with a mild roasted character. It is medium sweet up front, but things go a little off kilter at the end, with the bourbon burn exposing the beer's underweight malt body.

One could smother some braised brisket with a bourbon and perhaps fig glaze for an intensely rich dish. Otherwise, get the cheeseboard out and match it with aged cheddar and Gruyère plus sweeter blue cheeses such as Cambozola.

This 11% ABV beer is the barrel-aged big brother of the Uppsala-based craft brewery's standard Imperial stout that is brewed using four different malts (pilsner as the base, then dark caramel, chocolate, and black malt) and three different hops (Northern Brewer, East Kent Golding. and Fuggle).

DP

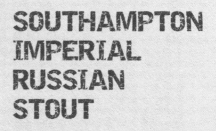

SOUTHAMPTON IMPERIAL RUSSIAN STOUT

SOUTHAMPTON PUBLICK HOUSE

Russian Imperial stouts, like India Pale Ales, are named after the region they were originally shipped to rather than the place where they were brewed. The flavors and alcohol content of these styles were born of necessity. High alcohol and high hop content act as natural preservatives in beer. Therefore, as demand for foreign beer grew internationally, brewers resorted to combining additional hops and fermenting with higher alcohol to ensure that their product could be shipped across longer distances. Made to last, IPAs and Russian Imperial stouts are still some of the most cellarworthy beers made.

Southampton Publick House brews an Imperial Russian stout every year, and it has attracted a cultlike following. Its relatively small production means high demand and few bottles left for the cellar. This bottle aged only about two weeks before it was popped open, still in its infancy.

It pours a dirty motor oil black with a dark coppery-brown head. The viscosity and weight of the beer are noticeable at first glance. The foam dissipates but never vanishes completely, leaving a fine lacing on the glass.

Some dried fruit, fig, and date were evident on the nose while the beer was still at a low temperature. Once it was a bit warmer, burnt coffee, licorice, and dried straw joined the bouquet. The alcohol (which is high at 10.5% ABV) seems to lift the aromas rather than overpower them. There were no apparent alcohol esters in the mouth.

The nine different malt varieties and an abundance of hops bring about a multitude of flavors that continue to develop as the beer warms. The generous hopping is nicely balanced by a strong roasted malt character. Boasting a smooth milky texture, the stout suspends notes of espresso, toffee, and caramel. Superfine bubbles barely tickle the tongue and allow these flavors to sing. The hops shine through in the superlong but not overly bitter finish. The brewer, Evan Addario, mentioned that the hop character in the stout will fade over time, allowing the malt profile to come to the foreground.

GC

SOUTHWARK OLD STOUT

SOUTH AUSTRALIA BREWING CO.

This award-winning foreign stout is brewed by South Australia Brewing (Lion Nathan Co.) in Thebarton, Australia. Brewed in the style of the old Imperial Russian stout, they've been using the same recipe for more than forty years. Southwark Old Stout remains to be, to this day, one of Australia's favorite dark beers and is highly thought of around the world.

This is a big, rich stout. Almost like a beer-port. It pours black and creamy. The roast coffee, roasted malt and dark chocolate, and dark fruits like plum and fig, make it an excellent nightcap. Rich, chewy, and complex.

SPEEDWAY STOUT

ALESMITH BREWING CO.

This stout is so dark, it's black. We're talking jet black with a dark tan head that leaves a thick lacing. The nose is sweet with toffee and dark chocolate with a touch of oaky vanilla that is almost bourbon-like. The dark color matches the dark chocolate and coffee taste, nicely balancing the bitterness with a fudge flavor. Its smooth and creamy texture hides the high 12% ABV dangerously well. As this beer warms up, the complex flavors round out very well, making it even tastier to drink as you near the bottom of the glass.

JC

ST-AMBROISE STOUT IMPERIALE RUSSE

MCAUSLAN BREWING

This is one of the darkest beers around. St.-Ambroise Russian Imperial Stout is brewed by McAuslan Brewing in Montreal, Canada. It has an absolutely midnight black body and a huge dark brown frothy head that laces and retains wonderfully. The aroma features sweet red grape, black licorice, roasted malt, and a hint of alcohol.

It begins with a remarkably sweet red grape taste; this is a unique flavor since some beers of this style tend to have a sour grape component to the palate. Black licorice and a general confectionery sweetness come rushing in through the middle, and the palate ends with a strong, dry bitter note. It's actually one of the most bitter beers of this style, which certainly makes it unique. There's a subtle alcohol warmth and accompanying dry flavor in the aftertaste, too. The roasted malt has a very unique dark chocolate and almost peanut butter taste. There is also a slight bourbon flavor.

There are many rare, exclusive, hyped Russian Imperial stouts, and there are definitely differences among them. St.-Ambroise Russian Imperial Stout is a very tasty beer that has no flaws.

For a pretty hefty beer, St.-Ambroise Russian Imperial Stout is a cinch to drink. It may be almost too drinkable because the mouthfeel is so soft and comfortable, the finish is so smooth, the texture is so soft, and the aftertaste is so pleasant. There's a touch of alcohol warmth and dryness, but it's very easily overlooked. It seemed to sit more heavily on the system than most 9.2% ABV beers do, but it's a perfect dessert brew.

CP

STONE FARKING WHEATON WOOTSTOUT

STONE BREWING CO.

This beer is brewed with rye, wheat malt, and pecans and partially aged in bourbon whiskey barrels. It has an opaque black body with no visible carbonation and pours to a small brown soapy head that retains and laces well. The aroma is surprisingly fruity, almost berrylike. There are sweet aromas of vanilla and licorice, though alcohol is quite prominent.

There's a long story behind this beer. From the unlikely trio of the actor Wil Wheaton, the alternative news website Fark.com creator Drew Curtis, and Stone CEO and cofounder Greg Koch comes an Imperial stout unlike any ever made. This is a one-off collaboration brew: an Imperial stout brewed with rye and wheat, with some of it aged in bourbon barrels. As seems to be the case with some Stone beers, you don't always get the rye or wheat, though the barrel aging is noticeable. Regardless, it's an excellent Imperial stout that tastes great.

Much like the nose, the palate is remarkably fruity, with not just grape as in so many other Imperial stouts but an almost berrylike (blue, red, and black) taste; this is odd since the beer isn't brewed with any of those additives. There's some licorice or aniselike spiciness through the middle, followed by deeply roasted barley and dry bitterness on the back end, probably from the rye, though there isn't a lot of rye taste per se. The alcohol is a major player in the palate, too, imparting a woody, vanillalike flavor throughout the drinking experience as well as significant warmth.

At 13% ABV, Stone Farking Wheat w00tstout is a beast of a beer. To call it robust is an understatement, yet you wouldn't go so far as to call it hot or difficult to drink. The alcohol is noticeable, but it's warm and smooth and works well with the body. The mouthfeel is soft and smooth, and the aftertaste is bitter but tolerable. You'll have no trouble drinking half a bottle, though any more than that would be a challenge.

A bottle of this beer probably would be amazing a few years from now, but since it was a one-off brew and bottles were scarce, it's doubtful you'll have the opportunity to find out. In the end, it's a great Imperial stout that can hold its own with a lot of other comparable brews.

CP

STONE IMPERIAL RUSSIAN STOUT

STONE BREWING CO.

This stout is opaque black of the deepest shade and forms a small, brown, foamy head that dissipates mostly but not completely, leaving minor lacing on the glass. It has an interesting aroma that's a combination of red grape, orange citrus, and chocolate syrup.

The taste makes good on the aroma's promise, delivering a delicious blend of chocolate, black licorice, red grape, some orange fruit, and just enough bitterness to balance it out. Chocolate syrup is quite prominent, as is some black licorice or root beer flavor but without any spiciness. There's some black cherry through the middle along with a slightly dank hoppiness coupled with some orange flavor. The hop character maintains the balance as the sweetness never becomes cloying. The alcohol fades into the background well, though it's still noticeable and ties all the flavors together. This is one of the best examples of the style.

The mouthfeel is soft, smooth, and slightly slick but not oily. It goes down remarkably easy and is only slightly dry in the aftertaste. The 10.8% ABV is quite efficient as the beer is still overtly strong, but its actual boozy character is mellow and easily tolerable.

CP

STORM KING IMPERIAL STOUT

VICTORY BREWING COMPANY

The story of Victory Brewing Company starts on a school bus in 1973 when fifth-graders Ron Barchet and Bill Covaleski met. Twenty-three years later, Victory Brewing Company opened its doors to the public on February 15, 1996. What was once a Pepperidge Farm factory in Pennsylvania became home to a 144-seat restaurant with a 70-foot-long bar and a full-scale brewery. In its first year, Ron and Bill brewed 1,725 barrels of beer.

Victory Storm King Stout is a Russian Imperial stout. Made with three imported 2-row malts and hopped with whole flower American hops, this 9.1% ABV beer is impressive. It's opaque black with a finger-high head that stays a good long while, and leaves gorgeous lacing. Cocoa and Grade B maple syrup in the nose let you know you're in for something serious. All this dark chocolate and those roasted malts explode underneath a canopy of massive hops aroma. A big block of a stout, complex and extremely well-balanced. Impressive!

TACTICAL NUCLEAR PENGUIN

BREWDOG

On Thursday, November 26, 2009, BrewDog set a record by creating the strongest beer in the world. Weighing in at an ABV of 32%, BrewDog's Tactical Nuclear Penguin beat the previous record of 31% held by the German beer called Schorschbräu.

This beer is all about pushing the boundaries; it is about taking innovation to a whole new level. It is about achieving something that has never before been done and putting Scotland firmly on the map for progressive craft beers.

According to BrewDog, "This beer is bold, irreverent and uncompromising. A beer with a soul and a purpose. A statement of intent. A modern day rebellion for the craft beer proletariat in our struggle to over throw the faceless bourgeoisie oppression of corporate, soulless beer.

"The Antarctic name inducing schizophrenia of this uber-Imperial stout originates from the amount of time it spent exposed to extreme cold. This beer began life as a 10% Imperial stout 18 months ago. The beer was aged for 8 months in an Isle of Arran whisky cask and 8 months in an Islay cask making it our first double cask aged beer. After an intense 16 months, the final stages took a groundbreaking approach by storing the beer at -20 degrees for three weeks to get it to 32%.

"For the big chill the beer was put into containers and transported to the cold store of a local ice cream factory where it endured 21 days at penguin temperatures. Alcohol freezes at a lower temperature than water. As the beer got colder BrewDog Chief Engineer, Steven Sutherland decanted the beer periodically, only ice was left in the container, creating more intensity of flavors and a stronger concentration of alcohol for the next phase of freezing. The process was repeated until it reached 32%."

TEMPEST IMPERIAL STOUT

AMSTERDAM BREWERY

This potent dark brew is one of the Imperial stouts made in Canada. The dark brown, almost black brew has a dark tan head and a thick, almost oily body. At 10%, the alcohol is definitely noticeable but is very well integrated. This is a brew with a wonderful intensity of flavor, like drinking a concentrated double espresso with a hint of soy and molasses. The even more potent Double Tempest aged in bourbon barrels checks in at an overwhelming 14% ABV.

TEN FIDY

OSKAR BLUES BREWERY LLC

It wasn't too long ago that the idea of good beer in a can was just absurd. Surely, cans are the domain of light, flavorless beer, right? That perception is slowly and rightfully changing, and a good deal of the credit goes to Oskar Blues in Lyons, Colorado. The Oskar Blues Grill and Brew Pub opened in 1997 and in 2002 became the first craft brewer in the United States to can its own beer. (Although other craft brewers had sold beer in cans, they'd had larger breweries do the packaging, and so Oskar Blues' claim that it is the first to can its own holds water.)

Rather than simply packaging light lagers and ales in cans, the brewery put big, bold beers in cans. The first to get the treatment, the hoppy Dale's Pale Ale, was followed quickly by the G'knight Imperial Red Ale. But the most audacious move was the brewer's next canned beer. Ten FIDY, a bold and boozy Imperial stout, went into cans in 2007. Though craft beer drinkers are a bit more acclimated to Imperial styles in cans these days, it was unprecedented at the time.

Oskar Blues' signature stout pours black without any light sneaking in around the edges; it would look as appropriate pouring from an oiler as from an aluminum can. The nose on Ten FIDY is intense. There's the coffee and chocolate that you expect from a Russian Imperial stout, of course, but there's also a noticeable alcohol bite at 10.5% ABV, and a citrus hop scent reminds you that this stout isn't from Russia but from the American West. The taste is supersweet up front, dominated by chocolate and even caramel, but the hops lend a dry bitterness to the finish. It's a viscous beer (again, motor oil comes to mind), but the inclusion of oats in the brew lends it the velvet smoothness of an oatmeal stout.

Ten FIDY doesn't just stand out as one of the few imperial stouts in a can; it stands among the best Russian Imperial stouts in the world.

JC

TOKYO INTERGALACTIC FANTASTIC OAK AGED STOUT

BREWDOG

This is BrewDog's oak-aged stout was inspired by a 1980s arcade game. BrewDog is always one for taking chances and doing outrageous things. Sometime it doesn't work, and sometimes it does. This is one of the times when it does.

This Imperial stout is brewed with huge amounts of specialty malts (Marris Otter, Dark Crystal, Caramalt, chocolate malt, roast barley), jasmine, and cranberries. After fermentation it is dry-hopped with a bucket-load of Galena hops before being aged carefully on French toasted oak chips.

There is nothing in moderation. This is a huge beer with big and dark molasses; roasty notes of coffee, caramel, and dark, red fruit; and big hops and immense body. With 18.2% ABV, it is a huge beer, with plenty of body and enough dash and élan to balance out its muscle.

VERDI IMPERIAL
BLACK JACK STOUT

BIRRIFICIO DEL DUCATO

Birrificio Del Ducato, based in Parma, Italy, was founded in 2007 and is one
of that country's most highly acclaimed breweries. It is situated in Roncole
Verdi, a small village in Parma County, the birthplace of Giuseppe Verdi
and the home of foods such as Parma ham and wines such as Lambrusco
and Malvasia.

Holding a BA in food science and technology, Giovanni Campari, a
former homebrewer, is the radical brewmaster, and Manuel Piccoli is the
brewery's executive visionary entrepreneur. As a result of their efforts,
Birrificio Del Ducato is a great success. The brewery is growing at a tre-
mendous rate, and its beers can be found in the United States, Canada,
Brazil, Norway, Sweden, Spain, and Japan.

Verdi Imperial Black Jack Stout is a stout that the company says
spends no less than eight months aging in whiskey barrels from Scottish
distilleries. Aromas of vanilla, licorice, dark chocolate, and peat harmoni-
ously balance with ethereal alcohol nuances. The mouthfeel is warm and
smooth, refined, and well-balanced.

According to Birrificio, "The idea of aging Verdi Imperial Stout in
whiskey barrels was inspired by an old Swedish importer of ours. One
day he gifted us a Swedish bourbon barrel, requesting to fill it with
Verdi Imperial stout and to name it Black Jack to follow up on a project

he had already started with other European breweries."

The beer's well-roasted smoothness is perfectly matched by the bourbon's ethereal notes and vanilla aromas. A single cask is used for every batch to extract the uniqueness of each barrel. Each beer is numbered and states on the label the region of origin of the distillery as well as the year of the barrel.

At 10% ABV this is not a beer to be trifled with. This is a big, smoky stout, probably owing to the peat smokiness of the whiskey barrels. Coffee and caramel come through, as well as vanilla and licorice. There is a hint of sweetness at the beginning of each sip, but the beer finishes more like a dry stout.

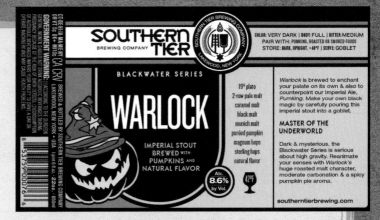

WARLOCK

SOUTHERN TIER BREWING COMPANY

This beer has a dark brown body with ruby red highlights. It pours to a small tan foamy head that mostly dissipates and leaves some lacing on the glass. There is a strong aroma of cinnamon graham crackers and pumpkin pie filling.

If there were no such thing as Southern Tier's Pumking, Warlock would be an amazing beer. Warlock is essentially Pumking with black malt thrown in for color. The mouthfeel is a little smoother and there are faint elements of chocolate and roastiness, but otherwise it's Pumking. But Pumking is a delicious beer, and so a slight variation of the palate is still delicious.

Right away there is a taste of liquid pumpkin pie. Cinnamon and pureed pumpkin along with all the usual zest create a sweet and spicy combination that awakens the palate. At the apex there's a hint of milk chocolate and perhaps some roasted malt, but it's quickly obscured by the strong dry bitterness of the Magnum hops. As the beer is going down, it reverts to its initial sweetness, but with less spice and a flavor akin to cola. Although the overall taste is great, it lacks a distinct stout character; you might not consider this a stout but a black pumpkin ale.

Although Warlock may have a palate similar to Pumking's, there is a noticeable difference in the mouthfeel. Pumking tends to be effervescent and crisp, whereas Warlock is calmer, smoother, and softer. The black malt gives it a slightly velvety texture, though the hops and spices linger on the tongue and are dry and slightly cloying. It doesn't feel nearly as heavy as its 8.6% ABV weight. You'll have no trouble drinking an entire bottle by yourself.

CP

WEYERBACHER XIII

WEYERBACHER BREWING CO.

There's a certain anxiousness that you get from drinking big beers—not the average 7 or 8% ABV India Pale Ale but a double-digit Imperial stout. You don't know where it comes from, but the best way to overcome a fear is to face it head on, which is what you do with Weyerbacher XIII. This is one of the heftiest beers you'll ever encounter, and you will be pleasantly surprised at how intimidating it isn't.

Weyerbacher XIII, which was brewed on the Easton, Pennsylvania, company's thirteenth anniversary, is one of the darkest beers around. Stouts tend to look black on the surface, but on closer inspection they're usually dark brown or ruby red. However, this brew is indeed jet black with the slightest hint of mahogany around the edges. Even the head is a shade of dark brown and fizzles out quickly like a glass of flat Pepsi or Coke.

The aroma contains three distinct smells: a sour grape/red wine–like scent, a dark chocolate scent, and of course alcohol. Unlike other Imperial beers, these elements add up to form a single aroma.

One of the reasons you might not be a fan of Imperial beers is the fact that many tend to have the same basic flavors in their palates. What separates Weyerbacher XIII from the others is just how much genuine taste is not only noticeable but easy to appreciate.

Upon the initial sip you get a taste of dark sour grapes that you might find in a red wine. It finishes with a surprisingly strong flavor of dark chocolate, followed by a lingering roasty aftertaste. The more you drink, the more the chocolate and roasted malts become prominent as the grape flavor is obscured.

The alcohol is very well masked, especially considering the 13.6% ABV. Unlike other Imperial or extrastrong beers in which the booze jumps out at you, it combines with the palate as a whole, giving it a slightly dry, somewhat sour flavor reminiscent of red wine. The taste is interesting since it's kind of like drinking red wine while eating a chocolate bar. As the beer warms, the flavors weaken for an overall dry, warm taste.

You expect Weyerbacher XIII to be a sipper from start to finish, and so you are shocked by how easy the beer is to drink. Since alcohol doesn't overshadow the flavors and meshes well with the palate, this isn't a beer with a boozy, jagged, bitter finish. In fact, it's almost quaffable when it's cold, although there is a noticeable warming sensation throughout the life of the drink.

The 13.6% ABV doesn't overwhelm. It's probably meant to be an after-dinner treat in and of itself, and in that respect it works. You'll feel buzzed and content but never bloated or intoxicated. Because of its potency, a one-time approach is the best drinking plan.

CP

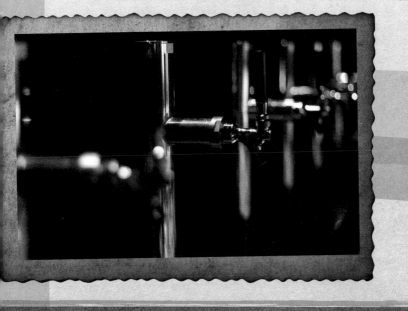

MILK STOUTS

Also called "sweet" and "cream" stouts, milk stouts are distinguished by the addition of lactose (or milk sugar) to the brew. The style's origins lay in the late nineteenth century when barkeeps and publicans would mix milk into stout. Along with giving the beer a sweet, creamy character, the addition was touted by servers as nutritious. Over time, the addition of milk to the final beer was phased out and replaced by milk added directly to fermenters, and eventually with lactose in favor of actual milk. Milk stout never regained its early twentieth century popularity in the UK (though Mackeson's version, introduced in 1907, endures to this day), but craft brewers in the US and big brewers in South Africa have found success with the style. Characterized by full-bodied mouthfeel and a sweetness that plays off stout's characteristic dark malts, the style pairs well with sweeter dishes, including barbeque.

2X STOUT

SOUTHERN TIER BREWING COMPANY

You've heard of double IPA, but what about a double stout? When you think of stout, you think of the regular version and the Imperial kind, but can't there be something in between? That's probably the idea behind Southern Tier's 2X Stout. It's a "Double Milk Stout" according to the label, a base style that should work well as a stronger stout but without the bulkiness of an Imperial size. It's a good beer but not as monumental as you'd think.

The beer has the typical stout facade of opaque black. It forms a small, dark-tan, foamy head that dissipates rather quickly and doesn't leave much lacing on the glass. There is a mild aroma with a scent reminiscent of the supermarket dairy aisle and candy bar chocolate. There's a very subtle hint of alcohol, too.

Milk stouts tend to be one of the popular types of regular, non-Imperial stouts, and so you can expect unique and impressive things with Southern Tier 2X Stout. It begins quite normally with a light bitterness typical of the usual stout. Slightly dry, slightly toasted malt flavor up front quickly gives way to a much sweeter element of licorice, candy bar choco-

late, and a hint of vanilla extract. There's a colalike sweetness with a faint taste to match. The palate becomes sweeter as the beer warms, but never to the point of becoming cloying or sticky.

For a big beer, Southern Tier 2X Stout has the body of something much smaller. The mouthfeel is rather light, but with a silky smooth texture. The aftertaste is mild and clean with just the faintest bittersweet flavor. The 7.5% ABV is only slightly detectable as far as taste and weight go, though this brew has more noticeable body than the average stout. It is very drinkable.

CP

BLACK RAT IMPERIAL STOUT

CELLAR RATS BREWERY

Black Rat's Imperial Stout has a black body with a tan creamy head that retains and laces quite well. It has a sweet aroma of cream and milk, plus minor dark fruit scents and a hint of vanilla.

From the label, you might think that this beer is a Russian Imperial stout, but after only a few swigs you can tell it's a milk stout. It's too sweet to be an RIS; the palate is a combination of traditional milk stout, lots of coffee creamer, and a little cola. There is mild bitterness throughout but no hop flavor per se.

It starts with subtle black licorice and then transitions to iced coffee with a lot of cream in it. The ending is even sweeter and has a distinct taste of milk . Not quite chocolate, not quite vanilla, it has just a hint of coffee flavor and bitterness plus roasted malts. The palate never expands beyond this, so it's consistently sweet but never cloying. Unfortunately, the vanilla in the nose does not carry over to the palate. Still, it's a satisfying dessert beer.

The first thing you notice is how comfortable and smooth it is in the mouth, with a soft, velvety texture but minor carbonation presence. It's not quite as thick as you'd expect and finishes cleanly with a lightly sweet aftertaste. If you were drinking Black Rat Imperial Stout blind, there's no way you'd know its 9.2% ABV as it has the weight of something much smaller and no alcohol presence at all. The high drinkability makes this beer appealing.

CP

CAFÉ ROYALE

ALEWERKS BREWING COMPANY

The AleWerks Brewing Company is situated in the heart of the early colony Williamsburg, Virginia. Established in 2006, it operates a direct-fired brick-clad Peter Austin brewhouse. Chuck Haines, a longtime proponent of fine beer, secured the property of the old Williamsburg Brewing Company in 2005, recruited a brewer, and started AleWerks.

This 5.4% ABV milk stout starts with two-row, crystal, and black malts and then adds lactose and American Fuggles hops. The brewers add Guatemala Antigua coffee to create a sense of warmth. There are big flavors of coffee, cocoa, milk sugar, and roasted malt. This is a big, creamy, smooth, full-bodied milk stout.

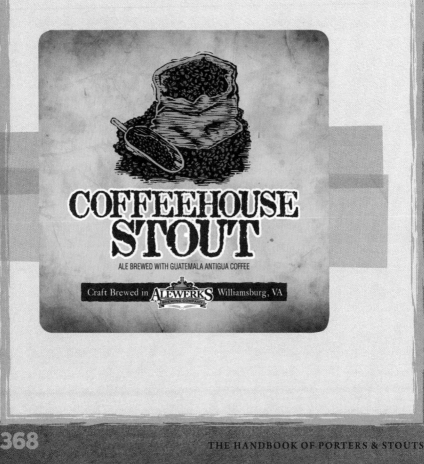

COFFEEHOUSE STOUT

ALE BREWED WITH GUATEMALA ANTIGUA COFFEE

Craft Brewed in ALEWERKS BREWING COMPANY Williamsburg, VA

FEAR MILK CHOCOLATE STOUT

BREWFIST ITALIAN ALES

At BrewFist Italian Ales, Pietro Di Pilato is the head brewer and Andrea Maiocchi is the head of sales and marketing. This Italian brewery was founded in 2010, and its products already can be found in the United States, the Netherlands, Sweden, Spain, Australia, and Finland.

This milk chocolate stout is brewed for men who are scared of dark beers. Sweet, complex, but very drinkable, it is made with pale, crystal, chocolate, pale chocolate, wheat, oat, Monaco, and Vienna hops for a substantial but soft body that is leveled with Magnum hops. Added milk sugars and cocoa beans make this beer very palatable and drinkable.

THE DUCK-RABBIT
MILK STOUT

DUCK-RABBIT CRAFT BREWERY

Duck-Rabbit Craft Brewery is a small microbrewery in Farmville, North Carolina, that began selling beer in August 2004. Its beers are beautiful, delicious full-flavored dark brews that are highly acclaimed and difficult to find. Duck-Rabbit Milk Stout is a traditional full-bodied stout brewed with lactose (milk sugar). The subtle sweetness imparted by the lactose balances the sharpness of the highly roasted grains that give this delicious beer its black color. This is a fantastic beer.

EMPOWERED STOUT

TRIGGERFISH BREWING

Empowered Stout is a milk stout–style beer brewed by Triggerfish Brewery in Somerset West, South Africa. A big English sweet stout, this brawny brew is empowered by a combination of five different malts and two hop varieties. The nose is filled with roasted coffee, bittersweet dark chocolate, dried fruit, raisins, and licorice. The beer's touch of sweetness is balanced by the roasted malts and the hops. Brown-black in color, with a lovely, dark beige head, this is a well-balanced example of a milk stout.

"...freakin'
Christmas
in a bottle.
Our Score: 100"
-BeerAdvocate

HARDYWOOD
RESERVE SERIES
THE ORIGINAL
Gingerbread
STOUT
IMPERIAL MILK STOUT BREWED WITH FRESH LOCAL GINGER AND HONEY

HARDYWOOD GINGERBREAD STOUT

HARDYWOOD PARK CRAFT BREWERY

Hardywood Park Craft Brewery is in Richmond, Virginia. An award-winning 9.2% ABV Imperial milk stout brewed with fresh baby ginger from Casselmonte Farm and wildflower honey from Bearer Farms, Hardywood Gingerbread Stout captures the terroir of central Virginia in a rich, creamy libation with a velvety mouthfeel and an intriguing evolution of flavors ranging from milk chocolate and vanilla to honeycomb and cinnamon to a snap of ginger in the finish. It is deep dark chocolate in color with a mahogany tint and a frothy caramel-colored head.

Hardywood Gingerbread Stout offers aromatics of holiday spice originating from the ginger, balanced with a generous dose of whole Madagascar bourbon vanilla beans and Vietnamese cinnamon. Milk sugar (lactose) contributes to the full body of this stout and tames its roasty character, and oats lend it a silky quality. This is a unique and delicious beer.

MILK STOUT NITRO

LEFT HAND BREWING CO.

As is the case with so many modern breweries, the story of Left Hand starts with a fortuitous encounter with a home brewing kit. Left Hand cofounder Dick Doore started brewing at home in 1990 and in 1993 picked up his college roommate and fellow cofounder Eric Wallace as a brewing buddy. Soon afterward, the duo incorporated as Indian Peaks Brewing Company (named for the local mountains), although that name didn't last long. Rechristened as Left Hand, the brewery opened its doors in early 1994. The duo launched with its flagship Sawtooth Ale and has been growing ever since.

For my money, there's not a beer on the planet that's as much fun to pour as Left Hand's bottled Milk Stout Nitro. Guinness may have the legendary "two part" pour, but advice for pouring the Milk Stout Nitro comes down to only two words, which happen to be written on the cap: pour hard. Rather than use a nitrogen widget as many other beers do, Left Hand's nitro beers are capped under pressure with nitrogen. To get the full, creamy effect of N_2, you've got to invert this stout and pour it aggressively. Surprisingly, it doesn't foam over but leaves a cascading, inch-thick tan head on the sumptuous stout. The stout has brown sugar, coffee, and a hint of vanilla on the nose and the same elements on the palate. With a lactose-assisted milky mouthfeel and flavor, Milk Stout Nitro is the love child of a stout and a latte with 6% ABV.

JC

MOO THUNDER STOUT

BUTTERNUTS BEER & ALE

Milk stouts are an often-overlooked gem of the craft beer community. They've got more flavor than a dry stout and are much more drinkable than the Imperial versions. If you want a milk stout brewed with a bit of authority, try Moo Thunder by Butternuts Beer & Ale. After all, this brewery is housed in a former dairy barn; surely some of that experience with milk has carried over.

BEER 12 FL. OZ. (355ml)

This beer produces a thick foamy off-white head, which quickly dissipates, leaving little lacing on the glass. It has the appearance one expects from a stout: jet black with a touch of ruby red highlights around the edges. The aroma is mild but rather complex with a distinct roasted malt scent as well as a touch of chocolate sweetness and a general dairylike smell (like when you walk down the dairy aisle at the supermarket).

Much like the aroma, the palate is mild but surprisingly multidimensional. Up front you're hit with a dairy sweetness that is reminiscent of chocolate milk. The roasted malts show up in the background and make for a gentle but noticeable bitterness. It's akin to burnt chocolate or maybe burnt toast but without the intense carbon flavor. The aftertaste is rather sweet, a little milky but also a little sour. The palate seems to diminish in flavor as you finish the beer. There is very little carbonation here, and so the flatness of the body seems to keep the flavors subdued. Perhaps a more lively body would lead to a more robust taste. Not that it's bad, just that the beer doesn't live up to its potential. Overall, the notes are good.

Owing to the fairly mild palate and the flatness of the body, Moo Thunder is a highly drinkable beer. In fact, it's one of the most quaffable stouts you'll ever encounter. The lack of bitterness to the mouthfeel combined with the slight sweetness makes it as easy to slug down. The lack of intensity in the body also makes it seem a little thin, but this is standard for a milk stout.

At only 4.9% ABV, it's also a highly sessionable beer. It would accompany dark meats very well or could be paired with a milk chocolate dessert.

Moo Thunder is a satisfying beer, and it's one of those rare instances in which having a mild palate is a positive attribute since it's more drinker-friendly that way. Some drinkers might prefer something more robust, but Butternuts intends for this beer to be a satisfying, easy-to-drink stout, and it has succeeded.

CP

NIPPLETOP MILK STOUT

LAKE PLACID CRAFT BREWING COMPANY

Nippletop has an opaque black body with no carbonation visible. It pours to an average-size, dark-tan, foamy head that retains and laces fairly well. It has a pretty standard sweet pub-style stout aroma with noticeable sweetness but is light on the roasted malt.

Lake Placid Nippletop Milk Stout is a strangely named beer. That's ironic considering that everything else about it is pretty much by the book. If you want an example of what a milk stout can be, this is a good one to go to. It seems to be brewed in the traditional style of a standard pub-style stout with the addition of plenty of lactose. It's quite sweet as that sugar is definitely the spotlight of the palate. There's a light sweetness with a slight dairylike character to it throughout most of the swig. Mild roasted malt bitterness on the back end helps balance it with just a hint of astringency or acidity. This is a no-frills milk stout, but it tastes good and it's to spec, making it plenty good enough.

There are two reasons to drink this beer: its sweet drinker-friendly taste and its drinker-friendly drinkability. The mouthfeel is soft, smooth, and comfortable. Drinking it down is no challenge. Rather than a little residual stout aftertaste, it finishes almost completely clean. This is a stylistic choice for sure. At only 4.9% ABV, it's right where it should be in terms of body and robustness. This is the type of beer you can session in the winter.

CP

PUGSLEY'S SIGNATURE SERIES MINT CHOCOLATE STOUT

SHIPYARD BREWING COMPANY

Made with a top fermenting English yeast, Shipyard uses Process Pale, Flaked Barley, Chocolate Roasted Barley, Rolled Oats, Whole Wheat, and Caramuniich II to make this beer, and it's hopped with Process, WGV, and Perle. Mint chocolate stout is a dark, silky beer with aromas of chocolate and licorice. Smooth chocolate and coffee flavors upfront lead to a spearmint finish.

RAVEN STOUT
MITCHELL'S BREWERY

Raven Stout is a milk stout–style beer brewed by Mitchell's Brewery in Knysna, South Africa. In 1983, Lex Mitchell started Mitchell's by brewing only two beers: Forester's Lager and Bosun's Bitter. They were meant for local distribution only, but Mitchell's Brewery has come a long way since then. They now have seven craft brews in their repertoire, which are distributed nationally and in key markets around the world.

Mitchell's claims that the beer pours as "black as a raven's wing." We're here to tell you it's true. It's a well-balanced sweet stout, with roasted coffee, burnt malt, and a nice dose of toffee and caramel. This 4%-ABV stout is straightforward and full-bodied.

ROYAL EXTRA STOUT

CARIB BREWERY

In 1960, the Caribbean Development Company Limited of Trinidad, formed Grenada Breweries Limited, a public company located in Grenada, West Indies. The company started production with Carib Lager in 1961, and by 2005, the brewery was licensed to produce Carlsberg Lager as well as Ginseng Up and Carib Shandy.

Royal Extra Stout was inherited from Walters' Brewery, Port of Spain, and was later reformulated by Carib Brewery to achieve its distinctively full-bodied texture and taste, with 6.6% ABV. Similar to brewing lagers, Carib introduces lager yeast in the production of Royal Extra Stout, but the fermentation time is much shorter than with lagers and takes place at a higher temperature. The beer is brewed with pilsner malt and black malt, sweetened with granulated sugar, lactose, and caramel, and finished with hops. Caramel is used in brewing as a flavor as well as a coloring agent.

The beer pours opaque black-brown. A nice foamy head occurs, and there is solid lacing throughout. Coco, vanilla, milk chocolate, and roasted coffee all come through, as well as a sizable dose of toffee. The beer is somewhat of a combination of an extra stout with a milk stout touch. The cocoa dominates, with flavors like milk chocolate. A very nicely balanced beer, as there's just enough bitterness to keep the beer from going off the tracks. Nicely balanced.

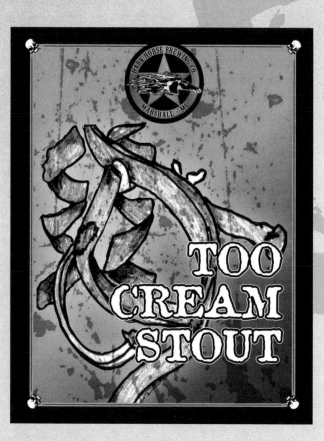

TOO CREAM STOUT

DARK HORSE BREWING COMPANY

This is beer number two from Aaron and Cally Morse of Dark Horse Brewing in Marshall, Michigan, who have created a whole line of high-end porters and stouts. This beer is made with milk sugar (lactose), which gives it a nice creamy mouthfeel that mingles with hints of chocolate and roasty flavors with a touch of dark cherries. The head is dark and thick and lingers. With an ABV of 7%, this beer is thick, rich, and creamy.

LA VACHE FOLLE IMPERIAL MILK STOUT

MICROBRASSERIE CHARLEVOIX

Microbrasserie Charlevoix brews fantastic Belgian-inspired beers in the heart of Baie-Saint-Paul, Quebec, Canada. They've been brewing since 1998, but in January 2009 their operations were transferred to new, more modern and efficient facilities to increase the production capacity to better meet demand. The name of this beer means "mad cow." This 5% ABV milk stout is a dark black beer with notes of chocolate and burnt barley and a dark beige head. It is sweetened with lactose, balancing the taste of coffee and black chocolate. It is basically a cross between an Imperial stout and a milk stout, unique and easy to drink.

WACHUSETT MILK STOUT

WACHUSETT BREWING COMPANY

This is the darkest beer they've ever brewed in Westminster, Massachusetts. It has a sweet, malty flavor and a creamy, full body. The smoothness comes from the addition of lactose (milk sugar) during the brewing. That, combined with roast coffee and chocolate tones, gives this beer a unique, rich flavor.

Founded in 1993 by former attendees of Worcester Polytechnic Institute, Wachusett Brewing Company is Worcester County's first and only brewery and has been well accepted by the town of Westminster. The company maintains a relationship with the founders' alma mater and has arranged for students in its Department of Chemical Engineering to earn college credits in cooperation with the brewery.

They first started brewing their milk stout in 2010 with six grains, oats, flaked barley, and lactose combined with hops such as Magnum, Northern Brewer, and East Kent Goldings.

When poured into a pint glass, this beer is the same color as Pepsi or Coke. The head is a nice foamy, creamy-tan color. Very nice lace stays up around the glass as you drink. The smell features dark chocolate, brown sugar, and some coffee.

There is a lot of malty sweetness in the first sip, but the hops balance this beer. It is not superheavy but has good gravitas and good carbonation. There is plenty of roasted malt, sweet and dark chocolate, and a touch of bitterness, with a smooth, refreshing finish. This is a very good example of what a milk stout should be.

Unlike chocolate, milk, and coffee stouts, where the eponymous flavors can come from roasted malt or additional sugars rather than the namesake ingredients, oatmeal stout is straightforward. First brewed in late nineteenth-century Britain, oatmeal stouts are characterized by the addition of raw or malted oats to the brew. The style's popularity in the twentieth century rose and fell alongside its sweeter sister, milk stout, before practically disappearing. Then in the late '70s American beer importer Charles Finkel of Merchant du Vin asked the Samuel Smith Brewery to whip up a contemporary take on the style. Since its resurrection, the style has found new life on both sides of the pond.

Flavor-wise, modern oatmeal stouts fall in a Goldilocks zone between a few other stout sub-styles—sweeter than the dry Irish stout, but not as sweet as the milk and cream stouts. The most distinguishing characteristic imparted by the oats is a velvet smoothness, though they also add the slightest cookie sweetness. The sweet-but-not-too-sweet flavor of oatmeal stouts puts them in the privileged position of pairing well with pretty much anything, from steak and stew to sweet desserts.

BARNEY FLATS
OATMEAL STOUT

ANDERSON VALLEY BREWING CO.

This dark stout has a light brown head that leaves a nice lacing on the glass. The chicory coffee nose is slightly smoky. The nose follows through to the taste, with notes of chocolate added to the chicory coffee. This beer is smooth and velvety from the oats in this easy-drinking, 5.8%-ABV oatmeal stout.

JC

BEER GEEK BREAKFAST

MIKKELLER APS

This oatmeal stout made with coffee is the kind of beer you treat yourself to for your birthday. There are a few variations of this beer, but this is the flagship version.

Beer Geek Breakfast has a pitch-black body without any traces of red. The very dark brown whipped cream–like head retains and laces extremely well. The light dairy-aisle aroma has minor notes of iced coffee. The nose is surprisingly tame, although it indicates that the taste will be more sweet than bitter.

Beer Geek Breakfast is one of those beers that starts off with a bang. The first few sips are incredible, with the strong flavors of a robust Imperial oatmeal stout. The light sweetness throughout the first half is very creamlike. Then suddenly the roasted malts appear out of nowhere for a big, bitter taste. Bitter dark chocolate also emerges between the two flavors and again as the roasty flavor transitions to a light iced coffee sweetness. This is a very impressive and tasty palate.

As you drink on, the sweetness mellows out and the coffee bitterness fades a little. It certainly remains a quality oatmeal stout through and through, but the overall palate seems better when it's not homogenized. The lack of real coffee flavor is a bit disappointing, although the coffee bitterness is plenty prominent.

The mouthfeel is soft, comfortable, and less thick than you'd expect. This beer psyches you out. It looks, smells, and tastes a little like an Imperial stout, but it's not since it's only 7.5% ABV. It's surprising how easy it is to gulp down and how velvety smooth the texture is. This is a good beer to have as a liquid dessert. Overall, Mikkeller Beer Geek Breakfast is a perfect example of a higher-end oatmeal stout.

CP

BEER GEEK VANILLA SHAKE

MIKKELLER APS

There's a growing movement in the world of craft beer termed "phantom" or, less politically correctly, "gypsy brewing." Whereas traditional brewers build their own facilities and contract brewers work in partnership with a single brewery, phantom brewers typically travel from brewery to brewery and create unique (and often one-off) beers. Mikkeller, founded by Danish homebrewers Mikkel Borg Bjergsø and Kristian Klarup Keller, is one of the earliest breweries of this type. In 2005, the pair scaled up from brewing at home to producing beer at the Danish microbrewery Ørbæk, which they then sold and distributed through a shop owned by Mikkel's brother Jeppe. Soon afterward, a successful stout put the brewers on the world stage.

Beer Geek Breakfast, a hearty stout brewed with oats and coffee, is the first beer that really got Mikkeller noticed in the United States. An oatmeal stout with French-press coffee added, the brew rocketed to stardom after being voted the world's best stout on RateBeer.com's beer forum. Since that original brew, the brewer's Beer Geek series has expanded to include Rauch Geek Breakfast (a smoked version), this Beer Geek Brunch Weasel (a version brewed with civet coffee), and this Beer Geek Vanilla Shake, a sweet version brewed with vanilla.

The booziest of the bunch at 13% ABV, Vanilla Shake is simply decadent. The flavor is close to that of the namesake dessert; it's easy to imagine a mad scientist brewer conjuring this beer from chocolate syrup, vanilla ice cream, and whipped cream. Not quite as thick as a milk shake, Vanilla Shake is still formidable on the palate, thick and creamy as all get out. Smart money says this brew would pair well with sweet desserts, but it's hearty enough to stand on its own.

JC

B.O.R.I.S. THE CRUSHER OATMEAL IMPERIAL STOUT

HOPPIN' FROG BREWERY

This stout is opaque black all the way to the edges with no signs of carbonation. It forms a very small, brown, soapy head that doesn't last very long but can be regenerated with a vigorous swirl (little to no lacing, though). The nose is black licorice, plus a clean rum alcoholic aroma and pure chocolate syrup or baker's chocolate.

Hoppin' Frog B.O.R.I.S. The Crusher Oatmeal Imperial Stout is a by-the-book stout. It's very straightforward, but the taste is plenty flavorful and appealing. It begins with a remarkably sweet colalike taste that gives way to a more traditional Imperial stout palate: deeply roasted malts, black licorice, bittersweet chocolate, and a hint of coffee bitterness and dryness. The alcohol is slightly prominent, imparting a dry rubbing alcohol effect as well as some richer, more vanilla- and rumlike flavors and gives

the beer a warming sensation. It is satisfying all around, but there's no wow factor.

The mouthfeel is surprisingly thin for such a big beer. It coats the mouth but leaves an aftertaste similar to what you get from eating too much chocolate, and some people may find it cloying.

Oatmeal tends to be used in stouts more for texture than for taste and is probably what accounts for this beer's velvety smooth body and easy drinkability. There is a definite alcohol presence, although a little more than one would expect for a 9.4%-ABV brew; however, this beer tastes better and becomes even smoother as it ages. It is good as a dessert beer or a nightcap.

CP

CRAFTSMAN OATMEAL CHOCOLATE STOUT

RENAISSANCE BREWING COMPANY

Headquartered in Blenheim in the heart of the province of Marlborough, New Zealand, the Renaissance Brewing Company is situated at the old Grove Mill on Dodson Street, the oldest commercial building in Blenheim. Over the years it has housed an ice cream factory, a malt house, two very famous wineries (Grove Mill and Whitehaven), and more recently a craft brewery.

Craftsman is the big brother to the popular Elemental Porter Ale. Building on the flavors of the crystal, brown, and black malts, the brewers added a portion of organic rolled oats for a silky smooth mouthfeel and then a small amount of cocoa nibs to the mash and brew kettle, plus a large addition of nibs to the fermenter. The beer then matured on those cocoa nibs.

This beer pours a superdark opaque-brown color. The head bubbles up at first but quickly settles into a mousse around the rim of the glass. Toffee, roasted oats, toasted almonds, cocoa, and rich dark chocolate explode out of the glass, with a hint of port.

Bittersweet chocolate and coffee fade, and the finish is somewhat dry, with a nice balance of bitterness. This is a lovely drinking stout that goes perfectly with fruit desserts, rich cakes, and cookies.

DIRTY STOP OUT SMOKED OATMEAL STOUT

TINY REBEL BREWING CO.

Tiny Rebel Brewing Co. is based in the Maesglas area of Newport, Wales. The brand-new 3,000-square-foot brew works is in the Maesglas Industrial Estate. The small brewery was founded in 2011 by two rebellious brothers-in–law, Gareth Williams and Bradley Cummings. What began as a hobby in a garage has become a dream come true. Their goal was to specialize in making retro beers with a modern twist.

Dirty Stop Out is a smoked, oat stout that has all the characteristics of a heavy night out: complex and dark with hints of smokiness and a perfumed aroma. A blend of nine malts matched with a firmly hopped spine makes this a very solid, confident stout. The 5% ABV makes it sessionable.

LÁGRIMAS NEGRAS OATMEAL STOUT

RAMURI CERVEZA ARTESENAL

Ramuri Lágrimas Negras ("Black Tears") Oatmeal Stout is an English-style, generally strong dark ale brewed in Baja California, Mexico. It has a lot of character and body. It is almost black in color, and its flavor profile is obtained from the same malt Ramuri uses in other beers, but with a lot of different levels of toasting. Lágrimas Negras Oatmeal Stout is flavored with the elixir of Moctezuma: xocolatl, considered by the pre-Columbian culture as the food of the gods. It contains a blend of malts, toasted oats, and lots of cocoa, and there is deep milk chocolate and roasted coffee in every sip. It is superdark with a creamy light head. It drinks smooth, with not a lot of bitterness and lots of chocolate.

OATMEAL STOUT

BROWN'S BREWING CO.

In 1993, Gary and Kelly Brown decided to turn a 150-year-old warehouse on a blighted river street in Troy, New York, into a fully operational craft brewery. Brown's Brewing Company became an instant success. Their River Street Taproom, is a mainstay of the city. They've earned a number of awards over the years, including a gold medal at the World Beer Cup in 2004, TAP New York's 2008 Matthew Vassar Brewers' Cup for the best brewery in the Hudson Valley, and a gold medal from the Culinary Institute of America for their pale ale. They've also won prestigious World Beer Cup gold and silver awards for their oatmeal stout and whiskey porter, respectively, and *Metroland* readers voted them best brewpub in 2008 and 2009.

There is no doubt that this is an impressive beer. The beer was created with two-row pale, black, chocolate, flaked rolled oats, caramel, and Willamette hops. The ABV is 5.25%.

The beer pours a deep, rich black with a mocha-colored thick head that seems to last a very long time. It has an impressive hang time with nice lacing, too. There's lots of chocolate on the roast; the roast comes in second. The body is full, smooth, and creamy. Oats and malt come through big. A nice roastiness is combined with good carbonation. This is not a heavy beer, which means you can have several without feeling over-full. It's a good-drinking oatmeal stout.

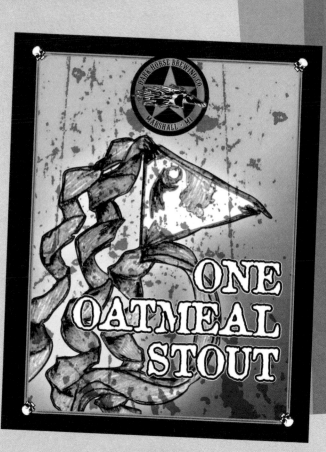

ONE OATMEAL STOUT

DARK HORSE BREWING COMPANY

Aaron and Cally Morse are brewing amazing things in Marshall, Michigan. They and their crew have created a whole line of high-end quality porters and stouts. Number one in a series of five porters and stouts produced to help ease drinkers through the cold gray Midwestern winters, this beer is full-bodied with hints of chocolate, roasted barley, and coffee flavors and a nice creamy head. This 8% ABV stout pours very dark and thick. It is slightly sweet and creamy. Highly rated, it is indeed very good and lives up to its hype.

THE POET

NEW HOLLAND BREWING CO.

The Poet is brewed by New Holland Brewing Co. in Holland, Michigan. The Poet is a classic oatmeal stout; there is nothing Imperial about this one.

It has an opaque black body with a dark-tan, frothy, and creamy head, with excellent retention and lacing. The aroma is typical of oatmeal stout with sweet dairy notes of heavy cream, chocolate milk, and slightly roasted malt aroma in the background.

The Poet has the palate of almost every solid oatmeal stout: It begins with a slightly sweet dairylike flavor, imparts a little bitterness through the middle, and finishes with a kick of roasted malts. It doesn't take any chances with the oatmeal-stout style. The back could have accentuated the malts more, though. There is only a slight flavor of coffee and dark chocolate. The initial sweet dairy flavors, especially chocolate milk and coffee creamer, are so prevalent that they carry the entire palate. It is sweet and satisfying to be sure. The mouthfeel is not as thick as you'd expect. It's soft with a faint dry aftertaste.

The best reason to drink this beer might be the ease with which is goes down. The mild, sweet palate and soft, velvety mouthfeel make for an extremely smooth finish. There is definitely a slight toasted taste and sensation that lingers, but it is easily tolerable and is quenched by the next sip. The 5.2% ABV body is commendable for its genuine flavor and sessionability. Overall, The Poet is tasty and highly drinkable.

CP

SHAKESPEARE OATMEAL STOUT

ROGUE ALES

One of the ways in which we measure our enjoyment of a beer is by how much we would like to drink of it. In the case of Rogue's Shakespeare Oatmeal Stout, simply drinking a 22-ounce bomber is not *nearly* enough. It has exactly what you look for in a beer: a strong flavor that caters to the discriminating beer drinker while also being easy to drink and surprisingly light in weight.

The beer pours a little rough and forms a nearly pitch-black opaque body with a thick, creamy head that lasts for quite a while and leaves a lot of lacing on the glass. Its scent was odd for a stout, with a deep roasted quality detectable in the nose as well as a significant hoppy component. So many stouts tend to be weak and flat in scent, but Shakespeare is quite vocal.

There's only one word that comes to mind when it comes to describing the taste of this beer: roasty. Stouts are often associated with having a dry, bitter flavor with some roasty quality. But in the case of Shakespeare Oatmeal

Stout, the opposite seems to be true. This is a beer whose roasty flavor is quite pronounced, balanced with a creamy core that mixes coffee and chocolate flavors to give it a subtle, smooth, sweet finish.

It's rare you come across a beer that is so intense in taste and still makes proper usage of its hoppy side. Usually, you associate an India Pale Ale with the high IBU rating of 69 that this beer has. That a stout can be this bitter and this tasty without coming off as bland and dry is quite an accomplishment. For a highly-hopped beer, it is surprisingly smooth and easy to drink. It does have a noticeable creaminess to its taste, which probably accounts for its smooth finish.

While stouts are often thought of as being "heavy" beers, this is not necessarily true (Guinness has only fifteen more calories than Bud Light). At 6% ABV, Shakespeare Oatmeal Stout is only slightly more potent than your average beer, but for such a dark beer it is surprisingly light on your system. That's another sign of quality, that it is not overwhelming to the drinker. Still, it is what you would consider a beer for serious drinkers only. The flavor is quite complex and intense, so it's better for sipping, not chugging. It should be drank as slowly as possible to savor the craftsmanship that went into making this such a great beer.

CP

ST-AMBROISE OATMEAL STOUT

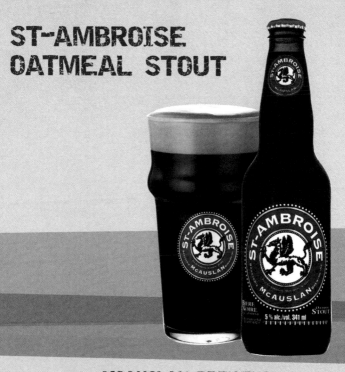

MCAUSLAN BREWING

Some beers are better in retrospect than in the moment. Others are great in the moment, but in retrospect you feel you romanticized it too much. However, St-Ambroise Oatmeal Stout, brewed by McAuslan Brewing in Montreal, Canada, is as great in the moment as it is in memory.

The beer pours smoothly and forms a thick layer of a tan, creamy head that lasts throughout the life of the drink and leaves some lacing on the glass. The body has all the makings of a classic stout with an opaque black body. No carbonation is noticeable, although the beer appears to have a more viscous body from the liquid and head alone. The aroma is light, sweet, and slightly malty.

St-Ambroise Oatmeal Stout is so sweet and rich that it works much better when drunk on its own, especially as a dessert alternative. This beer has a sweet, roasty taste with a distinct nutty finish. Chocolate, coffee, and even a bit of vanilla can be detected and combine to create a savory palate. It's balanced with maltiness to make for a spectrum of great taste.

St-Ambroise Oatmeal Stout is one of the easiest brews to consume, probably as a result of its overall robust body and seemingly low carbonation. It has a very soft mouthfeel despite maintaining a strong presence of hops. However, it does leave a slightly bitter aftertaste in the mouth.

Great beers like this show just how heavy stouts aren't. I'm not sure of the number of calories and carbs, but I was able to drink two bottles back to back after a big dinner without feeling full or overwhelmed. At only 5% ABV, St-Ambroise Oatmeal Stout is the type of beer that can be consumed quickly, easily, and in a mass quantity (if only it came in six- or twelve-packs rather than four-packs).

There are sweeter and even tastier stouts out there, but it's hard to find a quality stout that is this satisfying on so many levels. That's what makes St-Ambroise Oatmeal Stout such a great beer.

CP

STOCKYARD OATMEAL STOUT

TRADER JOE'S BREWING COMPANY

A variety of breweries contract brew for Trader Joe's, and Stockyard Oatmeal Stout and the rest of the Josephs Brau Brewing Company beers are made by the Gordon Biersch Brewing Company. If you want a by-the-book oatmeal stout, this is the one for you.

This beer has an opaque black body with a tan frothy head that mostly dissipates and leaves only minor lacing on the glass. Like every other brew of this style, there is a dairylike scent with a hint of chocolate and some subtle sourness.

The mildly sweet palate is closer to a porter than to a stout, though only discriminating tasters will be able to detect this. There's a hint of dark chocolate right as it finishes, plus a strange twangy character of almost sour grape. There's a hint of roasted malt on the back end but not a lot in the way of aftertaste.

The mouthfeel is not thick, and there's enough energy to keep it from feeling completely flat and watery. It goes down supersmooth, but the aftertaste is a bit too clean (it is slightly sweet, though). Stockyard Oatmeal Stout is exactly the kind of beer it should be at 5.2% ABV, something more suitable for sessioning than as a dessert beer.

CP

VELVET MERLIN

FIRESTONE WALKER
BREWING COMPANY

Velvet Merlin is black through and through with a few spots of ruby red on the bottom. The head is dark tan and creamy and frothy, with good retention and lacing. This beer is sweet-smelling with notes of chocolate candy, sugary coffee, and cream. It is not very roasty or toasty, though.

The taste is very close to that of Samuel Smith's Oatmeal Stout, with gentle sweetness in the beginning and middle. The ending and aftertaste feature slightly roasted malts with baker's chocolate and light coffee flavor and bitterness. The aftertaste is pleasant but doesn't last very long, which is fine in a more sessionable-type stout. The mouthfeel is noticeably soft with medium thickness. The carbonation is slightly higher than expected.

The first thing you notice before the taste is how velvety smooth Velvet Merlin is from start to finish. This beer just glides across the tongue. The 5.5% ABV makes it highly drinkable. Overall, this is a very impressive stout because it's so tasty and smooth. It's not the biggest Imperial stout you've ever had but is an excellent beer.

CP

WOLAVER'S OATMEAL STOUT

OTTER CREEK BREWING/WOLAVER'S

This beer is opaque black with no visible carbonation. It forms a dark-tan, foamy, frothy head with decent retention but light lacing. The aroma is slightly milder than that of the average stout, with sweet, milk, and dairy aromas along with hints of roasted barley.

Wolaver's Oatmeal Stout is not an amazing beer, but it's fun to drink. Brewers use oatmeal mostly as a sweetener and to create a smooth texture, and it's clearly worked well here. It begins with overt sweetness, almost tasting like a chocolate milk or cola. There is mild bitterness through the middle and the back end, with roasted malt and coffee flavor and an accompanying bitterness. At the end, the sweetness returns stronger than it began. It finishes a tad too clean with just a hint of burnt toast flavor and a residual dairy taste.

The mouthfeel is almost full-bodied in terms of consistent flavor but medium in terms of thickness. It is silky smooth with a fine carbonation fizz.

Beers like this remind you that there's a difference between stouts brewed with oatmeal and those brewed without it. The sweeter taste and very comfortable, soft mouthfeel and silky smooth finish make it quaffable. The 5.9%

ABV is right on in terms of flavor energy and overall weight. It's quite versatile and would make a good dessert beer or a session brew for a more experienced stout drinker.

CP

OYSTER STOUTS

For centuries, beer drinkers have recognized that sweet, briny oysters pair perfectly with the roastiness of a fine stout or porter. But how did the mollusks make the jump from beer bedfellows to brewing component? The key lies in calcium carbonate, a stellar beer clarifying agent that also happens to exist in high quantities in oyster shells.

In the 1800s, brewers found they could clarify their beer by pouring it over oyster shells. Over the decades, the process went from pouring finished beer over shells, to adding the shells directly to the boil while brewing, to adding oysters—meat and all—to the boil in the 1920s. The style was reportedly first brewed this way in the South Pacific, though by the mid-twentieth-century, brewers in England were also brewing with whole oysters. When craft brewing took off in the US, breweries on both coasts experimented with oyster stouts, complete with locally sourced sea life. Though there aren't many widely produced American versions of the style, it's popping up with more and more frequency.

While it's tempting to assume that there's something fishy about brewing with shellfish, brewers will quickly assure you that's not the case. Often built from a base of a dry or sweet stout, oyster stouts retain little (if any) of the salty character of their marquee ingredient. Downing an oyster stout, drinkers can expect notes of chocolate, roast malt, and just the slightest tang of astringent mineral. While the stouts are fine on their own, where they really shine is paired with (you guessed it) oysters. With the stout and oyster drawing out contrasting and harmonizing flavors in their partner, it's easy to see why the two have been associated for so long.

IMPERIAL LOUISIANA OYSTER STOUT

ABITA BREWING COMPANY

Founded in 1986, the Abita Brewing Company is nestled in the piney woods thirty miles north of New Orleans. In its first year, the brewery produced 1,500 barrels of beer. They outgrew the original site (which is now their 100-seat brew pub) and moved up the road to a larger facility to keep up with demand. Each year they now brew more than 150,000 barrels of beer and 9,000 barrels of root beer in their state-of-the-art brewing facility.

Abita Imperial Oyster Stout is made with pale, caramel, roasted, and chocolate malts. The roasted malts give the beer its dark color as well as its intense flavor and aroma. Oats are also added to give the beer a fuller and sweeter taste. Big wallops of toffee and chocolate come across the nose and palate, but there is nice balance provided by a solid dose of Willamette hops (not a lot, but just enough to provide balance and complexity). The bitterness complements the sweet, rich malt. Late in the brewing process freshly shucked Louisiana oysters are added to the boil. The salt from the oysters gives the beer a more intense aroma and mouthfeel. A very nice example of the style with an ABV of 8%.

ISLAND CREEK OYSTER STOUT

HARPOON BREWERY

Now this is a great story. First, let's talk about the oysters this beer is made with. Skip Bennett planted his first oysters at Oyster Creek Island Farm in 1992 after three years growing quahogs in Duxbury Bay. Skip was eventually joined in his adventure by Christian Horne, an oyster farmer from Maine, and shortly thereafter by Don Merry, the owner of a local fish market. Today, Island Creek Oysters' team includes seventeen employees in the wholesale company, additional farmers around the region, and a distribution arm that sells more than 100,000 oysters a week!

The idea for Island Creek Oyster Stout, part of the Harpoon's 100 Barrel Series, came to the brew team at Harpoon after years of enjoying locally harvested New England oysters and freshly brewed pints of stout with their friends from Island Creek Oyster farm. Once they decided to team up, the beer was brewed by Bill Leahy using Island Creek Oysters.

It pours dark, dark brown with a hint of red in it. Roasted barley and chocolate rye malts lend it a smooth mouthfeel and luxurious body. The roasted malt notes blend beautifully with the briny, mineral flavors of the Island Creek oysters. The oysters are faint, not intrusive. And the hops make a big difference on the end. A beautiful, impressive oyster stout.

MARSTON'S OYSTER STOUT

MARSTON'S PLC

Marston's is a British public house operator and brewer. It runs over 2,000 pubs in the United Kingdom and is the world's largest brewer of cask ale. Ninety percent of the profits come from its pubs. It was known as Wolverhampton and Dudley Breweries PLC until 2007 when it rebranded as Marston's. It owns five breweries and brands including Marston's, Banks's, Jennings, Ringwood, and Wychwood.

Contrary to what the name says it is, this is not a stout made with oysters. It is a stout meant to be drunk while *eating* oysters. Marston's uses unique yeast taken from the Burton Unions when brewing. According to some experts, this very aggressive yeast imparts a special taste associated with classic English stouts, making it clean and refreshing, but also meant to be drunk with food.

Latching onto the recent trends in brewing, but while holding onto many of its older traditions, Marston has updated their recipe to include the roastiness and chocolate profiles that are so popular in stout brewing today. They've also added English aroma hops, Fuggles, and Goldings to their Oyster Stout to complement the dark, roasted malt and ensure a well-balanced beer. It is brown-black in color with a cappuccino colored head. The nose promises chocolate, coffee, and dark red fruits—solid drinking stout.

OYSTER STOUT

THE PORTERHOUSE BREWING CO.

In 1989, Liam LaHart and Oliver Hughes opened the first Porterhouse Brewery, which specialized in importing various beers from around the world with a keen eye on Belgium. In 1996, they opened The Porterhouse in Temple Bar, which was Ireland's first brew pub (amazing, right?). In 1999, they opened a Porterhouse in Covent Garden, London, followed by one in Glasnevin, Dublin, in 2003. Then they purchased Lillie's Bordello and created Porterhouse Central on Nassau Street, Dublin, in 2004. Most recently they opened a bar on the southern tip of Manhattan in a marvelous historic tavern called Fraunces Tavern.

Their oyster stout is brewed using grains such as pale malt, roast barley, black malt, and flaked barley, and finished off with hops such as Galena, Nugget, and East Kent Goldings. According to the brewery, there is "More sweetness derived from fresh oysters shucked into the conditioning tank, what a way to go!"

At 4.6% ABV this oyster stout has a sweetness up front that finishes dry and is perfect to put down with a plate of oysters, or just to drink a few of. With such low alcohol, it's easy to order another . . . and another.

PEARL NECKLACE OYSTER STOUT

FLYING DOG BREWERY

Pearl Necklace has a dark, opaque black body. It forms a small, dark-tan, soapy head that mostly dissipates and doesn't retain or lace very well. There is a standard dry stout aroma of cola, the dairy aisle, lightly roasted malt, and a hint of coffee. Stouts have been a great pairing with oysters for a long time, but the making of oyster stouts dates back only to 1929. There have been many examples of this style. In the past, the oyster flavor was mild but noticeable and complemented the palate well. In the case of Flying Dog Pearl Necklace, the oysters' flavor is light. The core beer is a traditional dry stout that is a bit more robust than

Guinness and noticeably sweeter. There's almost a bit of anise or other root beer or colalike flavors. There's a slight milky taste at the peak, similar to that of a milk stout but nothing much in the way of roasted barley or coffee. The palate as a whole is satisfying and enjoyable.

Flying Dog Pearl Necklace, though extremely dark, is not even close to being an Imperial. The mouthfeel is light, thin, noticeably fizzy, but a bit refreshing across the tongue. The finish is clean, so it's easy to drink this brew fast or slow since it is not cloying. At 5.5% ABV it's technically a bit too big to session, though the mild palate and drinker-friendly delivery make it an ideal candidate for a waiver.

Flying Dog Pearl Necklace is brewed with local Rappahannock River oysters and is the perfect complement to oysters. The oyster taste is extremely light, but in the end you're left with a very decent stout.

CP

PERLE AI PORCI

BIRRA DEL BORGO

This beer has a solid black body. No light getting through there! The nose is faintly chocolate and caramel with a hint of possibly imagined brine. There are slight oyster and clam notes in the body, backing up a creamy stout with toasty coffee and strong mineral flavors. The salty finish leaves you thirsty for more of this 5.2% ABV oyster stout.

JC

ROCKY MOUNTAIN OYSTER STOUT

WYNKOOP BREWING COMPANY

This beer comes from Denver, Colorado, where the rarefied air does things to the brain and makes the softball-sized gonads of the average male cow look like a tasty treat. Bull testicles, or Rocky Mountain oysters, can be found all over Colorado but stayed out of beer until October 2012, when Wynkoop decided it would sack up and make a brew using that delicacy. Rocky Mountain Oyster Stout, which Wynkoop spokesman Marty Jones calls "another seminal moment in our 25 years of small-batch liquid art," has made its way into cans (sold in two-packs, of course).

Oyster stout is a real thing. Salty bivalves have long been matched with beer, their briny flavor for some reason perfect in a dry, roasty stout. Certain breweries have been adding oysters straight to the boil since the 1920s. Rocky Mountain Oyster Stout, however, was originally a joke. After

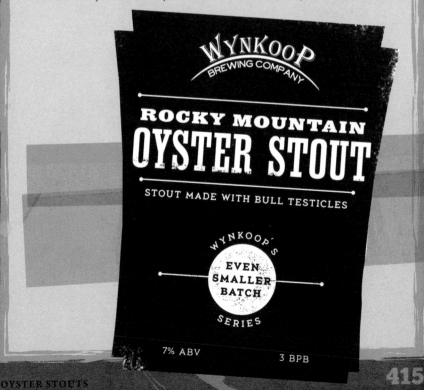

sampling a traditional stout made with oysters crafted by Odell Brewing Co., Jones got the guys at Wynkoop to post a video for April Fool's Day in which they claimed to have released a beer made with bull testicles.

As happens often on April 1, people took the video seriously. Wynkoop started getting e-mails from drinkers eager to taste the ballsy beer, and after much prodding, the brewers finally got teste enough to make a stout packed with bull balls a reality.

The recipe, which was developed by Wynkoop's head brewer, Andy Brown, uses Colorado base malts, roasted barley, seven specialty malts, Styrian Goldings hops, and a dash of sea salt, along with twenty-five pounds of freshly sliced and roasted bull testicles. The beer is brewed in tiny eight-barrel batches, meaning three whole huevos de toro make their way into each barrel. At 330 beers per barrel, this means every can of the inky liquid contains about one one-hundredth of a testicle.

Can you taste it? It's hard to say. The aroma certainly houses something savory deep in the background: a hint of umami akin to a well-marbled steak. But the other notes are better: salted caramel, milk chocolate, toasted bread, figgy dark fruits, and smoke. The flavor displays more of the same: bits of coffee, sweet cream, cocoa powder, vanilla, and ethanol are offset by an earthy hop bite and a raisiny finish. It's hard to tell if the very subtle gaminess is actually there or if you just want it to be. It doesn't really matter in the end; this stout would taste superb even without its ballsy adjunct.

ZF

THREE BOYS OYSTER STOUT

THREE BOYS BREWERY

Three Boys Brewery is a small, artisanal brewery in Christchurch, New Zealand. The brewery says of their oyster stout, "Doctors once prescribed stout as a revitalizing tonic, while brewers enhanced their potency with additional ingredients, like oysters, which had desirable properties of their own. The Three Boys Oyster Stout contains select malt and hops to produce a beer that is rich and complex. And, who knows, our addition of genuine Bluff oysters to this very special brew might be just what the doctor ordered."

If it doesn't have medicinal properties, it will absolutely make you feel better, regardless. It pours almost black with a nice khaki-colored head. Roasted coffee, chocolate, cocoa, and espresso dominate the palate, but the minerality and saltiness of the oysters come through slightly. Beautifully balanced and complex. An exceptional beer and an excellent example of the style.

Beyond the half-dozen recognized sub-styles of stout, there are brewers worldwide making new, bold takes on the storied dark beer. These range from adding unique ingredients (pumpkin in Cape Ann's Fisherman's Pumpkin Stout), to changing up the grain bill (Allagash Black, for example, is a wheat stout), to fermenting the beer with a Belgian yeast strain (such as in Ommegang's Chocolate Indulgence and Sam Adams' Thirteenth Hour). These riffs, experiments, and deconstructions of stout offer different perspectives on what a stout is while still retaining the deep, rich, roasty character that stout drinkers have known and loved for centuries. While some of these beers may prove popular enough to spawn a sub-style or two down the road, for the time being they remain idiosyncratic brews worth seeking out.

ABSTRAKT
AB:08

BREWDOG

Imperial stouts are almost without exception very dark brown bordering on black. That's always been the way of it: lots of dark malts makes the beer dark. Then this beer came along and upset the order of things. You wouldn't call it blond (strawberry blond, perhaps), but it certainly throws you off by pouring a deep orange-amber with a thick off-white head.

Now that your eyes have been deceived, it's time to trick your sense of smell. Coffee is the first thing that hits, sending your mind spinning back to a bottle of Mikkeller Koppi Coffee IPA, only this beer's more intense and sweeter. The aroma is of maple syrup, chocolate, oranges, oak, and the faintest hint of licorice. Despite its hefty ABV, there's no obvious booze. The nose is nothing short of glorious. You can sniff it for hours.

By now you're so confused anything could happen. This is a glutinous beer with a thick, warming body, and it's very sweet. There's more than a suggestion of an American barley wine with chocolate and coffee added. The finish has caramel and candy floss and is peppery; it ends a little hot.

What does one eat with a deconstructed Blond Imperial stout? Nothing at all, perhaps. It's massive enough to be enjoyed on its own in a snifter glass (remember to let it warm up to get the most out of it). However, the sweet syrup notes blended with chocolate and coffee make this a fascinating dessert and cheese beer. What about a black licorice crème brûlée or an odoriferous Gorgonzola, Stilton, or aged English cheddar?

Six key ingredients went into this truly novel beer: oats, licorice, heavily toasted oak chips, cocoa, coffee, and smoked malt. The oats help give the beer its incredibly thick, luscious mouthfeel, and the cocoa was grated into the beer after fermentation to allow it to stew. The beer then was aged on coffee beans to extract the flavor without transferring any of the color, and for good measure it also was aged on toasted oak chips for some roasted mellowness. For many reasons this is one of the most enjoyable BrewDog beers available.

DP

ALLAGASH BLACK

ALLAGASH BREWING COMPANY

Compared with the British Isles and the Baltic states, there's little history of Belgian takes on stouts and porters. Rather than a peerless take on the style, Belgian-style stouts usually combine the roasted dark chocolate flavors of an English or American stout with the spicy notes of a Belgian yeast and the sweetness of candi sugar. It's a style that's a great example of how Old World and New World brewing can combine to create something new and exciting.

It's little surprise that one of the best examples of this hybrid style comes from Portland's Allagash Brewing. The Maine-based brewery helped popularize Belgian-style beers in the United States, and over the last few decades it has steadily expanded its catalog to include more and more styles. Its take on a Belgian-style stout, brewed with barley, wheat, oats, roasted and chocolate malt, and caramelized candi sugar, debuted in 2007.

The opaque brew's intercontinental aspects play off one another perfectly at 7.5% ABV. Roast malt and caramel combine pleasantly on the nose, backed by subtle spice. The flavor is a complex trip, starting with coffee up front before coming around to a mocha finish. The oats used in the recipe provide a silky smoothness not unlike an oatmeal stout. Allagash occasionally puts out a bourbon barrel–aged version of Black, which adds wonderful oak and vanilla (not to mention whiskey) flavors to an already pleasant package.

JC

ALLAGASH
black
belgian
style
stout
7.5% Alc. By Vol.
OPEN CAUTIOUSLY: CONTENTS UNDER PRESSURE
1 PINT 9.4 FL OZ (750 ML)
FIRESTONE WALKER BREWING CO.
PASO ROBLES, CALIFORNIA 93446

THE BEER DIVINER GOT YOUR BACK

THE BEER DIVINER

This beer has an opaque black body. It forms a small, dark-tan, foamy head that doesn't completely evaporate and leaves some lacing on the glass. There is a strong vanilla aroma similar to cake batter—a generally sweet stout scent with hints of dairy.

Although Got Your Back is an Imperial coffee oatmeal stout, you get more of a vanilla flavor from it than anything else. It's reminiscent of Southern Tier's Crème Brûlée Stout, but without any cloying characteristics. This is a delicious dessert beer and is well balanced enough that no individual flavor overwhelms the palate.

It is much like a milk stout up front with a sweet dairy flavor, though this probably is due to the oatmeal with which it is brewed. A hefty bitterness breaks through in the middle of the swig, which is a touch dry and almost salty; this gives way to a smooth rush of vanilla sweetness. The list of ingredients is unusual and interesting: seven types of malts, two hops, decaf Sumatra French coffee, and a Belgian yeast strain are responsible for the palate, and they work together extremely well.

You'd never know Got Your Back was 9% ABV if you drank it blind. There is absolutely no alcohol presence in the nose or the taste, making this a highly drinkable beer. Even though it's brewed with Belgian yeast, it doesn't have a spastic, fizzy mouthfeel. Although it is on the thicker side, it's not a viscous stout and is quite comfortable in the mouth with only a mildly dry aftertaste. It goes down easy, making it an ideal sipper, though it also could pair well with the right meal.

CP

CASPER WHITE STOUT

JAMES PAGE BREWING COMPANY

Founded in 1986, JP's Craft Beers is now part of Stevens Point Brewing. It is one of the first craft beers to be put in cans, and in doing so, they ask you to throw your expectations about canned beer out the window.

People had questions when they decided to do a white stout, and the answers are good ones: "So how do you get a stout flavor in a light-colored beer? Since the black roasted malts typically used in stouts were not used, the flavor characteristics came from aging the beer for two weeks with coffee beans and cocoa nibs. They were enough to provide the chocolate stout flavor, but not darken the beer," explained writer Todd Haefer, in *USA Today*.

It's absolutely golden in color with big Pilsen malt flavor, and a touch of hops. The nose is butterscotch, white chocolate, vanilla cake, caramel, graham cracker, and shortbread. Full-bodied for such a lightly-colored ale, it has a nice, peppery finish. A hint of sweetness is balanced by a nice addition of hops. It's big, complex, and impressive, and at 6% ABV a very drinkable brew for a such a big, flavorful beer.

JP's casper™

WHITE STOUT
BEER WITH NATURAL FLAVOR ADDED

CHOCOLATE INDULGENCE BELGIAN-STYLE STOUT

BREWERY OMMEGANG

Ommegang Brewery, in Cooperstown, New York, has an exceptional reputation among those who like Belgian-style ales. With this background, it's not surprising that it does not have too many entries in the porter and stout category.

Chocolate Indulgence has an opaque black body with some carbonation visible at the edges. It pours to a large, dark-tan, foamy, head that laces and retains well. The surprisingly muted nose of generic Belgian yeast esters has notes of soap and perfume but no chocolate scent. This beer is lacking in overt chocolate as well as stout character, though the Belgian component is strong and interesting.

It seems that the first sip of any stout tends to be great, and so it is surprising that the first sip of this one is only average. Up front there's a standard Belgian flavor as well as a standard dark ale taste. It's not roasted malt per se; it's simply Belgian yeast esters. There's almost a smokiness as the beer continues downward with a zesty, almost soapy sensation. A faint hint of dark chocolate appears just as the beer finishes; it's very subtle and short-lived. There is additional bitterness in the aftertaste, along with a slight perfumelike character.

Although technically a big beer at 7% ABV, Chocolate Indulgence drinks like something much lighter. It doesn't have the thick, heavy, dense body of an Imperial stout but rather the character and delivery of a standard Belgian ale. There's plenty of carbonation and spiciness across the tongue, but it goes down smooth. If you are looking for a big chocolate bomb, this isn't it. If you're looking for something more subtle and restrained with a Belgian kick, this is your beer.

CP

DIRTY PENNY ALE

THE OLDE BURNSIDE BREWING COMPANY

This beer has an opaque, murky brown-black body that initially pours to a gigantic head. There's sediment on bottom of the bottle, and so it can be assumed it was bottle-conditioned. The tan, sodalike foamy head dissipates almost completely and leaves no lacing. There is a roasted malt plus peat scent, though this is not an aromatic beer per se.

The beer is a black and tan mixture of a Scottish ale and a California-style stout. Basically, it's an interesting pub-style beer. There does seem to be some astringency and tannins present that impart a sharp, dry bitterness and a somewhat phenolic character. This tastes like a homebrew, not a professional-grade beer. Still, the flavors are pretty decent and the sweetness and interesting use of flavor combinations are enjoyable. You could see this beer being good to excellent when fresh on tap, but a mystery bottle doesn't do it justice.

At only 5% ABV, it seems that Dirty Penny Ale is intended to be a deliberately sessionable beer. The body is thin but fizzy, though it finishes clean. It's no trouble to get down.

CP

FAT DOG IMPERIAL OATMEAL STOUT

STOUDT'S BREWING COMPANY

Stoudt's is a microbrewery and restaurant located in Adamstown, Pennsylvania. It was one of the commonwealth's first microbreweries, having been started in 1987 by Ed and Carol Stoudt. The restaurant, Black Angus Steakhouse, has been in business for half a century. For many years one of their most popular beers has been Fat Dog Imperial Oatmeal Stout, a British-style stout.

This is a hard beer to categorize. It merges the smooth and complex richness of an oatmeal stout with the assertive hoppiness of Imperial stout. The oatmeal also lends a creaminess to the overall texture. Fat Dog has an inviting silky-black color, a prominent roasted malt character, and a chocolaty, coffee-like finish. So tasty, you hardly notice the 9.2% ABV. It pours black, with a nice head and the coffee aroma is strong. Bitterness makes it refreshing, which is surprising given the big bodied nature of this dark, highly-acclaimed, chewy beer.

FISHERMAN'S PUMPKIN STOUT

CAPE ANN BREWING COMPANY

Every year features an endless parade of pumpkin-flavored products, but Fisherman's Pumpkin Stout by Cape Ann Brewing of Gloucester, Massachusetts, (as a contract brew with Mendocino Brewery) is unique. People like stouts and like pumpkin ales in moderation, but can the two styles be merged into one?

Fisherman's Pumpkin Stout is one of those beers that walk the tightrope between a genuine, unique brew and a novelty act. It wouldn't seem that pumpkin and stout could work together, but they do in the case of this beer, though that's not to say it's anything spectacular.

This stout has an opaque black body and a large khaki-colored frothy head that retains well but doesn't lace. It has a mild pumpkin ale aroma of cinnamon, nutmeg, and pumpkin with the slightly sweet dairylike scents often found in a milk stout.

The palate begins with two distinct stages. The first is by-the-book pumpkin ale with light spices and a gentle sweetness. It's definitely in the pumpkin potpourri style of beer, not the liquid pumpkin pie type. The second half is a by-the-book stout: a milky, velvety taste and texture with a quick burst of roasted malts and bitterness. But as you drink on, the two halves homogenize into one and create a pub-style stout with subtle pumpkin potpourri flavors. Not that this is bad, but when you combine two otherwise mild palates, you end up with one big mild palate; this does give the beer some uniqueness. The mouthfeel is medium-bodied, tepid, and soft with a milky texture and a mild dry aftertaste.

You'll have no idea that Fisherman's Pumpkin Stout is 7% ABV while you are drinking it. From the mild palate and complete lack of alcohol presence it seems like it would be closer to 4 or 5%. This beer should get extra accolades for masking its alcohol so well.

CP

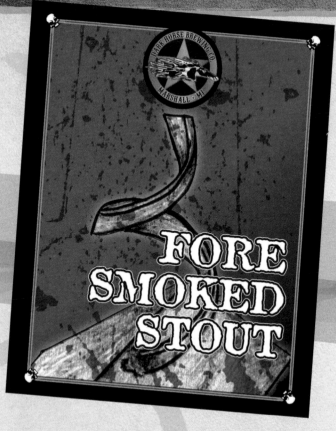

FORE SMOKED STOUT

DARK HORSE BREWING COMPANY

The number series from Dark Horse has a smoky entry. Number four is brewed with all malted barley and peat malt (smoked malt). It pours dark and has a big dark head that lingers. Fore Smoked Stout is full-bodied with chocolate and roasted barley flavors and a smoky, almost barbecue finish. The flavor starts with chocolate and cola and finishes with finger-licking barbecue. This is another impressive beer from Dark Horse.

FOUNDERS BREAKFAST STOUT

FOUNDERS BREWING COMPANY

Founders Breakfast Stout combines chocolate stouts, coffee stouts, and oatmeal stouts into a very good beer. The fact that it is able to do this as well as it does is commendable, and it's a tasty, palatable beer.

This beer pours like used motor oil; it's pitch black with no ruby red around the edges. It forms a small brown creamy head that leaves a little lacing on the glass. The aroma is exactly what you're used to in

a good stout: dark-roasted coffee and bittersweet chocolate with hints of dairy. It's not very potent in the nose, although each whiff is very pleasing.

The Founders brewery describes this beer as a "double chocolate, coffee oatmeal stout" on the label, but what does that combination of flavors actually taste like? It's much more akin to a traditional oatmeal stout than anything else. There is a silky, creamy, lactoselike sweetness up front with a strong coffee flavor in the middle and an aftertaste that is mildly bitter and dissipates quickly. This flavor combination is definitely pleasing, but there is a noticeable lack of chocolate, especially since it's advertised as "double chocolate."

As the beer starts to warm, the coffee flavor becomes more prominent in the finish and the bitterness lingers a bit longer. Once it warms up significantly, a dark chocolate flavor begins to make itself known. The combination of the oatmeal sweetness and the bitterness from the coffee and chocolate creates a great balance of flavor. As tasty as it is, the overall palate is milder than expected.

Imperial stouts tend to be an Achilles' heel of mine since they are so thick, rich, sticky, and bitter. However, Founders Breakfast Stout is amazing in how strong it isn't. The mouthfeel isn't like motor oil as is the case with so many other Imperial beers of this style, but quite soft and thin. The bitterness from the coffee and chocolate grows stronger as the beer warms, but never to the point of being obnoxious.

At 8.3% ABV this is a beer in which the statistics lie. There is virtually no indication of alcohol in the palate or in the composition other than the slightest feeling of warmth. Most beers this strong tend to be sippers or at least one-and-dones, but you could drink a few bottles of this one after dinner.

CP

GLUTENBERG IMPERIAL SOTOLON

GLUTENBERG AND CHARTIER CRÉATEUR D'HARMONIES

The Quebec-based microbrewery Glutenberg and Chartier Créateur d'Harmonies have formed a partnership to create the new Série Gastronomie, an innovative range of gastronomic beers. Designed to enhance culinary experiences and crafted with the aromatic science of world-renowned sommelier François Chartier, Glutenberg's Série Gastronomie offers a selection of seasonal beers that make it easy to create harmonious beer and food pairings.

Inspired by the aromatic explorations of Franç Chartier and his international bestseller *Taste Buds and Molecules*, Glutenberg's founders approached the sommelier to create a bold and ambitious partnership. The collaboration was an obvious one for the Créateur d'Harmonies when he realized that Glutenberg was open to using unexpected ingredients, allowing him to apply his principles to beer.

The Impérial Sotolon was created around sotolon, the central aromatic component found in maple syrup. It was made from millet, roasted buckwheat, Demerara sugar, molasses, maple syrup, grilled fenugreek, coffee, hops, and yeast. It was aged in old dark rum oak casks from the Guyanan producer El Dorado.

This 8% ABV blond stout is golden yellow in color. The head is light: not white but a creamy light beige. There are the notes of roastiness you expect from an Imperial stout as well as coffee and molasses and maple, but there are also figs, dates, soy sauce, and sugar with whiffs of rum. The maple comes across on the palate along with a lovely spiciness. The sweetness is balanced by some bitterness, and the 8% alcohol doesn't overpower the beer.

It was made to pair well with recipes that feature flavors such as maple, curry, balsamic vinegar, and soy sauce as well as dishes dominated by nuts, apricots, peaches, or coconut and, obviously, grilled or roasted beef. It is a perfect accompaniment to glazed ham or grilled pork. A very, very unique beer. Very little like it in the market place.

IMPERIAL PUMPKIN STOUT

LONG TRAIL BREWING COMPANY

Long Trail made its first batch of brews 1989. The brewery was known as the Mountain Brewers then, and made a modest forty-five barrels a year from the basement of the Old Woolen Mill in Bridgewater Corners, Vermont. The founder, Andy Pherson, in many ways blazed the trail for Vermont's notable craft brewing industry.

Long Trail Imperial Pumpkin Stout is part of Long Trail's Brush and Barrel series. There are pumpkin beers everywhere, and every fall there seems to be more and more of them. How many are exceptional? How many of them are even stouts?!

This is Long Trail's version of an Imperial Russian stout brewed with pumpkins, cinnamon, ginger, nutmeg, and cloves as well as malts such as 2-row, wheat, caramel 80L, and caramunicht and finished with Nugget, Mt. Hood, and Willamette hops. This is a classic brown malt stout with lovely highlights of spice and beautiful aromatics. And the 8% ABV is better hidden than you might suspect. A well-constructed seasonal beer.

LAVA SMOKED IMPERIAL STOUT

ÖLVISHOLT BRUGGH'S

Olvisholt is located in the southwest part of Iceland, in the middle of the most fertile agricultural area of the country. The Ölvisholt farm has been a conventional sheep and dairy farm since Iceland was settled more than thousand years ago. The active volcano, Hekla, is visible from the brewhouse door, and occasionally eruptions are visible from the Ölvisholt farm. The label for Lava resembles this view from when an eruption occurs. The idea is that the name is supposed to suggest an explosion of flavor. And it doesn't disappoint.

Lava, a smoked Imperial stout, is quite a unique experience. It's made with classic malts, including six types of barley malt and one type of wheat malt, and hopped with First Gold and Fuggle hops. It's not a demure beer at 9.4% ABV. The touch of smoke is a compliment, even for those who may not normally enjoyed smoked beers. Dark, dark brown in the pour with chocolate, roasted malt, and smoke coming across big time on the nose, this is a big, impressive hybrid of styles, but no doubt a winner. It is one of the most highly acclaimed beers in this style.

JC

MEAN OLD TOM
MAINE BEER COMPANY

The Maine Beer Company in Freeport, Maine, makes some of the most serious beers in the Northeast, but they have a wicked sense of humor. The inspiration for this vanilla stout was the owner-brewer's uncle: "I think it was the summer of '76, I was 5 years old and my uncle Tom came to paint our house. It was in the tiny town of Louisiana, Missouri, on the mighty Mississippi River, where he would take me to stroll the roadside ditches to gather one man's junk (beer cans). I named this beer in honor of his magnificent treasure (his beer can collection) and his spirit for fast cars, tough motorcycles and mean smiles."

This 6.5% ABV American-style stout is made using malts such as American two-row, chocolate, roasted barley, Midnight Wheat, Caramel 40, and flaked oats and hops that include US Magnum and Centennial. It then is aged on organic vanilla beans. The beer gives off intense notes of coffee and dark chocolate that subtly lead up to luxurious natural vanilla. Flaked oats help the beer achieve its sensational silky mouthfeel. Fantastic!

MERRY MAKER
GINGERBREAD STOUT

SAMUEL ADAMS,
THE BOSTON BEER COMPANY

Admit it. You saw this in the store and said to yourself, "Really? Ginger-bread and beer?" But this has become a very popular style. Made by the popular Boston Beer Company, this 9%-ABV, rich, aromatic, dark-ginger-bread stout is a real crowd pleaser during the holidays. The gingerbread aroma comes announcing itself out of the glass with big, loud church bells. It pours pitch black, and exhibits a delicate sweetness balanced with hearty dark roasted malts and a touch of wheat. The beer was brewed with 2- row pale malt blend, wheat, Special B, Paul's roasted barley, and flaked oats and finished with East Kent Goldings and Fuggles hops. So it's got a well-made, quality back bone of a more normal stout. But no matter where you go in this beer, the intense spices of cinnamon, clove, nutmeg, and ginger add that unmis-takable holiday touch. This is an excellent example of what a gingerbread stout can be.

MONK'S STOUT

BRASSERIE DUPONT

Brasserie Dupont is a brewery in Tourpes-Leuze, the center of West-Hainaut, Belgium. The current brewery was founded in 1950 and is still found on a working farm that dates back to 1759. Since the 1980s, when they began being distributed in the US, they've been best known for their Saison Dupont. That beer provides a link to the historic farmhouse ales of the region. Now, they are making a Belgian stout! And the beer writers of the world lit up the board in surprise.

"Dupont has done it again. They've brewed the first true Belgian interpretation of stout, not a simple recreation of the style. Dark, dry and quenching, as only Dupont's active and attenuating yeast can make it," wrote Jason Baldacci on *Chicagoist*.

"What's surprising about this beer is that while it's a stout, I'm instantly reminded of Saison Dupont. The grassy barnyard notes that make Saison so identifiable, and for me, such a perfect summer beer shine through without a problem," wrote Mario Rubio on *Brewed for Thought*.

It pours pitch black. A nice tan head develops, which lingers nicely and leaves a lovely sheet of lacing on the sides of the glass. The taste has lots of roasted malts, roasted coffee, burnt caramel, and hints of plum or fig jam and nutty finish. Thin for a stout, but still good mouthfeel, and excellent balance. At 5.2% ABV, it's easily drinkable.

THIRTEENTH HOUR

SAMUEL ADAMS, THE BOSTON BEER COMPANY

When it comes to beer buying, a cool bottle will win my purchase almost every time. So it was with the Samuel Adams Barrel Room beers. The beautiful vessels designed to look like the wooden barrels in which these limited brews were aged came onto the scene in 2011 but were available for purchase only in Boston.

Four beers make up the Barrel Room Collection: New World Tripel, Stony Brook Red, American Kriek, and Thirteenth Hour. All take inspiration from the Belgian practices of blending and aging beers for wild and flavorful results, but Thirteenth Hour is unique in that it implants Belgian flavors into a very English creation: stout.

The thirteenth hour is also known as the witching hour, the time of day when witches, demons, and ghosts appear and black magic is most effective. The name refers not only to the dark juju created by combining the roasted flavors of a stout with the spicy character of a sour Belgian ale but also to the thirteen ingredients used to brew the beer. It combines several different malts (Samuel Adams two-row pale malt blend, Caramel 60, Munich 10, Special B, and Carafa III), Hallertau Mittelfrueh hops, two different brewing sugars, Kosmic Mother Funk, Belgian yeast, and champagne yeast for bottle conditioning.

The result is a brew that's as deathly black as the midnight hour. In a tulip glass, the obsidian brew is topped with a super-frothy layer of cocoa-colored bubbles that look as thick and inviting as pancake batter. The stoutlike appearance is belied by the nose, however. Place the nostrils close and you'll get a dose of Belgian dark fruits: raisins, figs, and dates. Vanilla, black pepper, and a hint of acidity swirl in the rich background.

All Barrel Room Collection beers contain Kosmic Mother Funk, an ale that's fermented with wild yeasts and bacteria and then aged in oak tuns for over a year. The KMF is blended into the Barrel Room beers in varying amounts, lending them new layers of funky flavor. In Thirteenth Hour, this wild ale contributes herbal spice and a mild tanginess that grabs the back of the tongue.

More impactful on Thirteenth Hour's flavor is the extended barrel aging. The Barrel Room name isn't arbitrary: Each beer in the collection was aged in special oak barrels originally used to make brandy. The containers traveled far to get to New England. The oak, which originated in Eastern Europe, was used for brandy making in Italy. Coopers in Portugal took the barrels apart and then flew to Boston to reassemble them by hand. From these elements, Thirteenth Hour gets heaping helpings of rich, sweet red grapes and oak to blend with the underlying stout flavors of smoky peat, chocolate, vanilla, and coffee. The brandy almost makes the brew seem more like a Belgian strong dark ale than a stout.

The Belgian stout is a weird style on its own, and Thirteenth Hour is a fine example of how these flavors play off one another. Pick one up if you want an interesting taste.

ZF

YABBA DHABBA CHAI TEA PORTER

JAMES PAGE BREWING COMPANY

James Page loves to brew things other aren't. Here, the Stevens Point, Wisconsin–based craft brewer is making a porter with Chai Tea. Anise combined with a six-malt blend, make this a hands-down discovery in beer. Seriously bold flavors of chai including ginger, cinnamon, clove, and cardamom all come across in the nose and across the palate. A mild roasted beer with an impressive aroma, medium body, and a light at 5.5% ABV. A reach, but fun for the adventurous.

CONTRIBUTORS

Stephen Beaumont

Once described as "beerdom's Brillat-Savarin," Stephen Beaumont is one of the world's most authoritative voices on beer as well as a widely recognized writer on spirits, food, and travel. As co-author of *The World Atlas of Beer* and *The Pocket Beer Guide* (both with Tim Webb), as well as the author of six other books about beer, Stephen has amassed an unparalleled understanding of what's going on in the fast-paced and expanding world of beer today. If there is good lager or ale to be had, whether in San Francisco or Singapore, Montreal or Milan, Stephen knows about it, and has most likely sampled it!

When he is not writing about or tasting beer and spirits, Stephen travels the world talking about them, at a beer dinner in Dallas, a seminar in São Paulo, or a competition in Brussels. He has worked with a large number of corporations, including Starwood Hotels and Resorts, Crystal Cruises and Scenic Tours, and appears regularly at conferences such as VIBE and the International Wine, Spirits and Beer Event. Stephen writes regular columns for publications as diverse as the spirits quarterly *Whisky Advocate*, the foodie favorite *City Bites*, and the beer bi-monthly *Ale Street News*. He also serves on the editorial tasting panels of both *Taps* and *All About Beer* magazines, and he contributes regularly to a variety of other magazines.

Joshua M. Bernstein

Joshua M. Bernstein is a beer, spirits, food, and travel journalist. Over the last fifteen years, he's written for scores of newspapers, magazines, and websites, including *Bon Appétit*, *Men's Journal*, *Details*, *New York*, *Saveur*, *The New York Times*, and *Imbibe*, where he is a contributing editor overseeing beer coverage. Additionally, he is the author of *Brewed Awakening* and *The Complete Beer Course*. As a beer expert, he has been featured on NPR's Marketplace and Beer Sessions Radio. He lives in Brooklyn, New York, with his wife, daughter, and dog. You should come to New York City sometime and take one of his homebrew tours.

Julia Burke / JB

Julia Burke is a freelance writer with a passion for beer, wine, and food. She grew up in western New York, where she fell in love with the region's emerging craft beer industry and the Niagara Escarpment wine region. Her work has been featured in *Great Lakes Brewing News*, *New York Cork Report*, Skepchick.org, and *Isthmus*, the alternative weekly newspaper of Madison, Wisconsin, where she currently resides. The first beer she ever loved was Flying Bison's oatmeal stout.

Josh Christie / JC

Josh Christie's writing has appeared in print in the *Portland Phoenix*, the *Maine Sunday Telegram*, and other publications and online as a featured columnist at RateBeer.com. He lives in Yarmouth, Maine, with his wife, cat, and steadily growing beer cellar. He is the author of *Maine Beer: Brewing in Vacationland*.

Greg Clow

Greg Clow is the publisher and editor of *Canadian Beer News*, the premier online source for news from Canada's beer and brewing industry. He is also a regular contributor to *TAPS Magazine*, Canada's only national beer publication, and an occasional host of beer dinners and other tasting events in and around Toronto.

Martyn Cornell

Martyn Cornell is a journalist, author, and one of the leading authorities on the history of British beer and the development of British beer styles. His publications include Beer: *The Story of the Pint* (2003) and *Amber Gold and Black: the History of Britain's Great Beer Styles* (2010). His awards for his writing on beer, food, and travel include Beer Writer of the Year (2003), Beer and Food Writer of the Year (2005 and 2012), Beer Blogger of the Year (2011), and Beer and Travel Writer of the Year (2000 and 2013). His blog, zythophile.wordpress.com, is one of the best-read and most influential blogs on beer in the UK.

Campbell Gibson / CG

After graduating from Binghamton University with a degree in English, general literature, and rhetoric, Gibson found his way back to Long Island Wine Country. After working various jobs he found himself behind a winery tasting bar. Immersing himself in all things local, he joined the *New York Cork Report* as the Long Island Beer Correspondent and posts weekly beer reviews.

Zach Fowle / ZF

Zach Fowle is a Certified Cicerone and a BJCP-certified beer judge who has written about beer for the *Phoenix New Times* and *Draft Magazine*. As a consultant for craft beer bar franchise World of Beer, he has trained hundreds of staff and members of the public on beer knowledge. His weekly column about beer can be found at phxfood.com.

Darren Packman / DP

Darren Packman is considered one of the most passionate and influential figures in the Swedish beer industry today. Darren, a trained journalist who moved from his home in southeast England to Sweden back in 2000, has worked professionally with beer for sixteen years and traveled the world educating people about it. In 2009, he started the *BeerSweden* blog which quickly grew to become Sweden's most popular beer site. In 2011 he also founded the BeerSweden Forum, now the country's most active online beer community. He is the Svenska Ölfrämjandets Guldpin winner for 2011 for his contribution to beer culture in Sweden and is one of the founders and vice-chairman of the Skandinaviska Ölskribenters Förening (Scandinavian Beer Writers Association). Darren is a veteran of hundreds of beer talks across Europe and America and delivers fast-paced tastings laced with English humor and crammed full of useful (and sometimes not so useful) facts and information about the world's most popular alcoholic drink. In 2013, he started his very own craft brewery, Beer Studio. His ambition is to build a world-class local brewery and bring the craft beer revolution to the City of Birches!

Chad Polenz / CP

Chad Polenz has been a craft beer enthusiast for well over a decade and has been publishing reviews on a near daily basis at his website ChadzBeerReviews.com since 2008. He first tried something other than "fizzy yellow beer" during his active duty days in the US Navy when he visited other countries and realized there was more to beer than marketing and performance value. Chad was one of the first people to produce video beer reviews on YouTube, which has now become a worldwide trend. In 2013, he began writing about beer for the *Times Union* newspaper of Albany, New York. Chad is also an avid homebrewer and an officer in the Albany Brew Crafters homebrew club. He has both entered and judged over a dozen homebrew competitions with several of his brews winning style categories as well as Best in Show. When he's not drinking, reviewing, or making beer, Chad makes a living as an IT professional specializing in Windows server administration.

Josh Rubin / JR

Josh Rubin, a native of Toronto, is the beer columnist for the *Toronto Star*, Canada's biggest daily newspaper. He also contributed to the *Oxford Companion to Beer*. When he's not sipping stouts and porters, he's got a soft spot for single malt, good bourbon, and a well-made negroni.

ACKNOWLEDGMENTS

Thanks to my friends, family, and co-workers for their support of my writing endeavors, and to scores of brewers for donating both their time and the fruits of their labor to this project.

—Josh Christie

I would like to thank God, my family, the readers of the *Beer Nut* blog, everyone involved with the Albany Brew Crafters, and especially all the readers and watchers of all my text and video reviews, respectively. I couldn't have gotten this far without your support, so thank you all very much!

Thanks also goes out to the many, many people who helped bring this book to life: John Whalen at Cider Mill Press, Carlo DeVito for gathering up so many of the pieces, Alex Lewis for keeping everyone on track, Alicia Freile and Corinda Cook for their gorgeous designs, Eric Lowenkron for his outstanding editorial work, and Katherine Furman for piecing it all together.

A big thanks is also due to the breweries and the kind souls who work at them for providing many of the wonderful images on these pages.

—Chad Polenz

PHOTO CREDITS